THE ESSENTIAL
JAMES GARNER

THE ESSENTIAL
JAMES GARNER

Stephen H. Ryan
Paul J. Ryan

ROWMAN & LITTLEFIELD

Lanham • Boulder • New York • London

Published by Rowman & Littlefield
An imprint of The Rowman & Littlefield Publishing Group, Inc.
4501 Forbes Boulevard, Suite 200, Lanham, Maryland 20706
www.rowman.com

Unit A, Whitacre Mews, 26-34 Stannary Street, London SE11 4AB

British Library Cataloguing in Publication Information Available

Library of Congress Cataloging-in-Publication Data

Names: Ryan, Stephen H., 1961– author. | Ryan, Paul J., 1964– author.
Title: The essential James Garner / Stephen H. Ryan and Paul J. Ryan.
Description: Lanham : Rowman & Littlefield, 2018. | Includes bibliographical
   references and index. | Includes filmography.
Identifiers: LCCN 2017054685 (print) | LCCN 2017059356 (ebook) | ISBN
   9781442278219 (electronic) | ISBN 9781442278202 (hardback : alk. paper)
Subjects: LCSH: Garner, James—Criticism and interpretation.
Classification: LCC PN2287.G385 (ebook) | LCC PN2287.G385 R93 2018 (print) |
   DDC 791.43/092—dc23
LC record available at https://lccn.loc.gov/2017054685

♾™ The paper used in this publication meets the minimum requirements of
American National Standard for Information Sciences—Permanence of Paper for
Printed Library Materials, ANSI/NISO Z39.48-1992.

Printed in the United States of America

For
Isabella Anne Ryan
Anne Herkins Ryan
Anne Rea Freeman

CONTENTS

ACKNOWLEDGMENTS

First and foremost, we want to thank and acknowledge our family. Each of them has supported us not only in the writing of this book but in countless other ways whose value can't be measured.

Thanks to our mother, Anne Herkins Ryan (the epitome of a renaissance woman).

Thanks to our father, John L. Ryan Jr. (one of the most intelligent men we've ever known).

Thanks, admiration, and love to our incredibly supportive sisters:

Aryna Ryan, who led the creative way when her first book was published a few years ago
Amy Ryan Rued, who has been an unwavering source of inspiration and encouragement
Alicia Ryan Karanian, who may not realize how much she means to us

Likewise, to our equally supportive brothers:

John L. Ryan III, who has sustained us in various ways, *all* of which are truly appreciated
Michael G. Ryan, a master of social media who never fails to herald our accomplishments

No one could ask for better siblings, and we're grateful to each of them.

Thanks also to Neil Battiste, Jack Rued, John Karanian, Joyce Ryan, and Hagit Glickman.

Thanks as well to our nieces and nephews: Meghan, Rachel, and Jordan Karanian; Taylor and Spencer Ryan; Thomas H. Ryan; and Jacob Ryan.

A special thanks to Gigi Garner for graciously reviewing the proofs and providing input.

—Stephen and Paul

• • •

First, of course, is my coauthor and brother Stephen. We talked about writing a book for many years. It was Stephen's idea to write one about my favorite actor and that product sits in your hands (or on your e-reader). We share a very similar sense of humor, and boy did we need it creating this book—and to get through being brothers so close in age.

Thanks to James Garner, who not only inspired this work, but provided us with countless hours of entertainment, both before and during the writing of this book. When Garner passed away in 2014, several family members and friends called or texted me to confirm I heard of this, knowing how much I had admired Garner's work. Thanks to those same friends who no doubt would have supported me on this project had I disclosed to them my efforts on making this book a reality.

And then there is my pride and joy, and my only child, Isabella Anne Ryan, who no doubt will pen a book all her own one day. She was supportive in her own way with the writing of this book, including helping me with some of the sections. I would like to believe I will inspire her all her life.

—Paul J. Ryan

• • •

Although Paul and I have acknowledged our siblings, nieces, and nephews, I wanted to pay a particular shout-out to my brother-in-law John Karanian and to my nieces Meghan, Rachel, and Jordan, whose close proximity has meant much to me over the years. I've said it to them in person but I reiterate it here: I admire their gifts of empathy and kindness, no doubt instilled in them by Alicia and John K.

I also feel especially close to my nephew, Spencer "Are You Finished with the Book Yet?" Ryan, who shares my irreverent sense of humor ("What do you mean by that, Brian?").

And thanks to my delightful nieces Taylor and Isabella, whom I'm proud to say are also my goddaughters. Each in her own way is a special young lady, and I continue to marvel at their accomplishments.

A great deal of thanks goes to my brother Paul, who gave me the motivation to finally write something more substantial than marketing copy for a book.

Thanks to my colleagues at Rowman & Littlefield (née Scarecrow), present and past, who make my job a little bit more manageable, and sometimes fun, in particular Jayme Bartles, Neil Cotterill, Sally Craley, Bethany Davis, Kicheko Driggins, Glenda Green, Lara Hahn, Jackie Hicks, Deb Hudson, Christen Karniski, Edward Kurdyla, Kim Lyons, Kate Powers, Kelly Rogers, Jon Sisk, Piper Wallis, Devin Watson, Dustin Watson, Lois Wesley, Jessica Wetzel, and Patricia Zline.

Special thanks to Jessica McCleary, production editor extraordinaire, not to mention, friend. After working together for fifteen years and on roughly five hundred books, it doesn't necessarily get any easier, but it does get done—one way or another! Thanks for making me look better!

Thanks also to my authors/series editors Cynthia J. Miller and Bob Batchelor. After being the recipient of your acknowledgments more than a few times, I'm grateful for the opportunity to return the favor.

Last but not least, thank you to a great group of supportive friends who have been there for me at one time or another, and continue to champion me in his or her own special way: Becki Chalmers, Andrea Freeman, Leil Garner, Rick Hall, LeVan Hawkins, Nicholas Kelly, John Lee, Kevin McGettigan, Laura Mitchell, Kiev Murphy, Thomas Murphy, Karen Randell, Jesus Rosario, and Lisa Talenti.

And to Anne Freeman: No Hallmark card can capture what your friendship means to me! Thanks and love always!

RIP Erin Drew, Evie Powers, Maggie Ryan, and Martha Ryan.

—Stephen H. Ryan

INTRODUCTION

It could be said that James Garner had three careers on-screen: as a television star, as a movie star, and as a made-for-television movie *actor*. In his more than five decades of film and television roles, Garner is best remembered as the star of two very successful television series, *Maverick* and *The Rockford Files*. It's indisputable that *Maverick* made the actor a star, but television in the 1950s—particularly westerns—made stars out of many actors. Taking control of his career, Garner parlayed television stardom into big-screen successes. Between the end of his *Maverick* run and the start of *The Rockford Files*, Garner appeared in more than twenty films, including classics and near classics like *The Great Escape*, *The Americanization of Emily*, and *Support Your Local Sheriff!* From the 1950s to the present, Hollywood has typically confined an actor to one medium or the other, whether by design or chance. Although it's more commonplace today for actors to cross back and forth between mediums, James Garner achieved that balance decades ago. After *The Rockford Files* concluded its run in 1980, Garner appeared in fifteen more features, along with steady appearances in television films and series. In all, James Garner appeared in more than forty feature films over the span of fifty years, from *Toward the Unknown* in 1956 until *The Ultimate Gift* in 2006.

Apart from *Maverick* and *The Rockford Files*, Garner was a series regular on five shows and appeared on seven others as a guest star or featured performer. He also starred in three miniseries (*Space*, *The Streets of Laredo*, and *Roughing It*) and more than twenty television movies, including revivals of his two most enduring roles, Bret Maverick and Jim Rockford.

But all of those are credits for James Garner, the *actor*. He also kept busy behind the camera, first as the head of his own production company, Cherokee Productions, beginning with the 1964 World War II thriller *36 Hours*. In all, Cherokee Productions was associated with ten films in Garner's career, as well as the entire run of *The Rockford Files*. Garner also formed production companies aside from Cherokee, primarily for television films, beginning with *Promise* in 1986. These ventures resulted in several highly regarded films and even brought Garner his second Emmy, not for acting but as a producer of *Promise*.

Though Garner was admired by critics and fans, he was also admired and respected by his colleagues. In addition to his Best Actor Oscar nomination for *Murphy's Romance*, he was nominated for four Screen Actors Guild awards, twelve Golden Globes, and fifteen Emmys (including two nonacting nominations). Over the course of his career, Garner won three Golden Globes and two Emmys, including one as lead actor in *The Rockford Files*. But perhaps the most meaningful accolade the actor received was for his body of work, recognized by the Screen Actors Guild in 2005 when they bestowed upon him their Lifetime Achievement Award.

● ● ●

Understandably, James Garner will be best remembered for his two iconic television roles of Bret Maverick and Jim Rockford. This is good, because one really can't imagine either *Maverick* or *The Rockford Files* as being nearly as successful—or enduring—if Garner had not headlined both programs. *Maverick* made Garner a star, but Garner made *Maverick* a success, which in turn bred his stardom. Nearly fifteen years after Garner quit *Maverick*, he brought his star quality—honed for more than a decade in feature films—back to the small screen, and made *The Rockford Files* a success. With all due respect to the writers and directors who helped produce those programs, those shows would not be nearly as memorable if some other actor had played those lead roles. James Garner was—and always will be—Maverick. And perhaps even more so, he is Jim Rockford. And that fact, while not exactly a bad thing, doesn't give James Garner his full and proper due.

And that is where this book comes in.

In *The Essential James Garner*, we look at the entirety of the actor's career. Of course, we acknowledge key episodes from his two most familiar shows—*Maverick* and *The Rockford Files*—as well as the underappreciated

Nichols. But, more importantly, we focus our attention on the dozens of films that merit proper consideration—not just the ones that casual fans of the actor are familiar with, but long-neglected gems that also deserve a look. This includes his work on the small screen, when he appeared in a number of critically acclaimed made-for-television films that are as memorable as his feature films—and in a few cases, those films were as important as any work he did on the big screen.

We have kept the film summaries brief, eschewing plot points for a simple overview, lest we spoil the viewer's enjoyment of the film by revealing too many details.

We have also summarized the reception each film received, including reviews from various publications, box office results, and acknowledgments from his peers, in particular the Emmy, Golden Globe, and Screen Actors Guild organizations.

While we have provided snippets of critical reviews, we know that critics are not always discerning, not always consistent, and not always right. And indeed, we found ourselves disagreeing with them several times, but not always in the actor's favor. For example, one film that received fairly decent reviews when it was released did not make our list of essentials for two reasons: (1) we were not impressed with the film overall (in fact, viewing the movie proved to be a pretty miserable experience), and (2) the film wasted Garner's skills—he did not contribute much to the film, because frankly, the script didn't allow him. But he was not alone in that regard. Nearly the entire cast—including a pair of Oscar-winning powerhouses—appeared off their game, done in by a script and direction that gave them very little to do—or worse, forced them to access their melodramatic impulses. Painful.

But being negative is the not the goal of this book.

Our aim is to point out the highlights of Garner's career and encourage readers to discover or revisit the best that Garner had to offer, on screens both small and large, particularly those that were not given their proper due, not just by critics, but audiences as well. And yes, even by Garner himself. In his memoir, *The Garner Files*, which was published in 2011, the actor evaluated many—though not all—of his projects. In a few cases, his assessments were much harsher than either critics' or his fans', including the authors of this book. On the other hand, we found a few films the actor remembered with fondness as not being quite the gems that we had hoped for. Some films he neglected to mention at all, and rightfully so—and some, we wished he had mentioned, to see if his assessment equated to ours. In a prolific career of forty-plus films, hundreds of television episodes, and possibly even more commercials—there are bound to be some lows interspersed with the highs. This book is about the highs.

And finally, we elaborate on why we feel the film in question merits inclusion as a James Garner essential. To be considered such, there are two key criteria:

1. The film is enjoyable to watch, whether you're a particular fan of Garner's or not. It's as simple as that.
2. Garner's performance makes the film worth watching even if the movie does not meet the first criteria. In many cases, Garner's performance contributed to the first criteria, of course. In other cases, he was one of the bright spots in an otherwise uneven film—making the viewing experience a rewarding one.

In our opinion, many films meet both criteria.

But we don't stop there. Part of the pleasure of this endeavor has been to really examine the merits of Garner's contributions to each film, not as some stuffy academic exercise, but as a way of processing how his participation elevated the work. It's an oversimplification to say that Garner's genial manner and affable nature are why viewers enjoy his television shows and films. It goes deeper. Indeed, this venture became even more rewarding as we reviewed the films toward the latter part of his career—as he transitioned from a star to something much more significant.

Sure, some of the films are included in this volume because they capture Garner at his charming best. Others are cited for their cultural impact, even if Garner himself did not play a key role, such as early films like *Sayonara*. The best of the best are those films with an enduring impact, thanks in no small measure by Garner's participation.

Our star rating system is simple, from one star (don't waste your time) to four stars (a classic). While we have included a filmography that rates everything, our pick for the essentials must earn at least two and half stars. And yes, this is a subjective rating, so some viewers might disagree with our choices, arguing that a film deserves better—or possibly worse. And we get that. There are a number of two-star films that we still admire, but they just didn't make the final cut. That doesn't mean we don't think they're not worth watching—they simply aren't *essential* viewing.

A note to readers: we make no distinction between Garner's feature films and his made-for-television movies, primarily because many of those TV ventures contributed to the actor's legacy. Indeed, soon after *The Rockford Files* concluded its run in 1980, the actor began a "new" career in television films, a transition that showcased the type of acting that few knew he was capable of, perhaps even Garner himself. The first of these films, *The Long*

Summer of George Adams, heralded a string of critically acclaimed performances that also brought the actor several nods from both the Emmys and the Golden Globes, not to mention the Screen Actors Guild. Little wonder that we regard many of these films among the highlights of Garner's career.

Of Garner's forty-six feature films, twenty-one television films, and seven television series, we shine the spotlight on thirty-one: twenty-eight films and three series. The films are listed chronologically, from *Shoot-Out at Medicine Bend* in 1957 to *The Notebook* in 2004, a span of nearly fifty years, followed by the series. Take a look at what we think is among James Garner's best—and why. We hope you'll enjoy the reading—and watching—as much as we enjoyed the writing.

THE CAREER
OF JAMES GARNER

James Garner enjoyed a five-decade career in entertainment, one that encompassed television shows, feature films, made-for-television movies, and commercials—not to mention swimsuit modeling and even a stint on Broadway. Though he took to acting a little later in life compared to most who pursue a career in Hollywood or on the stage, he quickly made up for it. Almost exactly two years after his on-screen debut, Garner was headlining his own series, *Maverick*, which was an instant success. That rapid ascent could be attributed to any one of several serendipitous factors, but all of them are meaningless without acknowledging the chief reason: James Garner's irresistible charm and his ease in front of the camera, honed very quickly over the course of two years.

Like a number of fellow actors since the early 1950s—including superstars Steve McQueen and Clint Eastwood—Garner first made a name for himself in television westerns. For Garner, guest parts in a number of Warner Bros. westerns eventually led to *Maverick*, as well as a few supporting roles in feature films for the studio.

But before these, James Bumgarner made his first professional appearance on Broadway, in the 1954 staging of *The Caine Mutiny*. The actor recalled learning much from the experience, in part because his was not a speaking role. As one of the judges presiding over a military trial, Garner spent each performance listening, absorbing, and reacting—acting tools he would sharpen in the months and years to come. He also watched how the play's star, Henry Fonda, conducted himself, on stage and off, which resonated with Garner throughout his life.

After *The Caine Mutiny*, Bumgarner returned to the Los Angeles area where his Hollywood career kick-started almost by happenstance. One evening, the young actor crossed paths with a Hollywood director, Richard L. Bare, in a bar. Bare prided himself on spotting talent and thought the young man had presence. When later casting *Cheyenne*, a new western he

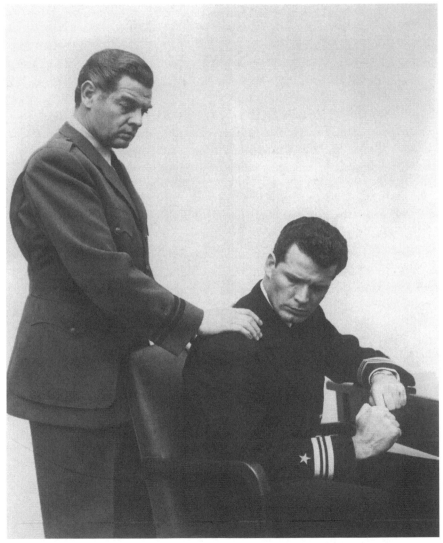

Garner with Robert Lowery in the stage version of *The Caine Mutiny* (1954). *Photofest*

was about to direct, Bare recalled the young man and thought he might be a good fit for the part of a Union Army lieutenant in the show's first episode. But Bare did not know the actor's name. After three days of searching, the director finally tracked down Bumgarner through mutual acquaintances and offered him the role. Filming his first television scene went fine, and the dailies were screened for the studio head, Jack Warner. After viewing the raw footage, Warner asked the show's producer, Bill Orr, who was the actor playing the army lieutenant. According to Bare, Orr replied, "A new kid by the name of Jim Bumgarner." Warner's reply? "Take the 'Bum' out and give him a seven-year contract."[1]

Both *Cheyenne* and Garner made their television debuts on September 20, 1955. On the episode "Mountain Fortress," Garner plays Lieutenant Brad Forsythe, a member of an army troop that is besieged twice—first by Indians and then by a band of outlaws staving off the same band of Indians. For the record, James Garner's first line of dialogue is "White men. How many?" which he delivers a bit woodenly. He fares better later in the episode, showing a little bit more of his charm while spending a tender moment with Ann Robinson, who plays his fiancée.

A few months later, in January 1956 to be exact, Garner made his second on-screen appearance, again in *Cheyenne*, again as an army lieutenant, and again providing one half of a romantic pairing. But this time, his role is much more prominent, receiving third billing behind star Clint Walker and fellow guest star Richard Denning. In a bit of unplanned symmetry, Garner featured in the final episode of the first season, on May 29, 1956, playing a character named Bret. He's no maverick, though, but instead a preacher headed to California to establish a church. But he's not your average preacher, either. He's not above fisticuffs to defend a lady's honor, nor does he shy away from guns when Indians attack the train full of settlers. And like the two previous episodes, romance is in the cards for his character.

Subsequent appearances in 1956 included first-season episodes of *Conflict*, an anthology program. In December of that year Garner appeared on another anthology program, *Zane Grey Theater*. In a curious bit of repeat casting, he played yet another lieutenant in yet another western-set drama. In February of 1957, the actor would make a fourth and final appearance on *Cheyenne* during the program's second season.

In the meantime, James Garner made his film debut in October 1956— and in Technicolor, no less—in the William Holden vehicle *Toward the Unknown*. Not a bad start! Garner's character—Lieutenant Colonel Joe Craven—is one of the men under the command of Holden's Major Bond. In this film, it's striking how much James Garner is like . . . James Garner. His

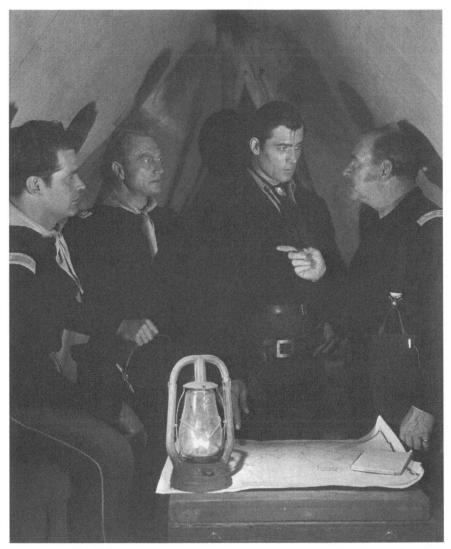

Garner's second television appearance during the first season on *Cheyenne* (1955). From left: Garner, Richard Denning, series star Clint Walker, and Ray Teal. *ABC / Photofest © ABC*

character is a likable and dedicated professional with a sense of humor. Ulti-mately, the role is fairly small but Garner makes his presence known. A week later, Garner's second feature arrived in theaters. Unfortunately, *The Girl He Left Behind* was somewhat of a demotion. Not only is his sophomore film in black and white, but the military figure he plays has a much lower rank—that of a private. And instead of supporting a star of Holden's caliber, Garner played second fiddle to another Warner Bros. contract player. Tab Hunter plays a peacetime draftee who stubbornly resists his stay in the army, making enemies of just about everyone, especially Garner's character. Garner doesn't even get to share the screen with the female lead, Natalie Wood, in a film that's not sure if it's a romantic drama or a military comedy. It's not a terrible film, but Wood is just about the only one who stands out, playing a young woman who is frustrated by her boyfriend's refusal to make a man of himself.

Shoot-Out at Medicine Bend, Garner's first western feature, though a fairly lighthearted one, starred Randolph Scott. Again, Garner appears in uniform—this time as an army sergeant—and again he finds romance among the drama. He also stands out among the cast in easily his most engaging performance to date.

The studio then gave Garner a role in his highest-profile film yet, playing a supporting role to Hollywood icon Marlon Brando in *Sayonara*. In this film about military men fraternizing with the locals while stationed in Japan, Garner wears a uniform, of course. But he doesn't do much more than that. Although he delivers a decent performance, the role offers little reward. Besides Brando's character, the central figure in the film is played

In his first film, *Toward the Unknown*, Garner shares the screen with Hollywood legend William Holden, along with Virginia Leith and Karen Steele. *Warner Bros. Pictures / Photofest © Warner Bros. Pictures*

by Red Buttons, who flaunts regulations by marrying a Japanese girl. A critical success, the film earned several Academy Award nominations (winning four) and was also recognized by the Golden Globes. For the latter, Garner was designated as Most Promising Newcomer (Male)—which he shared with future B-movie regular John Saxon and Patrick Wayne, son of Hollywood legend John. Small role or not, *Sayonara* put Garner in the spotlight.

And then came Bret.

By the fall of 1957 westerns were as ubiquitous on the small screen as they were in movie theaters. Of the top ten programs during the 1957–1958 season, half were westerns, including number one *Gunsmoke*. ABC's top western was *The Life and Legend of Wyatt Earp* starring Hugh O'Brian, a square jawed, six-foot actor. Also on ABC was *Cheyenne*, starring another square-jawed actor, six-foot-six Clint Walker.[2] *Cheyenne* was a property of Warner Bros. television, and no doubt both the studio and ABC network were eager to duplicate their successful westerns with another tall, good-looking face poking out beneath the brim of a cowboy hat. Garner was a "mere" six foot two when he was tapped for the role of part-time gambler and occasional con man Bret Maverick.

When *Maverick* debuted on Sunday night, September 22, 1957, there was nothing to suggest that it would distinguish itself from the other westerns on TV screens at the time—other than it was the only one on all three networks that aired Sunday evenings. ABC was the network with the most westerns in its lineup that season: *Cheyenne* and *Sugarfoot* alternated weekly episodes during the same time slot on Tuesday evenings, followed by *The Legend of Wyatt Earp*, which was then followed by *Broken Arrow*. On Wednesday, the network had *Tombstone Territory*, on Thursdays *Zorro*, and on Fridays *The Adventures of Jim Bowie* and *Colt .45*. NBC's two westerns, *Tales of Wells Fargo* and *Wagon Train*, aired on Monday and Wednesday nights, respectively. CBS clustered its westerns on the weekends, first with *Trackdown* and *Dick Powell's Zane Grey Theatre* on Fridays, and then *Have Gun—Will Travel* and *Gunsmoke* back-to-back on Saturday evenings.

Within the first three minutes of the first *Maverick* episode, "War of the Silver Kings," the show establishes the lead character, Bret, as a gambler, but also as a bit of a con man. However, his first deception is a clever little stunt that does nothing more than put himself in a favorable light and he doesn't cheat anyone out of money. Later in the episode, his character is shown to be a principled individual, intent on righting a few wrongs. However, he achieves this with further deception and by exploiting the human nature of the town millionaire, a greedy card cheat who isn't above hiring

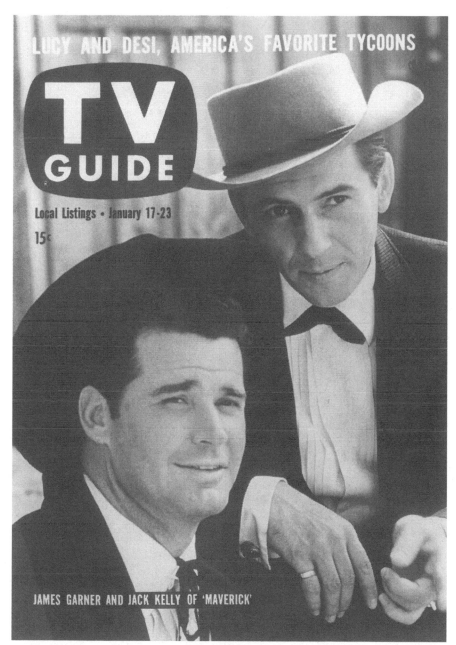

Garner's second appearance on the cover of *TV Guide*, with Jack Kelly: January 17, 1959 (Garner's first cover was in November 1957). *Photofest*

assassins. It's an entertaining debut for the series, establishing the show's lighthearted approach to the genre as well as showcasing the good-humored leading man. However, many of the early episodes provide standard western fare, and little of the playful humor for which both Bret and the series became known.

Several episodes into the first season, actor Jack Kelly joined Garner, playing Bret's brother Bart.[3] Because the show took longer than a week to produce, the studio alternated episodes between Bret and Bart, not unlike the ABC's decision to alternate episodes of *Cheyenne* and *Sugarfoot* during the 1956–1957 season. The eighth episode introduced Bart and was the first of several episodes in which both brothers were involved. However, when Kelly headlined the episode, Garner—as Bret—would often appear at the beginning to introduce the story (though Garner didn't receive screen credit).

ABC placed the one-hour program in the 7:30 p.m. time slot, with its first half hour in competition against CBS's well-established comedy *The Jack Benny Show* and NBC's new sitcom *Sally* starring Joan Caulfield and Marion Lorne. Both shows were followed at 8:00 by variety programs led by two powerhouses: *The Ed Sullivan Show* on CBS and *The Steve Allen Show* on NBC. Pretty soon it was clear that viewers who tuned into *Maverick* for its first thirty minutes were disinclined to miss the second half of the show.

Maverick was an immediate hit, stealing viewers away from three very high-profile programs, which took a hit in the ratings. While Benny, Ed, and Steve were able to weather the storm brought on by newcomer Bret, *Sally* was not so lucky. Though she arrived on the scene a week before Bret, the following autumn *Sally* was nowhere to be seen.

By its second season, *Maverick* was a top ten program in a western-heavy schedule. That season the show ranked behind *Gunsmoke*, *Wagon Train*, *Have Gun—Will Travel*, and *The Danny Thomas Show*, one of only three non-westerns in the top ten.[4] Garner was now a household name, with his face appearing on several magazines, including *TV Guide* and Hollywood gossip rags. The series was so popular that it inspired a comic book that ran for nineteen issues.

Contracted to Warner Bros.—as Garner learned—was a double-edged sword. On the plus side: a regular paycheck. And as paychecks went in the 1950s, $500 a week was more than good, especially compared to salaries earned by regular folk. Working for a studio also meant that bigger and brighter possibilities, such as feature film opportunities, loomed on the horizon. The downside? As a contract player, Garner was subject to the whims of the studio bosses, who could assign any projects they chose—even if those roles did not appeal to the actor. It also meant that big screen or small, the studio was not obligated to increase an actor's salary except when a contract was up for renewal. Garner wasn't the first Hollywood performer to bristle under Warner's terms. During the height of the studio system, Bette Davis and Olivia DeHavilland resisted the confines that Warner Bros. imposed on them, both arguing that they shouldn't be required to work in inferior films. Davis lost her case in 1936, but DeHavilland prevailed in 1943.

The third season was Garner's last. To take up some of the slack for Garner's disappearance, Roger Moore was brought on to play Bret and Bart's cousin Beauregarde (Beau)—a Texan who had emigrated to England and brought back with him a British accent.[5] The casting ploy worked reasonably enough, and the show survived two more seasons after Garner's departure—though it never returned to the top thirty.

In the end, Garner appeared in almost half of the show's 124 episodes, though some of his 60 appearances were little more than prologues in which Bret kicked off the narrative of a tale that featured his brother Bart.

Before Garner left *Maverick*, he was called to the big screen in two features, *Darby's Rangers* and *Up Periscope*, both military roles. But returning to feature films after his success on *Maverick* brought the actor to a new and welcome status—feature film leading man. Sort of. While Garner received top billing—as well as the title role of a real-life World War II hero in *Darby's Rangers*, the film plays out like an ensemble piece. Indeed, the various rangers are given as much if not more screen time than Garner's Darby, and their romantic—and occasionally comic—entanglements take up as much of the running time as their daring exploits. *Up Periscope*, in which the actor split top billing with Edmond O'Brien, was a step up from *Darby's Rangers*—in both quality and screen time—but Garner is not entirely center stage in this film either.

After Garner won his suit against Warner Bros., he was free to pursue more high-profile parts. In 1960, for the first time in his career, Garner's lead role had nothing to do with the military or the Wild West. *Cash McCall* was not only a contemporary film; it was a romantic comedy-drama set against a rare backdrop for film: the corporate world. Garner's character, McCall, is a shrewd businessman who finds himself romantically drawn to the daughter of one his takeover targets, played by Natalie Wood and Dean Jagger, respectively. It's a smart film that doesn't always take itself seriously.

Cash McCall started a string of features for Garner, and he would not return to the small screen in any meaningful way for more than a decade. After *McCall*, he filmed *The Children's Hour*, his first serious drama, in which he provides support for the two leading ladies, Audrey Hepburn and Shirley MacLaine. This underrated film was followed by the utterly forgettable

Boys' Night Out, a movie that reeks of 1960s comic contrivances, in which no one comes off looking good—least of all Kim Novak, whose suspect acting skills were matched by her "contributions" as a costumer for the film, for which she received screen credit.

After *Boys' Night Out*, Garner starred in a trio of films that secured his movie star status. Perhaps the most significant of these was the World War II prison drama-thriller *The Great Escape*. Based on a memoir by Australian Paul Brickhill, the film recounts a massive escape effort by prisoners of a German prisoner of war camp. The ensemble effort necessitated an ensemble cast, so that no one actor stood out among any of the others, though Steve McQueen, James Garner, and Richard Attenborough received top billing. For Garner, the role of Hendley the scrounger was all too familiar, since he had served a similar role while serving during the Korean War.

It was probably inevitable that Garner would be paired up with the screen's number one leading lady, Doris Day. *The Thrill of It All* was a satire of television, chiefly the commercial aspects, but also the dramatic offerings that the still fairly young medium proffered to its undiscerning viewers. Who else better to write such a film than Carl Reiner, a man who had achieved enormous success on television—both in front of the camera and behind it. Reiner won two Emmys for Sid Caesar's variety programs of the 1950s, and then created his most enduring achievement: *The Dick Van Dyke Show*. *The Thrill of It All* was a triumph for Reiner and his costars, whose on-screen chemistry led to another pairing, the less endearing *Move Over, Darling*.

Before frolicking again with Doris, however, Garner returned to financial shenanigans similar to those he perpetrated in *Cash McCall*, but the humor in *The Wheeler Dealers* is played much more broadly. His costar, Lee Remick, holds her own in a comedy that upends the world of modern art as much as it satirizes Wall Street. Garner and Remick make a good pair, and though some of the scenario is absurd, it's an enjoyable way to pass two hours.

And then came Charlie.

Garner reenlisted in another World War II film, his fourth overall and first since *The Great Escape*. As with the previous film, the role he plays in *The Americanization of Emily* relies on his scrounging skills—but for a different purpose: to appease the demands of the capricious admiral he serves. In *Emily*, Garner plays Charlie Madison, a resourceful "dog-robber" who is somehow able to secure a wealth of goods and perishables in England while its citizens struggle with their meager rations. Although it was not a commercial success, *Emily* still stands out as one of the greatest antiwar films ever produced. It was also Garner's favorite among his films, and for good reasons: it's an outstanding film propelled by a magnificent screenplay, which the cast—particularly Garner—serves with distinction.

In the psychological thriller *36 Hours*, Garner's Major Jefferson Pike is yet another character whose resourcefulness is put to the test. The movie was Garner's fifth and final World War II film—and second in a row specifically focused on D-day. It was also the first film in which the actor took on an additional role—that of producer. Aiming to take more control over his career, Garner established his own production company, and in honor of his partial Native American background, named the venture Cherokee Productions. Most of Garner's films that followed over the next decade would be produced by Cherokee, often in coordination with other studios.

Between 1965 and 1968, Garner made eight films—comedies, dramas, adventures, and westerns—of varying distinction, or lack thereof in some cases. Some, like *Mister Buddwing* and *Duel at Diablo*, offered intriguing premises or featured unusual casting choices, but didn't live up to their promise. Others, like *How Sweet It Is!* and *The Pink Jungle*, were just flat-out bad. During that four-year stretch, the most successful film was John Frankenheimer's *Grand Prix*. Often a thrilling showcase of elite racing, the film features an international cast of acting legends as well as a sprinkling of real-life drivers. At a running time of nearly three hours, though, the film drags on longer than it should.

Garner ended the decade with a pair of films that in some ways captured the spirit of his two most beloved shows: *Support Your Local Sheriff!* is a comic western reminiscent of *Maverick*, and *Marlowe* is a neo-noir featuring an acerbic private eye, not too far removed from Jim Rockford. Despite somewhat tepid reviews both films received from critics at the time, *Support Your Local Sheriff!* and *Marlowe* firmly belong among James Garner's best features. *Sheriff!* is often cited as a favorite among the actor's fans, while *Marlowe*, in particular, deserves revisiting—perhaps not by Raymond Chandler or noir purists, but certainly for fans of Garner who haven't seen the film.

After *Marlowe*, Garner went west for three consecutive films, beginning with *A Man Called Sledge*. As the actor professed on more than one occasion, Henry Fonda was something of a role model, ever since Garner was cast in the stage version of *The Caine Mutiny*. Whether in comedies, dramas, or other genres, Fonda often played the wholesome, likeable lead. But in 1968, he was lured by spaghetti western maestro Sergio Leone to play a despicable villain in the film *Once Upon a Time in the West*—an acting choice that may have inspired Garner to take on the role of *A Man Called Sledge*, a criminal seeking gold treasure. Unfortunately, *Sledge*'s director, actor Vic Morrow, was neither Italian nor experienced enough behind the camera to produce an effective film.

Support Your Local Gunfighter followed. In addition to Garner, the movie features many cast members and the same director of *Support Your Local Sheriff!* However, *Gunfighter* is not a sequel, and perhaps because of this, the film is not as entertaining as *Sheriff!* (and doesn't deserve an exclamation point, either).

The third western in a row for Garner was not only the most offbeat western for the actor but one of the most unusual westerns ever produced. *Skin Game* centers on two men, one white and one black, traveling the Kansas and Missouri territories conning slave traders of their money. The scheme is fairly simple: Garner's character, Quincy, poses as a trader and "sells" a black man (played by Louis Gossett Jr.) to the highest bidder. Soon after money has passed hands, the slave, Jason, escapes. But in reality, Jason is a free black man in equal partnership with Quincy. The best friends share the proceeds of their sales evenly. It's an unusual arrangement to say the least, and certainly an unconventional premise for a Hollywood film. It's unlikely such a plot would be acceptable now, and given the film's sometimes uneasy balance between comedy and drama, it must have been a risky venture. But the film works, in no small part because of the camaraderie between Garner and Gossett.

In the fall of 1971, Garner's next venture brought a new wrinkle to the western genre, when he returned to television to star in *Nichols*. Set not quite so distant in the past as most westerns, *Nichols* takes place in 1914, where the landscape that is usually trod by horses is slowly giving way to cars and motorcycles. When the series debuted on September 16, 1971, Garner had good reason to think the show would be successful. Created by Frank Pierson, whose screenplays for *Cat Ballou* and *Cool Hand Luke* had been nominated for Academy Awards,[6] *Nichols* took a wry approach that sprinkled lighthearted humor among the serious moments. Despite the show's star and the creator's pedigree, the program lasted just one season, and its final episode (which featured a plot twist in anticipation of a second season) aired in May of 1972.

After the cancellation of *Nichols*, Garner returned to features, first as a small-town police chief in California, *They Only Kill Their Masters*, followed by a pair of family-friendly films for Disney. Both *One Little Indian* and *The Castaway Cowboy* costarred Vera Miles, and both were box office failures.

And then came Jim.

Jim Rockford was an ex-convict. Wrongfully convicted of a crime, he served a five-year sentence before getting pardoned. In an effort to steer as far clear of the police as he can, Rockford specializes in cold cases, jobs that he hopes won't involve the authorities.

The show began with a pilot, "Backlash of the Hunter," that aired in March of 1974, but the series officially debuted Friday, September 13, 1974, on NBC, almost exactly seventeen years after the debut of *Maverick*. The show premiered in the Friday 9:00 p.m. time slot and remained there more or less for its entire six seasons.[7] In its first season, the show was the highest ranked debut for a drama, and for the 1974–1975 season, it was ranked number twelve overall and the third highest drama in the country (behind two CBS programs: *The Waltons* at number eight and *Hawaii Five-0* at number ten).[8]

Each episode begins with footage of Rockford's desk, on which lays an unfinished hand of solitaire, a picture of Rockford's father, Rocky, and a black phone (555-2368).[9] The phone rings and Rockford's answering machine picks up, playing a familiar message: "This is Jim Rockford. At the tone, leave your name and message. I'll get back to you." In a television first, the opening sequence was altered in each episode[10] as a variety of callers left messages, some funny, some threatening, and not a few that made it clear Rockford was a man of often meager means.

Along with Noah Beery Jr. as Rocky, the show's other regular was Joe Santos as Rockford's friend on the police force, detective (then ultimately lieutenant) Dennis Becker. Throughout the show's run, a few other characters appeared from time to time, most frequently Stuart Margolin as Jim's fellow ex-convict and perpetual con man Angel Martin, and Gretchen Corbett as Beth Davenport, Jim's lawyer friend, who sometimes was called upon to bail him out of jail or defend him in court. Becker's superior at the police department, Lieutenant Chapman (James Luisi), made life difficult for Rockford, which sometimes required Becker to intervene on Jim's behalf—often against his better judgment. The minor and sporadic role of Captain McEnroe was played by Garner's older brother Jack.

The Rockford Files ended abruptly, halfway through the show's sixth season, when Garner had to call it quits. The show had taken a physical toll on its star, who played in nearly every scene, which would have worn out most actors. But many of those scenes required the actor to engage in physically challenging sequences, from fistfights to chases. The actor endured several operations on his knees and by the series' end, he was also suffering from an ulcer—one that dealt the show its final blow. The final season ran only twelve episodes, slightly more than half the usual run.[11]

Midway through the run *of The Rockford Files*, Garner joined the league of actors-turned-spokespersons, when he began filming television commercials.

Once more—intentionally or not—he followed the lead of his role model Henry Fonda, who had joined the spokesperson brigade in the early 1970s. And like Fonda, who shilled for GAF, a film processing company at the time, Garner pitched for camera and film giant Polaroid. Although the first few commercials featured only Garner, the campaign really took off when actress Mariette Hartley joined the promos. Their unmistakable chemistry proved so successful that the pair appeared in more than two hundred different commercials for the camera brand. In some ways, the ads were too successful, since many viewers assumed that Garner and Hartley were a real-life couple, which forced Hartley to sometimes don a T-shirt that read "I am not Mrs. James Garner."

In addition to his Polaroid work, Garner starred in a number of commercials for Mazda, including one that features his older brother Jack and another with his daughter Gigi. Garner also provided voice-over narration for other companies, including Chevrolet, picking up the stint for the company's "Like a Rock" campaign after the death of his *Great Escape* costar James Coburn in 2002.

After *The Rockford Files* concluded its six-season run, Garner made two fairly forgettable films, both with Lauren Bacall. The first, *HealtH*, was an ensemble comedy directed and cowritten by American iconoclast Robert Altman. Since the release of *M°A°S°H* in 1970, Altman produced some of the most idiosyncratic films of the decade, to varying degrees of success. Unfortunately for Garner—as well as for Carol Burnett, Bacall, and Glenda Jackson, who were all Altman neophytes sharing the screen with the director's regulars Paul Dooley and Henry Gibson—the film was not a success. Despite game performances from Garner and company, the film fell flat, both critically and commercially—a shame since the role of Harry Wolff seemed a good fit for the actor. Bacall and Garner followed this flop with the manipulative thriller *The Fan*—about a Broadway actress who is stalked by a fanatic. In the wake of slasher movies like *Halloween, Friday the 13th*, and, yes, even *Dressed to Kill*, viewers were probably terrified that something particularly gruesome would befall one of the two stars, an on-screen decimation that would reduce the film to exploitation levels. It seemed very likely such a scene would happen to Garner, since his character seems almost destined for the ax. Without giving too much away to anyone who might find pleasure in watching this weak thriller, viewers are spared from such gratuitous violence—though not every actor who appears in the film is spared.

After these two disappointments, Garner returned to series television in the role that made him famous. *Bret Maverick* debuted in December of 1981 but sadly did not last into the following fall season. In fact, the series didn't even complete the usual full season run, finishing with just eighteen episodes. But during that time, several actors from *The Rockford Files* reunited with Garner, and even Jack Kelly made an appearance as Bart Maverick in the final episode.

And then came George.

With nearly three dozen films and two iconic series behind him, the actor ventured into somewhat uncharted territory. Whether James Garner acknowledged it or not, there were three pivotal years in his career: 1957, the year *Maverick* debuted and made him a star; 1974, the year *The Rockford Files* premiered; and 1982, the release of Garner's second made-for-television movie.[12] Though *The Long Summer of George Adams* is not the best movie Garner made for the small screen, it anticipated a string of television films that allowed the actor to embrace more nuanced roles in high-caliber productions. A new golden age for the medium was dawning, heralded by the arrival of *Hill Street Blues* in 1981, and followed the next year by two of the greatest programs in television history (both set in Boston)—the comedy *Cheers* and the hospital drama *St. Elsewhere*. Television movies were also growing up, and Garner played no small role in the development of quality specials in that era.

For Garner, George Adams established a new template: characters imbued with flaws and weaknesses that were on a different level than any previous roles he had portrayed, on large screen or small. These were characters who could stumble, who could fail, who could lose their moral compass, and yes, could even die. Maverick and Rockford were the roles that fans will remember best of their beloved *star* James Garner. For the *actor* James Garner, the complex, challenging roles he played in television movies, miniseries, and films beginning in the 1980s are those for which he should be appreciated as well. *The Long Summer of George Adams* represented the beginning of this distinguished new phase in the actor's career.

Though *The Long Summer of George Adams* marked a turning point for Garner, he was by no means finished with feature films. In fact, almost two months to the day after his first made-for-television film aired, the actor appeared on the big screen in his first—and only—musical, albeit a nontraditional one. *Victor/Victoria* was a commercial and critical triumph that paired Garner with his *Americanization of Emily* costar Julie Andrews. Set in 1930s Paris, the gender-bending film features Andrews in double drag as a woman posing as a man who dresses up as women for her nightclub act. Garner shines as a Chicago mobster who falls for Andrews's character—which also forces him to question his sexuality—but in a comic manner that provides much of the film's humor.

After filming the regrettable *Tank*, Garner appeared in his second made-for-television movie, *Heartsounds*, offering another impressive performance. Garner and costar Mary Tyler Moore portray real-life couple Harold and Martha Lear, who cope with Harold's mortality after he suffers a massive heart attack. The film received Emmy nominations for both the leads as well as one for Outstanding Drama/Comedy Special of the year.

Two more television projects followed *Heartsounds*, both adaptations of best-selling novels: First came the HBO production of Joseph Wambaugh's *The Glitter Dome*, featuring cringeworthy dialogue, much of it sprinkled with not ready for network television language. This was followed by Garner's first miniseries, the small-screen rendering of James Michener's epic novel *Space*.

And then came Murphy.

Garner had played romantic leads before, but at the age of fifty-seven, he may have assumed—and perhaps reasonably—that such roles were behind him. *Victor/Victoria* was a mere three years earlier, but Julie Andrews, Garner's leading lady, was well into her forties when filming that musical began. There was no mistaking *Murphy's Romance* for what it was—a May–December pairing of Garner and his costar, Sally Field, nineteen years his junior. Despite the age difference, the two exhibited the kind of magnetism such a film needed. Garner, always a charismatic performer, displayed all of his charms in the film, and even Field was not immune to his gravitational pull. The actress would later wistfully recall that of all her leading men, Garner was the best kisser.

Murphy's Romance was followed by another triumph, perhaps the crowning achievement of Garner's television movie career, and in more ways than one. In *Promise*, the actor plays a carefree man who must face responsibility late in life—taking care of his schizophrenic brother after their mother dies. James Woods plays the younger sibling who turns Garner's life upside down as they grapple with the realities of mental illness. Both actors deliver powerful performances, which earned them Emmy and Golden Globe nominations for Lead Actor. Woods took home the prize both times, but Garner was not left empty-handed. As a producer of the film, he received an Emmy for Outstanding Drama/Comedy Special, and the program also won the Golden Globe for Best Miniseries or Motion Picture Made for Television.

It was back to the big screen next and the opportunity to revisit a character he had played twenty years before, as well as another chance to work with his *Victor/Victoria* director Blake Edwards. Unfortunately for all involved, *Sunset*'s intriguing premise of situating the western lawman Wyatt Earp in silent-era Hollywood fell flat.

The actor rebounded with two highly acclaimed television movies, both for Hallmark Hall of Fame. In *My Name Is Bill W.*, Garner reunited with his *Promise* costar James Woods to portray the two men who founded Alcoholics Anonymous, William Wilson and Robert Holbrook Smith ("Dr. Bob"). The film's primary focus is on Wilson, which relegates Garner to a supporting—but pivotal—role. As with *Promise*, the program received an Emmy nomination for Outstanding Drama/Comedy Special, and the two actors were nominated as well. And once again, Woods walked away with the Emmy statue.

The following year, 1990, Garner and Hallmark collaborated on their third production, *Decoration Day*. In addition to the usual sterling performance by Garner, the film featured a fine supporting cast, including Judith Ivey, Bill Cobbs, Laurence Fishburne, and the incomparable Ruby Dee. Both Garner and the film received Golden Globe awards, while Dee was awarded the program's sole Emmy.

Three disappointments followed, the short-lived series *Man of the People*, in which Garner plays his third politician; an Eddie Murphy comedy called *The Distinguished Gentleman* in which Garner—again as a politician—provides what amounts to little more than a cameo; and then a supporting role in an allegedly true story of alien abduction, *Fire in the Sky* (although Garner is quite good as a jaded investigator).

The trio of failures was followed by a trio of successes, two of which earned Garner some of the best notices of his career and a third that became his most commercially successful film.

In his first film for HBO since *The Glitter Dome* nearly ten years before, Garner employed his charming persona to play real-life scoundrel F. Ross Johnson, the subject of the *New York Times* best seller, *Barbarians at the Gate*. Adapted for the small screen by one of Hollywood's finest scribes, Larry Gelbart (*M°A°S°H*, *Tootsie*), *Barbarians* recounts how Johnson waged a buyout war for Nabisco in the early 1980s. Garner sunk his teeth into the black comedy, which highlighted the absurd greed of all involved. His performance earned the actor yet another Emmy nomination, and he also received his second Golden Globe for Best Actor.

Garner followed *Barbarians* with his fourth and final Hallmark Hall of Fame special, an adaptation of Anne Tyler's Pulitzer Prize–winning novel *Breathing Lessons*. The quiet film follows a Baltimore couple during a weekend in their lives. Playing Garner's spouse was Joanne Woodward, the Oscar-winning actress of *The Three Faces of Eve* and wife of Garner's longtime friend Paul Newman. Yet again, Emmy and Golden Globe nominations followed for Garner—as they did for his costar Woodward, who won the Globe as well as a Screen Actors Guild award.

And then came Bret Maverick. Again.

But this Maverick looked different, younger. Or did he? While the film was a vehicle for superstar Mel Gibson, it would have been criminal to not secure Garner for a significant role—although that almost wasn't the case. The part of Marshal Zane Cooper was originally offered to Paul Newman, who no doubt would have offered a fine performance—but it just would have been wrong for Garner not to play that part. Released in the summer of 1994, *Maverick* debuted at number one at the box office and ultimately grossed more than $101 million.

And then came Jim Rockford. Again.

Following the triumph of *Maverick*, Garner revived his other iconic role in a series of television movies. On November 27, 1994, nearly fifteen years after the last episode of *The Rockford Files* was broadcast, Jim Rockford returned. In a clear indication that the networks were drawing heavily on nostalgia to attract viewers, the *Rockford* redux wasn't the first, the second, or even the *third*—revival of a former show that month. Three weeks earlier, "*Cagney and Lacey*: The Return" had been broadcast, followed by a Perry Mason mystery a few days later, then a *MacGyver* movie on November 24 (and yet another revival, "*Spenser*: The Judas Goat" aired on December 1).

The first of the *Rockford* movies, *I Still Love L.A.*, featured a few cast members from the original series, notably Joe Santos as Jim's friend on the police force, Lieutenant Dennis Becker, and Stuart Margolin as perpetual con man Angel Martin, as well as Garner's older brother Jack as Captain McEnroe. One notable absence was Noah Beery Jr., who had played Rockford's father, Rocky. Beery was too ill to appear in the revival, having undergone brain surgery in September of 1994. Indeed, he would pass away on November 1st, three weeks before the first revival film aired. Other guest actors from the original series would reprise their roles in one or more of the eight television films, including Gretchen Corbett who played lawyer Beth Davenport, James Luisi (Captain Chapman), Tom Atkins (Commander Diehl), Pat Finley (Becker's wife, Peggy), Kathryn Harrold (Megan Dougherty), and Rita Moreno (Rita Kapkovic).

Besides the cast, many behind-the-scenes figures associated with the show also returned: Stephen J. Cannell, who cocreated the series with Roy Huggins and wrote three dozen of the episodes, also wrote two of the movies and collaborated on the story of the final film, *If It Bleeds . . . It Leads*. Juanita Bartlett, a writer and producer for the series, wrote three of the films and worked with Cannell on the final film. The remaining two films were written by former *Rockford Files* writer and producer David Chase, who would later create the critically acclaimed series *The Sopranos*.

While Garner assumed his Rockford persona was a welcome sight, the films were not very successful at capturing the flavor of the series, though some came closer to others. Of them, the second film, *A Blessing in Disguise*, is perhaps the most disappointing, despite earning Garner a Screen Actor's Guild nomination. On April 20, 1999, nearly twenty-five years after Jim Rockford made his first appearance—and four and a half years since the first television movie aired—Garner bid adieu to his most iconic role.

Between the second and third *Rockford Files* revivals, Garner returned to the genre that served him so well in his career, the western. However, unlike western film legends like John Wayne, Garner's vehicles featured a much lighter touch, from the thoroughly enjoyable *Support Your Local Sheriff!* to the big-screen version of *Maverick*. Dramatic westerns such as *Duel at Diablo* (1966), *Hour of the Gun* (1967), and *A Man Called Sledge* (1970) did not suit the actor nearly as well as the comic variety. *Sledge* may have dampened Garner's desire to play it straight in a western so thoroughly that he didn't star in another one for nearly three decades. When Garner did return, it was in the 1995 miniseries *Streets of Laredo*, the sequel to the critically acclaimed miniseries *Lonesome Dove*. And though the three-night adaptation of the Larry McMurtry novel was nothing to be ashamed of, it came far short of the Robert Duvall–Tommy Lee Jones original. And Garner's portrayal of Woodrow Call, the role that Tommy Lee Jones originated, evidenced a curious decision on Garner's part—to mimic Jones's speech patterns throughout. For an actor like Garner who already had a signature style, it was an unusual—and somewhat distracting—choice.

A more entertaining venture for Garner came the following year when he was paired with screen legend Jack Lemmon. In *My Fellow Americans*, the two played rival ex-presidents on the run for their lives. Though slim on plot, the film boasts more than a few laughs thanks to the amusing exchanges between the two leads—sparring like old pros and proving that Garner's on-screen rapport was not limited to his leading ladies.

Between his first *Rockford Files* movie in 1994 and the last in 1999, Garner also appeared in two more television movies—*Dead Silence* for HBO and *Legalese* for TNT, the latter earning him a Screen Actor's Guild award nomination—and another feature film, *Twilight*. Despite a cast of Oscar heavyweights—Paul Newman, Susan Sarandon, Gene Hackman—as well as a three-time Oscar-winning writer-director Robert Benton (*Kramer vs. Kramer*, *Places in the Heart*) at the helm and a screenplay by Richard Russo (a future Pulitzer Prize winner for *Empire Falls*), the film was not a success. It's a shame because the film, while operating on low energy, is still an intriguing neo-noir.

Garner's final film of the century (or 1990s at least) was a television movie that reunited him with beloved costar Julie Andrews. *One Special Night*, which aired on November 29, 1999, was the story of two individuals experiencing similarly sad transitions: Andrews played a doctor whose husband has just recently died, while Garner was contending with his ill wife's deteriorating condition. Caught unexpectedly in a snowstorm, the two spend the night in an abandoned farmhouse, at first bickering with each other, but then finding a common ground that binds them. Though the film displayed Hallmark-ish qualities, they were of the Hallmark Channel kind—treacly and obvious—rather than the prestige of the specials *Promise* and *Decoration Day*. Nonetheless, the opportunity to see the two actors with such good chemistry work together for a final time was a welcome one.

In the new century, Garner appeared in only four features, beginning with a reunion of sorts with Clint Eastwood, fellow Warner Bros. contract player–turned–screen legend and director. Despite the presence of the two pals, along with Tommy Lee Jones, Donald Sutherland, and an exceptional cast of supporting actors, *Space Cowboys* is noteworthy only for seeing the four leads naked from behind. With an average age of sixty-five years among them, perhaps the movie should have been rated R.

This box office failure was followed by a trio of manipulative melodramas that neither blemished nor enhanced Garner's career, with maybe the exception of a romantic drama that still makes some viewers swoon.

First came the 2002 adaptation of the *New York Times* best-selling novel *Divine Secrets of the Ya-Ya Sisterhood* by Rebecca Wells. Unfortunately, the film included at least two too many actresses from across the pond slipping into unconvincing southern accents. But miscasting the usually stellar Maggie Smith and Fionnula Flanagan is just one of problems with the film. On the one hand, Garner was given so little decent material to work with, the role could have—and probably *should have*—gone to a lesser-known name. On the other hand, allowing the otherwise great Ellen Burstyn to go so over the top in her performance more or less sinks the film. Overall, the only actress who emerged somewhat unscathed was Ashley Judd, who plays Burstyn's younger self—though even she has to suffer in some ridiculously haphazard flashbacks.

Two years later, Garner appeared in yet another big-screen adaptation of a best-selling novel set in the south, Nicholas Sparks's *The Notebook*. Like *Ya-Ya*, this film features several flashbacks, but the viewer is kept in suspense until the very end, not knowing which actor plays the younger version of the elderly Duke, as portrayed by Garner: is it James Marsden, who at least somewhat physically resembles Garner, or is it Ryan Gosling, who retains his contemporary locks despite the 1940s setting?

Unfortunately, the much better written book, *Divine Secrets*, became a lousier film, while the weaker novel, *The Notebook*, was adapted into a marginally better film—although there are many who swear by both films, rather than swearing at them.

Aside from the features, Garner kept busy in the new century with several television projects, including a four-episode stint on *Chicago Hope*; a short-lived animated series for NBC called *God, the Devil, and Bob* (Garner played God in an apparently blasphemous show); a one-hour drama, *First Monday*, that fared no better; a TV movie, *The Last Debate*; and mini-series *Roughing It*. In the latter production, Garner plays Mark Twain who delivers a commencement speech for his daughter's high school graduation. He's quite good, of course, but only appears intermittently as the film brings to life recollections of his youth.

In 2003, Garner was invited to join the cast of a comedy series, which offered the actor a new challenge: performing live in front of a studio audience. *8 Simple Rules*, which had originally been called *8 Simple Rules for Dating My Teenage Daughter*, needed to be retooled after the series star, John Ritter, died suddenly of a heart condition at the age of fifty-four. In order to fill his void, Garner and comedian David Spade were brought on board a few episodes into its second season. Garner joined the series first, as the father of Cate, Katey Sagal's character, and several weeks later, Spade was added to the cast as Cate's nephew. Although Garner had made sporadic appearances on talk shows and even occasionally appeared in a comic skit or two for a live audience, *8 Simple Rules* was something else altogether. The reworked series was only modestly successful, ultimately getting canceled at the end of the third season. In all, Garner appeared in forty-five episodes.

Fifty years after he appeared in his first feature, *Toward the Unknown*, James Garner would film his last. If the title of the first feature Garner made suggested an apt portent for the actor's burgeoning career, then his final film's title—*The Ultimate Gift*—seems wholly fitting to his fans: through forty-plus features, twenty made-for-television movies, and hundreds of television episodes, the actor had gifted audiences with performances that charmed millions of viewers. It's a shame that the film itself couldn't live up to its title. With its contrived plot, maudlin story line, continuity lapses, and sentimentality, *The Ultimate Gift* comes across as the manipulative tearjerker it no doubt aspired to be. However, the film is not a complete wash. The production allowed Garner and Bill Cobbs, his *Decoration Day* costar, to reunite—however briefly—and despite the obvious and unimaginative screenplay, the performances are serviceable. The acting highlights do not come from the veterans, however, but by nine-year-old Abigail Breslin as a young girl dying of leukemia. That same year Breslin would give an unforgettable performance in *Little Miss Sunshine*, for which she received an Oscar nomination—and both films demonstrate that her talent was genuine. But is her performance and the knowledge that this was Garner's swan song enough motivation to watch the film? Probably not.

While *The Ultimate Gift* may have been Garner's last live-action role of note,[13] it was not his last work overall. During his final decade of work, Garner lent his voice to half a dozen projects, not only *God, the Devil, and Bob* in 2000, but to animated features and shorts, including *Atlantis: The Lost Empire* (with Michael J. Fox and Leonard Nimoy) in 2001.

James Garner's final acting gig was voicing a character for *The Return of Black Adam*, an animated short about the origin of superhero Captain Marvel. Garner portrays an ancient mystic whose power transforms young Billy Batson into the adult superhero.

So, the man who started his professional acting career as a character seen but not heard—as a part of a military tribunal in *The Caine Mutiny*—ended his career in a role in which he can be heard, but not seen.

• • •

Garner once stated that he didn't make "futuristic" or horror movies. The statement was made after he had been in the motion picture business for twenty-five years and still had another twenty-five more or so to go, so it would be understandable if the actor eventually made some choices that would invalidate such a remark. However, other than voice work for a very few animated fantasy and science fiction films at the tail end of his career, Garner remained true to his declaration. And he certainly never made any horror films, which is often the last resort for actors whose careers are on the wane.

The other option many actors consider after they no longer contend for leading man roles is to play villains. If he were offered such parts, Garner might have declined because he knew that his performances were rooted in one thing most villains lack: humanity. He might also have passed on such roles because he understood that most actors who take on such parts are inclined to hammish eccentricities, which was not Garner's style. Viewers gravitated to Garner for his likeability and charm, so for the sake of his fans, it was better to see the actor participate in calculated sentimental dramas than to play an over-the-top part in a cringe-inducing thriller. To be sure, the actor sometimes intentionally cashed in on his charm to play less-than-respectable characters—in *Barbarians at the Gate* and *Legalese*, for example—but subverting his charisma was essential to the enjoyment of those films. Otherwise, the actor rarely played the bad guy in the twilight of his career, a testament not only to the innate decency of his characters but to the man himself.

In November of 2010, Garner's final work, *The Return of Black Adam*, was released on DVD, fifty-five years after the actor's television debut in September of 1955. Over that half century plus of work, the actor filmed forty-six features, twenty-one made-for-television movies, and three miniseries, and appeared in more than 300 television episodes, including 45 of 8 *Simple Rules*, 52 of the original *Maverick*, and 120 (plus the pilot) of *The Rockford Files*.

Such numbers speak to his prolific output. Other numbers speak to the quality of his work: three Golden Globe awards out of twelve nominations, two Emmys from fifteen nominations, four nominations from the Screen Actors Guild, and a nomination from the Academy of Motion Picture Arts and Sciences. Perhaps the most important acknowledgment that came from his peers was the lifetime achievement award he received from the Screen Actors Guild in 2004.

The recipe for Garner's initial success is not particularly complicated: he was a handsome man who could also act, and for the most part, the roles he undertook possessed a charming, sometimes disarming demeanor that drew immediate attention to him. His longevity in the business—nearly six decades—may not be terribly difficult to fathom either: he never lost the qualities that endeared him to fans nor the instinct to take on roles that both fortified and enhanced his reputation. Even as he aged and his looks were inevitably compromised by time, he retained another, imperceptible but vital characteristic: integrity. His fellow actors and colleagues in the film and television industries often testified to this. In Hollywood, he was an actor who was admired for his skills in front of the camera, but also behind the scenes, and in the way that he comported himself, on set and off.

James Garner passed away on July 19, 2014, four months after his eighty-sixth birthday. Upon his death, tributes to the actor poured in from everywhere. Newspapers summed up his career with testimonials from peers, fans, and critics—both as a performer and as a decent human being. Sally

James Garner as Jim Rockford. *NBC / Photofest* © *NBC*

Field, his *Murphy's Romance* costar, stated, "There are few people on this planet I have adored as much as Jimmy Garner. I cherish every moment I spent with him and relive them over and over in my head. He was a diamond."[14] In the social media rush of tweets declarations came from both those who worked with him and those who emulated him.

But beyond the accolades and tributes, there remains the most important component of his legacy, the work he left behind. One could admire him for *Maverick*. Or for *The Rockford Files*. Or one could focus on the memorable performances in some truly great films like *The Great Escape* or *The Americanization of Emily*. Or one could just consider the lesser-known gems or his underappreciated performances: *The Children's Hour*, *Marlowe*, and *Skin Game*, to name a few. Or one could simply appreciate the television films he made in the 1980s and '90s—from *Heartsounds* to *Breathing Lessons*—that for some viewers are just as vital as anything else in his distinguished career.

Fortunately, there's no need to isolate any of these works, since much of the actor's output is readily available to view and savor, on DVD and streaming choices. While many of these can stand alone as a proof to his skills, their collective whole stands as a testament to the endearing and enduring legacy of James Garner.

PART I

FILMS AND MADE-FOR-TELEVISION MOVIES

❶

SHOOT-OUT AT MEDICINE BEND

(1957)

★ ★ ½

Director: Richard L. Bare
Screenplay: John Tucker Battle, D. D. Beauchamp
Producer: Richard Whorf. *Director of Photography:* Carl Guthrie. *Music:*
    Roy Webb. *Editor:* Clarence Kolster. *Art Director:* Stanley Fleischer.
    Set Decorator: Ben Bone. *Costume Designer:* Marjorie Best
Cast: Randolph Scott (Captain Devlin), James Craig (Ep Clark), Angie
    Dickinson (Priscilla King), Dani Crayne (Nell Garrison), James Garner
    (Sergeant John Maitland), Gordon James (Private Will Clegg)
Studio: Warner Bros.
Release Date: May 4, 1957
Specs: 87 minutes; black and white
Availability: DVD (Warner Archive Collection)

SUMMARY

Three army men—a captain, a major, and a private—pose as members of
a Quaker community after their uniforms are stolen. They plot retaliation
against an unscrupulous businessman whose sale of faulty firearms has led
to several deaths.

BACKGROUND

In the fall of 1956, James Garner made his feature film debut in *Toward the Unknown*, which was soon followed by *The Girl He Left Behind*. In both films, his screen time was fairly limited, but he supplemented these with more work on the small screen. Before the release of his third feature, the actor appeared in a handful of television episodes, which included two anthology series—*Conflict* (three episodes) and *Zane Grey Theatre* (one episode)—along with a final appearance on the western *Cheyenne*. In May of 1957 Garner was assigned his most prominent movie role yet, that of Sergeant John Maitland, in *Shoot-Out at Medicine Bend*. Notably, it was also his first western feature.

The film reunited Garner with director Richard Bare, who was instrumental in bringing Garner in front of the camera, when he suggested the young actor for a role on *Cheyenne*'s first episode. An admittedly no-frills director, Bare had begun his directing career in 1942 overseeing a series of comic shorts ("So You Want to Be . . ." with fictional host Joe McDoakes) that ran for more than a decade. These led to several episodes of television westerns, including *Maverick*. In the mid-1960s, Bare settled into a steady job as director of *Green Acres*, a rural comedy starring Eddie Albert and Eva Gabor, helming all but 4 of the program's 170 episodes.

Randolph Scott, the film's star, had been a veteran of Hollywood for nearly thirty years before filming *Shoot-Out*. At the beginning of his career, Scott had appeared in a variety of film genres, until the Virginia native settled into westerns, which he starred in almost exclusively from the late 1940s. After *Shoot-Out*, he appeared in five more films—all westerns—before retiring. Many believe Scott's final film, *Ride the High Country*, directed by Sam Peckinpah, to be the finest of his career.

Hired for the lead female roles were Dani Crayne and Angie Dickinson. Though both actresses were younger than Garner, they had as many—if not more—credits to their résumés, particularly Dickinson, by the time *Shoot-Out* was filmed. Crayne had even appeared with Garner before, in an episode of the anthology series *Conflict* ("The People against McQuade"). Gordon Jones was another veteran of westerns, having starred in several B films during the 1930s before taking on the leading role of *The Green Hornet* in a 1940s serial.

The film's suave villain was played by James Craig, who had a strong resemblance to screen legend Clark Gable. Though Craig never attained the stardom achieved by the "King of Hollywood,"[1] he did provide able support

Army men posing as Quakers in a lighthearted western with Garner, Gordon Jones (center), and Randolph Scott. *Warner Bros. Pictures / Photofest © Warner Bros. Pictures*

in a number of memorable films of the 1940s, including *Kitty Foyle* with Ginger Rogers, *The Devil and Daniel Webster* (a.k.a. *All That Money Can Buy*) with Walter Huston, *The Human Comedy* with Mickey Rooney, and *Our Vines Have Tender Grapes* with Edward G. Robinson and Margaret O'Brien.

Under contract to Warners, Garner was obligated to appear in his third film for the studio, at the rate of $500 a week. At the time, he probably didn't mind. The film would give him more screen time, and the exposure would breed more familiarity with audiences. Though Garner would eventually bristle under such terms—and eventually sue the studio—the experience would benefit him in the short run.

RECEPTION

While most of the major newspapers and magazines declined to review the film, regional papers around the country offered brief assessments. Referencing the film's star, *The Bridgeport Telegram* said the film, "offers outdoor adventure and action in the Scott tradition."[2]

COMMENTARY

When production began on *Shoot-Out at Medicine Bend* in November 1956, it was under the title "Marshal of Independence." Oddly, the film's scenario does not reflect either title accurately, but such was—and still is—how Hollywood often operated. Apt title or not, as a film with no other motive than to entertain, *Shoot-Out* succeeds. One of the reasons this film moves along briskly is the relatively short running time of eighty-seven minutes. In truth, the film plays like an extended episode of a television series, but that does not make it any less enjoyable. This is a western with a moral center, a charming but deadly bad guy, and a righteous lead determined to put an end to the villain's heinous activities.

Yes, Randolph Scott is the star. But Garner, in his first significant supporting role, is a star *in the making*. While the film has the trappings of standard western fare, it also features a playful sense of humor, allowing Garner to shine in a blend of the two genres—a precursor of things to come. It's not quite *Maverick*, of course, but nonetheless, *Shoot-Out* offers more than the typical Hollywood western. Garner does not account for all of the humor, however; character actor Gordon James and even leading man Scott engage in enough mirthful behavior to produce genuine laughs during the film, in between the action and romance, of course. For western purists, perhaps, the film is not gritty enough. For the rest of us, we can enjoy it as a not-quite-yet-in-his-prime Garner apprenticeship.

And though Garner's role in *Shoot-Out* was not a leading role, it did offer the actor significant screen time. The credits alone demonstrate Garner's rising status. From seventh billing in *Toward the Unknown* and eighth in *The Girl He Left Behind*, Garner was now up to fifth in *Shoot-Out*, though one could argue that it should have been third, after Scott and James Craig, who played the villain in the film. But Garner's name comes after the two ingenues, Angie Dickinson, whose star would rise over the next decade, and Dani Crayne, whose short career would come to a halt after one more film in 1957 (*The Story of Mankind*, as Helen of Troy).[3]

Garner and Gordon James, who report to Scott's Captain Devlin, are consistently featured throughout the film, and it's their interactions—along with Scott—that keep viewers' attention. Indeed, it's hard to take your eyes off of Garner. He's both tough and mischievous in the film, and with his army pals he engages in an amusing deception that isn't quite a con—but presages the Maverick character that would make him famous. *Shoot-Out* serves as a good introduction to James Garner before stardom came calling.

2

SAYONARA

(1957)

★ ★ ½

Director: Joshua Logan
Screenplay: Paul Osborn, based on the novel by James A. Michener
Producer: William Goetz. *Director of Photography:* Ellsworth Fredricks, ASC.
    Music: Franz Waxman. *Editors:* Arthur P. Schmidt, AE, Philip W.
    Anderson. *Art Director:* Ted Haworth. *Set Decorator:* Robert Priestly.
    Costume Designer: Norma Koch
Cast: Marlon Brando (Major Gruver), Patricia Owens (Eileen Webster),
    Red Buttons (Joe Kelly), Miiko Taka (Hana-Ogi), Ricardo Montalban
    (Nakamura), Martha Scott (Mrs. Webster), Miyoshi Umeki (Katsumi),
    James Garner (Captain Bailey), Kent Smith (General Webster),
    Douglas Watson (Colonel Crawford), Reiko Kuba (Fumiko-San)
Studio: Warner Bros.
Release Date: December 5, 1957
Specs: 147 minutes; color
Availability: DVD (MGM); Blu-ray (Twilight Time)

SUMMARY

Major Gruver is an air force pilot stationed in post–World War II Japan, where officers and enlisted men alike are strongly discouraged from fraternizing with the local women. At first Gruver toes the company line, disapproving of his fellow officers' flaunting of the rules and especially of his crew chief, who intends to marry one of the locals. But soon the major is entranced himself, not only by an actress who is beginning to warm up to him but also by Japanese culture. While Major Gruver and the others risk reprimands from their superiors, the women are subject to the racist behavior of less sympathetic Americans.

BACKGROUND

Before he became known as a novelist of sweeping historical epics like *Hawaii*, *Poland*, and *Texas*, James Michener had written more intimate works and had even received a Pulitzer Prize for his collection of stories, *Tales of the South Pacific*. That book would ultimately be adapted into the hit musical *South Pacific* with songs by Richard Rodgers and Oscar Hammerstein II. Joshua Logan, who had contributed to the stage musical, and screenwriter Paul Osborn collaborated on the film version of *South Pacific*, but before doing so, they brought to the screen another Michener work, the somewhat autobiographical novel *Sayonara*.[1]

Left to right: Garner, Reiko Kuba, Marlon Brando, Miyoshi Umeki, and Red Buttons celebrate. *Warner Bros. Pictures / Photofest © Warner Bros. Pictures*

Cast in the lead role of Major Gruver was Marlon Brando, who only a couple years earlier had played an Okinawan native in the film *The Teahouse of the August Moon.* That bit of yellow casting[2] in a broad comedy may have played well to American audiences in the mid-1950s, but some critics were less enchanted. Stung by their reaction to his performance, the actor looked at *Sayonara* as "a chance to redeem himself, to make a valuable film about America's blighted racial history."[3] The part also earned him $300,000, just *slightly* more than Garner's $500-a-week take as a contract player for Warners. According to Garner, Brando became his acting coach, in lieu of the film's director, Logan, who didn't provide the young actor much guidance.

Audrey Hepburn was the studio's top choice for the role of Hana-Ogi, the young actress who steals Gruver's heart, but Warners could only afford one star, so Brando was in and Hepburn was out. Instead, Seattle native Miiko Taka was hired for the movie in her film debut. The role of Joe Kelly, the smitten airman, went to actor and comedian Red Buttons, whose on-screen credits at the time could be counted on one hand. At least one Japanese native was in the principal cast, another newcomer, Miysohi Umeki, who plays Kelly's fiancée. Along with Garner and his fellow neophytes, the film featured Hollywood veterans Martha Scott, Kent Smith, and the regrettably casted Ricardo Montalban.

RECEPTION

Variety praised the film, calling it "a picture of beauty and sensitivity" and declared that "Joshua Logan's direction is tops." The reviewer also found Brando "wholly convincing as the race-conscious Southerner whose humanity finally leads him to rebel against army-imposed prejudice." Indeed, the film is successful for suggesting "the notion that human relations transcend race barriers."[4]

Bosley Crowther in the *New York Times* credited Brando for providing "eccentricity and excitement to a richly colorful film." But Crowther also cites other cast members' contributions with terse adjectives: Red Buttons ("excellent"), Miyoshi Umeki ("droll"), Kent Smith ("stolid"), and Patricia Owens ("sleek"). Garner is not mentioned in the review, but Crowther does call out Montalban as "not up to giving the illusion of being a Japanese theatre star."[5]

The film received ten Academy Award nominations, including Best Picture, Best Director, Best Adapted Screenplay, and three acting nods, including Best Actor for Marlon Brando. The film ultimately received four Oscars, including two for the supporting cast (Buttons and Umeki).

Of the six Golden Globe nominations the film received, it lost four: Best Motion Picture—Drama, Best Director, Best Actor—Drama, and Best Supporting Actress (Umeki). The two awards it did win: Best Supporting Actor for Buttons and Most Promising Newcomer—Male for Garner.[6]

In most of the major categories at the Oscars and the Golden Globes, the film lost out to a movie with a very different take on military relations with the Japanese: *The Bridge on the River Kwai*. The David Lean World War II epic was also the highest-grossing film of 1957, followed by the soap opera *Peyton Place*, and then *Sayonara*, which ultimately grossed $23 million.[7]

COMMENTARY

Sayonara is the only film in Garner's career to receive an Academy Award nomination for Best Picture, and was the most Oscar-honored film among the actor's credits. Despite its award-winning legacy, the 1957 film has not aged particularly well. Although Marlon Brando is regarded as one of the greatest actors of the twentieth century, he seems wrong for the role of a Southern officer—or at the very least, his choice to play the officer as a Southerner (not originally called for in the script) does not come off particularly well. And Garner's role, which is small and almost unnecessary, could have been played by any capable actor.

So why include this among Garner's essential films? In part, because of the aforementioned Oscar nominations, the reviews the film received upon its release, and even the high regard others hold for the film. Who are we to argue? But we will say this: for a film whose central theme is about racial intolerance, *Sayonara* stumbles with the usual racist faux pas, particularly in the casting of Ricardo Montalban—an Hispanic actor—as a revered Kabuki performer. This Hollywood gaffe is no less offensive than Mickey Rooney playing a Japanese character in *Breakfast at Tiffany's*—and perhaps more so. While Rooney's character in the 1962 film is obviously a ridiculous stereotype, Montalban plays a character whose very being is to embody a country's cultural contribution. Why wasn't a Japanese actor employed for this modest but significant role? At least the film's budget prevented the studio from hiring Audrey Hepburn to play Hana-Ogi, the young actress that Brando's character woos.

But the film's racist missteps are not limited to the casting of Montalban. According to *The Encyclopedia of Racism in American Films*, although the film was "widely lauded for its pointed critique of 1950s anti-Asian racism in the United States . . . *Sayonara* unfortunately reinforces other kinds in equal proportion. It plays, in particular, to Orientalist fantasies of Asian (and specifically post-defeat Japanese) women as not only sexually entrancing but also implicitly available to, even eager for, white men."[8]

To be sure, *Sayonara* does have some highlights, particularly the film's attempts to expose viewers to Japanese culture. Indeed, Brando's character is a stand-in for the audience as he is introduced to the particulars of Japanese life and attitudes. Most of these are handled in a delicate, respectful way—Montalban's appearance notwithstanding—at least for the era in which it was produced. It is the film's message of acceptance, ultimately, that redeems *Sayonara* from its Hollywood conventions. It's just a shame the filmmakers couldn't wholly practice what they preached.

As for Garner, he is fine in the film, displaying the affable nature that viewers would come to appreciate and that would help make him a star. But in some ways, he's window-dressing, since he isn't given much to do, except act as a conduit between Brando's Major Gruver and Hana-Ogi. But so be it. If the role brought him greater exposure to audiences—no doubt aided by the welcoming hands of the Hollywood Foreign Press—and thus expedited his ascent to stardom, who are we to complain? The success of *Maverick* loomed on the horizon, and with this film, Garner would say sayonara to supporting roles for the next three decades.

3

UP PERISCOPE

(1959)

★ ★ ½

Director: Gordon Douglas
Screenplay: Richard Landau, based on the novel by Robb White
Producer: Aubrey Schenck. *Director of Photography:* Carl Guthrie. *Editor:* John Schreyer. *Art Director:* Jack T. Collis
Cast: James Garner (Lieutenant Kenneth Braden), Edmond O'Brien (Commander Paul Stevenson), Alan Hale Jr. (Pat Malone), Carleton Carpenter (Lieutenant Phil Carney), Andra Martin (Sally Johnson), Frank Gifford (Ensign Cy Mount), Edward Byrnes (Mate Ash), Bernie Hamilton (Weary)
Studio: Warner Bros.
Release Date: March 4, 1959
Specs: 111 minutes; color
Availability: DVD (Warner Home Video)

SUMMARY

Pearl Harbor, 1942. Lieutenant Braden, a navy frogman, flies in from California and reports for duty on the SS *Barracuda* under the command of Paul Stevenson. The commander has just returned from a mission in which a young seaman was killed. Stevenson is racked with guilt by the incident, for which his crew blames him, so he is ill at ease with their next mission: convey Braden to a Japanese-occupied island, where the lieutenant hopes to obtain secret codes from a radio transmitter. Along the way, the submarine encounters other perils, while Braden and Stevenson clash.

BACKGROUND

Up Periscope was based on a novel by Robb White, who had written several adventure stories aimed at young readers. The film adaptation was meant to be a starring vehicle for Tab Hunter, Garner's fellow actor under contract to Warner Bros., but Hunter turned down the project—as did Garner initially. Edmond O'Brien, who had won the Academy Award for *The Barefoot Contessa* just a few years before, signed on to play the guilt-stricken commander. The supporting cast included Alan Hale Jr. (a dead ringer for his father Alan Hale, best known for playing Little John in *The Adventures of Robin Hood*), Andra Martin, Carleton Carpenter, and Edd Byrnes, a fellow Warners actor who had guest-starred in a couple of episodes of *Maverick*. In smaller roles were future broadcaster Frank Gifford—still a running back for the New York Giants when *Periscope* premiered—and an uncredited Warren Oates, who would ultimately star in several films of the 1960s, '70s, and '80s, including classics *In the Heat of the Night* and *The Wild Bunch*.

Vice Admiral Charles A. Lockwood, USN (retired), and the author of the book *Hellcats of the Navy*, served as technical adviser to *Up Periscope*. Like most Hollywood films, liberties were taken with the action and military protocol, but at least consulting Lockwood gave the film the appearance of authenticity.

Filming began in July of 1958, between the first and second seasons of *Maverick*.

RECEPTION

Writing for the *New York Times*, A. H. Weiler notes that *Up Periscope* "seems to run a familiar and somewhat undramatic course." However, the critic is not entirely dismissive of the film, nor its leads, remarking that O'Brien "very properly behaves like a nervous man beset with more problems than is normal," and Garner "does also a normal job of understated derring-do."[1]

COMMENTARY

Despite receiving top billing in *Darby's Rangers* the year before, Garner starred in his first true feature leading role in *Up Periscope*. The episodic *Rangers* focused as much on the love lives of several enlisted men as it did on the missions, making it more of an ensemble film. *Up Periscope*, likewise, features scenes that focus more on the submarine crew and its commander than on Garner's character. This is not really a flaw of the film, since the narrative serves at least two purposes: build tension as the submarine approaches its destination *and* allow the commander to achieve redemption and earn back the respect of his crew. So while Garner's character takes a backseat to the action in the first half of the film, much of the screen time in the latter half centers almost entirely on his character.

Ultimately the film belongs to Garner and O'Brien, and as their two characters prepare for their mission, the actors square off against each other in convincing fashion. While the more experienced O'Brien gives a polished performance, Garner holds his own against the veteran actor. Other standouts in the cast include actress Andra Martin. Despite her small, and in some ways curious, role, Martin makes an impression as Garner's love inter-

Garner on a mission to secure radio codes from a Japanese transmitter. *Warner Bros. Pictures / Photofest © Warner Bros. Pictures*

est. She appears briefly in the beginning of the film but conveys her character's inner turmoil with conviction. As more details about her are revealed to both Garner and the audience, her performance is even more assured. While the filmmakers might have been tempted to give her more screen time, for either her looks or acting ability, they wisely abstain from any such contrivances. Otherwise, they might have produced a film that stretches credulity, like the unfortunate *Darby's Rangers*, which gets bogged down in its ridiculous romantic vignettes.

Other actors who offer fine support include Alan Hale Jr. and Carleton Carpenter, although the latter expressed contempt for the finished film. Like Garner, who called the movie "a piece of crap,"[2] Carpenter was just as disdainful, nicknaming the movie "Up Your Periscope." The actor recalled that "it was fun to make but not so hot to see."[3] However, both actors are overly dismissive of the production.

By no means is *Up Periscope* a great film, but it's a decent adventure story with credible performances and an engaging, if not entirely gripping, story line. It deserves a viewing, if only to see Garner take command of the big screen for the first real time.

4

CASH McCALL

(1960)

★ ★ ★

Director: Joseph Pevney
Screenplay: Lenore Coffee, Marion Hargrove, based on the novel by
    Cameron Hawley
Producer: Henry Blanke. *Director of Photography:* George Folsey, ASC. *Music:*
    Max Steiner. *Editor:* Philip W. Anderson
Cast: James Garner (Cash McCall), Natalie Wood (Lory Austen), Nina Foch
    (Maude Kennard), Dean Jagger (Grant Austen), Henry Jones (Gilmore
    Clark), Roland Winters (General Andrew Danvers), Linda Watkins
    (Marie Austen), Edward G. Marshall (Winston Conway), Edward C.
    Platt (Harrison Glenn), Otto Kruger (Will Atherson), Edgar Stehli
    (Mr. Pierce), Parley Baer (Harvey Bannon)
Studio: Warner Bros.
Release Date: January 27, 1960
Specs: 102 minutes; color
Availability: DVD (Warner Home Video)

SUMMARY

A corporate raider named Cash—yes, that's his first name—McCall buys
underperforming companies, turns them around, and then sells them. One
of his prey is Austen Plastics, a company run by the father of Lory Austen,

a woman with whom Cash had a brief fling. While pursuing Austen Plastics, Cash rekindles his interest in Lory, which both intrigues and threatens him.

BACKGROUND

Cash McCall is the second film adaptation of a novel by Cameron Hawley, a former advertising executive who wrote often about the business world, first in short stories and then in longer works. His first novel, *Executive Suite*, was adapted into a 1954 film starring William Holden, Barbara Stanwyck, Fredric March, June Allyson, Walter Pidgeon, and Shelley Winters.

The screenplay for *Cash McCall* was cowritten by Lenore Coffee, who had been writing for Hollywood since the silent era. Her cowriter, Marion Hargrove, had first achieved success with a collection of articles about his experiences in the army, *See Here, Private Hargrove*, which was brought to the screen in 1944. Hargrove would be associated with several Garner projects: he wrote the novel *The Girl He Left Behind*—the film version of which featured Garner in one of his first roles—and later wrote several episodes of *Maverick* as well as contributed to Garner's 1962 film *Boys' Night Out*.

The film was directed by Joseph Pevney, a former actor, whose most significant on-screen credit was probably the 1947 John Garfield boxing film, *Body and Soul*. Pevney helmed several minor Hollywood films in the 1950s culminating in *Tammy and the Bachelor* in 1957. After *Cash McCall*, he made a few more films and then turned to television, where he directed episodes of *Bonanza*, *Star Trek*, and the small-screen version of *Executive Suite*. He also directed one of the final episodes of *The Rockford Files* ("The Big Cheese").

According to Raymond Strait, *Cash McCall* "was tailor-made for Garner,"[1] who began working on the film around the same time he received his first Emmy nomination. Garner was under contract to Warner Bros., which owned *Maverick*, and the studio was simultaneously grooming the actor for feature films. In addition to appearances on several Warner programs such as *Conflict* and *Cheyenne*, *McCall* was the actor's sixth feature film for the studio. Strait observed that Garner dropped more than ten pounds for the role of Cash and "never looked better than he did in the finished film."[2]

Also under contract with Warners was Natalie Wood, who was not pleased to be making the film. Wood had fought with the studio for better roles, which resulted in her getting suspended for several months. She only agreed to make *McCall* in part because "each month that she remained on suspension added another month to the duration of her contract."[3] The actress was also eager to star in Elia Kazan's next film, *Splendor in the Grass*, and the studio held the film out as a carrot, as long as she made *Cash McCall* first.

This was the second film in which Wood and Garner appeared together, after *The Girl He Left Behind* in 1956, in which Garner had a small, but somewhat pivotal role.[4] Although Wood was not yet twenty-one when she filmed *Cash*, she already had appeared in more than twenty-five films, including the classics *Miracle on 34th Street*, *Rebel without a Cause*, and *The Searchers*. Ten years older than his female costar, Garner had fewer film credits. Despite this, he received top billing for a film that represented only his second true lead, following *Up Periscope* the year before.[5]

In addition to Garner and Wood, the cast included a pair of film veterans who would become familiar faces on television—E. G. Marshall (*The Defenders*) and Edward Platt (*Get Smart*)—as well as Henry Jones, the actor who would share the big screen with Garner more than any other actor.

For two cast members, Dean Jagger and Nina Foch, *Cash McCall* was the second screen adaptation of a Cameron Hawley novel they appeared in, following *Executive Suite* in 1954. Jagger—who plays Wood's father, Grant Austen—made his feature film debut in 1929, just as the silent era was beginning to fade, and finished his career with a guest appearance on one of the greatest dramas of television's silver age, *St. Elsewhere*, in 1985. Near the midpoint of his career, the actor received an Academy Award for the 1949 Gregory Peck film *Twelve O'Clock High*. For actress Nina Foch, *Executive Suite* signified one of the highlights of her film career. She earned the film's only Oscar nomination for acting and received a Best Supporting Actress award from the National Board of Review.

RECEPTION

Cash McCall received mixed reviews, most of which praised the two leads if not the film itself. Howard Thompson, in the *New York Times*, called the film an "amusing movie exercise that now and then touches solid ground." Thompson also singled out Garner's performance, saying that the actor "balances the extremely youthful-looking terror of American industry . . . with an engaging personality and a ribald glint."[6] Other publications were also kinder to Garner than they were to the film. The *Hollywood Reporter* found the actor "surprisingly believable in this sort of role,"[7] and the *Motion Picture Herald* declared, "Whatever it is that makes a top-money-making star—James Garner has it."[8]

Although neither Garner nor Natalie Wood were enthusiastic about filming *Cash McCall*, their appeal as a pair cannot be disputed. *Warner Bros. Pictures / Photofest © Warner Bros. Pictures*

COMMENTARY

While *Cash McCall* can be viewed as a light romantic drama, it also denoted the latest big-screen depiction of the corporate world, not merely as a vehicle for the characters but as the central focus of the film. *Cash* followed on the heels of notable business-oriented films of the 1950s, such as *Woman's World* and *Executive Suite* in 1954 and *The Man in the Grey Flannel Suit* and *Patterns* in 1956. For actress Foch, her role in *Cash* was not nearly as progressive as the character she portrayed in *Executive Suite*. The ending of *Suite* makes a fairly bold statement about women in corporate America at the time, but in *Cash McCall*, produced five years later, women are not as favorably depicted. In particular, Foch's character in *Cash* is less sympathetic and less forward thinking than the role she played in the earlier film.

During the first few years of his feature film career, Garner was primarily cast in adventure films such as *Toward the Unknown*. No doubt, the studio and filmmakers behind *Cash McCall* sought to capitalize on Garner's genial nature—not to mention, good looks—a trait more in line with his *Maverick* role than with his two previous features, *Darby's Rangers* and *Up Periscope*. As the first film to truly test whether Garner's appeal would translate from the small screen to paying customers, *Cash McCall* excels in showcasing the actor as a romantic lead. Despite playing a corporate plunderer, Garner as Cash charms many of the other characters—female and male alike—which no doubt helps him succeed on multiple fronts.

Garner and Wood also play well off each other and generate real chemistry, despite the actress's lack of enthusiasm for the film. Garner didn't think highly of *Cash McCall*, either, claiming it was "not much of a movie, but I liked Natalie Wood."[9] It's understandable that Wood wasn't thrilled with playing second fiddle to Garner, and in a role that serves as little more than his romantic foil. After all, she had been steadily building a career for more than a decade, making the rare transition from child stardom to leading lady, while Garner had far fewer credits and—*Maverick* notwithstanding—not particularly stellar ones. Cash is, after all, the title character, so the film relies on its leading man to, well, *lead*, and Garner achieves this, making Wood's role secondary to his. The actress is not alone on the second tier, but must share the distinction with Dean Jagger, who plays not merely her father but the man whose life's work is targeted by Cash.

While the movie is certainly not a weighty drama, it is not a fluff piece of fantasy, either. Of course, the film's viewers want to see the romantic leads wind up together, but they are also invested in the fate of Austen Plastics. Unless Cash succeeds in "acquiring" both Lory and her father's company, the film could not come to a wholly satisfying resolution. The conflicts in the film are focused on the machinations that keep Lory—and Austen Plastics—out of Cash's reach, whether those collusions are devised by others or manifested by Cash himself. In the end, Cash's gains are the audience's gains as well.

5

THE CHILDREN'S HOUR

(1961)

★ ★ ★

Director: William Wyler
Screenplay: John Michael Hayes; adaptation by Lillian Hellman, based on the
   play by Lillian Hellman
Producer: William Wyler. *Director of Photography:* Franz F. Planer, ASC. *Music:*
   Alex North. *Editor:* Robert Swink, ACE. *Art Director:* Fernando Carrere.
   Set Decorator: Edward G. Boyle. *Costume Designer:* Dorothy Jeakins
Cast: Audrey Hepburn (Karen Wright), Shirley MacLaine (Martha Dobie),
   James Garner (Dr. Joe Cardin), Miriam Hopkins (Miss Lily Mortar),
   Fay Bainter (Mrs. Amelia Tilford), Karen Balkin (Mary Tilford),
   Veronica Cartright (Rosalie Wells)
Studio: MGM; Mirisch Corporation
Release Date: October 27, 1964
Specs: 107 minutes; black and white
Availability: DVD and Blu-ray (Kino Lorber)

SUMMARY

At an all-girl boarding school run by two young women—Karen and
Martha—a scheming young girl tells her grandmother a malicious lie:
Martha and Karen are engaged in a lesbian relationship.

BACKGROUND

Before *The Children's Hour* reached the screen in 1961, the property had been around for more than twenty-five years, first as a play, then as a Hollywood film. Lillian Hellman first wrote the play in 1934, when it landed on Broadway. Despite the sensational nature of the story—in an era when homosexuality was rarely discussed, much less out in the open—the play was a hit and ran for nearly seven hundred performances. Months before the show closed on Broadway, it debuted as a Hollywood film under the title *These Three*. The film starred Miriam Hopkins and Merle Oberon as the pair of schoolteachers, but the accusation leveled in the play is replaced by one about sexual misconduct between Martha and Joe Cardin, Karen's boyfriend—essentially turning the story into a heterosexual love triangle. Twelve-year-old Bonita Granville, who plays the pivotal role of the young girl who stirs the pot and makes lives miserable for the three adults, earned an Oscar nomination for Best Supporting Actress—the first year the category was offered (she lost to Gale Sondergaard, who played another despicable character, in the film *Anthony Adverse*).

In the 1930s, sensitive subject matter could be undertaken more easily on a New York stage than in a studio film, particularly after moral groups like the National Legion of Decency demanded that Hollywood clean up its act. By 1934, Hollywood was capitulating to the moral strictures of Will Hays and the Motion Picture Production Code of Dos and Don'ts. So the depiction of lesbian behavior—or even the suggestion of it—was verboten by the time *The Children's Hour* was adapted to the screen. By the beginning of the 1960s, however, provocative fare had been appearing on the big screen more regularly, as filmmakers made a case for more realistic scenarios. Films such as *The Man with the Golden Arm* and *Anatomy of a Murder* reflected a new, grittier cinema, suggesting that the subject matter of Hellman's play could be finally portrayed on-screen. But that didn't make the film any less scandalous.

When William Wyler directed the original screen version, he was still at the start of his career, steadily building a reputation in Hollywood. In 1936 Wyler's career took a leap forward, with *These Three* followed by *Dodsworth*, which received several Oscar nominations—including Best Director—and *Come and Get It*, another multiple Oscar nominee. By the time Wyler undertook the 1961 version, his reputation was more than firmly established, not just as an accomplished director but for his dictatorial style.

In the twenty-five years between the two productions, Wyler's iron-fisted control on the set resulted in three Oscar-winning Best Pictures: *Mrs. Mini-*

ver (1942), *The Best Years of Our Lives* (1946), and *Ben-Hur* (1959)—an honor unmatched to this day—and all three earned him a statue for Best Director. That same tyrannical manner ultimately benefitted his casts. Not only have his films received the most Academy Award nominations for acting (thirty-six) and the most acting Oscars (fourteen), but Wyler was the first person to direct Oscar-winning performances in all four acting categories, an achievement he secured when Fredric March picked up the prize for Best Actor in 1947 for *The Best Years of Our Lives*.[1] That accomplishment has been replicated only twice since, by Hal Ashby and Martin Scorsese.[2]

Remakes are a Hollywood staple and always have been—even before the end of the silent era—but why would a director care to revisit a property he had *already* brought to the screen? The practice was rare but not unprecedented. Cecil B. DeMille oversaw both the silent version of *The Ten Commandments* in 1923 and the technicolor, effects-laden remake in 1956. Alfred Hitchcock made two versions of *The Man Who Knew Too Much*, first as a 1934 Gaumont production in England and again in 1956 with the full support of Universal Studios, including a wealth of resources and two of Hollywood's biggest stars—James Stewart and Doris Day. And in a bit of coincidence, Wyler's fellow three-time Oscar-winning director, Frank Capra, also revisited one his 1930s originals, in the same year as *The Children's Hour*. Capra's swan song, *Pocketful of Miracles*, was a remake of his 1933 film *Lady for a Day*.

But for Wyler, the lure of remaking an earlier film must have been more than just working with a bigger budget, since the new film, like its predecessor, was produced in black and white, and unlike *The Ten Commandments* or even Wyler's own *Ben-Hur*, didn't require special effects to improve upon the original.

Wyler felt that he and Hollywood had underserved the original play by not adhering to its key conflict, the exploration of a taboo subject that could finally be brought to the screen. According to Wyler's biographer Jan Herman, "Wyler had always been irked about sanitizing the original—for the Hays office, for Goldwyn, for the need to conform to the social climate."[3]

Securing Hellman to adapt the play to the screen proved fraught with obstacles, so Wyler approached two screenwriters associated with some of Alfred Hitchcock's greatest films about undertaking the work. John Michael Hayes had collaborated with the suspense master on three of his films, most notably *Rear Window*, an adaptation of a Cornel Woolrich short story. More recently, Ernest Lehman had written for Hitchcock what many consider the director's greatest film, *North by Northwest*. In the end, Hayes was contracted for the work and therefore had the unusual distinction of helping two directors remake their own films, since he had previously adapted *The Man Who Knew Too Much* for Hitchcock.

Audrey Hepburn had been the first star cast in the film. The film allowed the actress to reunite with the man who not only had brought her to the attention of the world but also coaxed an Oscar-winning performance from her in *Roman Holiday* (1953). After Hepburn signed on to play Karen, Shirley MacLaine was hired to play Martha. Unlike Hepburn, MacLaine had not worked with Wyler before, but working with many of Hollywood's greatest directors was not a novelty to her. By 1961, the actress had appeared in films directed by Vincente Minnelli, Billy Wilder, and Hitchcock, whose *The Trouble with Harry* (with a screenplay by Hayes) was her film debut. For the role of the gullible grandmother, another Oscar-winning alum from Wyler's past, Fay Bainter, was brought on board. And then came Garner, who saw the film as an opportunity for growth. The actor disclosed that he took the part of Joe Cardin (played in the earlier film by Joel Mc-Crea), not because the role interested him, but for the prospect "to be in good company."[4]

Wyler and Hellman were not the only ones from the original production to take part in the remake. Miriam Hopkins, who played the original Martha in *These Three*, was cast in the remake as Lily Mortar, Martha's aunt. Casting the part of Mary Tilford, the student who sets the tragedy in motion, proved difficult, since the actress who had originated the role on-screen, twelve-year-old Bonita Granville, had been so disturbingly good. The part eventually went to Karen Balkin, who had played another conniving child in a stage version of *The Bad Seed*. Mary's classmate, the easily influenced Rosalie, is played by Veronica Cartright, an actress who would master desperate characters in a number of thrillers to come, including Alfred Hitchcock's *The Birds* (1963) and Ridley Scott's *Alien* (1979).

RECEPTION

While Bosley Crowther from the *New York Times* had virtually nothing good to say about the movie, *Variety* was much kinder, calling the film a "crackling production." The reviewer was particularly fond of the two leads, marveling at Hepburn's "memorable portrayal" while calling MacLaine's performance "almost equally rich in depth and substance." Fay Bainter "comes through with an outstanding portrayal of the impressionable grandmother" and "James Garner is effective as Hepburn's betrothed."[5]

Solid performances from Shirley MacLaine (left), Audrey Hepburn (center), and Garner make *The Children's Hour* an underrated drama of the early 1960s. *United Artists / Photofest © United Artists*

The film did not succeed at the box office. According to Tino Balio, "The marquee value of the stars, the adult theme, and Wyler's direction could not save the picture," which "lost $2.8 million on a gross of $3 million."[6]

Despite the lack of glowing reviews and failure at the box office, the film was not ignored during awards season. Wyler was nominated for Best Director by the Directors Guild of America, and the film also received three

Golden Globe nominations—one for Wyler's direction, one for MacLaine as Best Actress in a Drama, and another nod to Fay Bainter for Best Supporting Actress. The film also received five Academy Award nominations—for Bainter as Best Supporting Actress; Best Sound; and in the black-and-white divisions, Best Cinematography, Best Art Direction/Set Decoration, and Best Costume Design. Ultimately, the film did not receive any awards.

COMMENTARY

The strongest critique from reviewers about *The Children's Hour* is that despite the changing social climate—which had allowed the filmmakers to retain the content, even if they couldn't use the word *lesbian*—the movie still handles the topic too timidly. And of course, when viewed through a contemporary lens, some critics consider the film's treatment almost quaint. But these assessments are unfair, both then and now. The truth is such topics were still taboo, for the filmmakers and the audience. If you replace the lie with something truly heinous, the impact on the characters remains no less devastating.

According to Steven DeRosa, John Michael Hayes's biographer,

> Wyler and Hayes initially agreed that in modernizing Hellman's play, they should concentrate on the effect the lie has on the main characters rather than on the hysteria it causes in the town.[7]

Shirley MacLaine later acknowledged that the screenwriter "had not pulled any punches in the script,"[8] but Wyler later edited out scenes that clearly depicted Martha's feelings for Karen, which may have diluted the film's impact.

In hindsight, though, most films—or other means of artistic expression—from bygone eras that tackle a difficult subject are bound to be viewed hypercritically by a contemporary audience. It's easy to criticize, or even laugh at, a film whose take on a subject is unsophisticated by modern-day sensibilities. But dismissing *The Children's Hour* because it didn't explicitly embrace the subject of the gossip is, in effect, missing the point. The film is still a skillfully rendered depiction of how gossip, however near or far from the truth it might be, can ruin lives. And *that* was the true theme of Hellman's play, not the scandal of a forbidden relationship.

Notwithstanding *The Great Escape* and *The Americanization of Emily*—which were entertainments set against the backdrop of war—*The Children's Hour* is probably the weightiest of the actor's feature films. Indeed, many of the films that Garner appeared in that did tackle heavier subject matter did so in less direct terms, so calling them dramas would be inaccurate. *The Great Escape* is a thriller, *The Americanization of Emily* is a satire, and *Skin Game* is a dramedy.

Not until Garner began his third "career" of television films did he tackle serious subjects that could be characterized as straightforward dramas: *Heartsounds* (1984), about a husband coping with failing physical health; *Promise* (1986), about mental illness; and *My Name Is Bill W.* (1989), about alcoholism. But in features, Garner stuck to genres like westerns, thrillers, and comedies, with very few dramas in between. Dramas may not have been in Garner's wheelhouse as much as thrillers and comedies during the 1960s, but that doesn't mean he was any less capable of delivering credible performances in them. And given the critical success of his weightier television films, it appears that either Hollywood finally caught on to his dramatic skills, or, more likely, Garner himself eventually felt the need to stretch.

And though Garner's role in *The Children's Hour* is in support of the film's two stars who carry the heavier lifting—Shirley MacLaine in particular—the actor demonstrates his capability of handling dramatic material. Besides the three leads, there are two other standout performances: Fay Bainter runs away with the film as a woman who too easily takes a child's word simply because the young girl is her relation. But when Mrs. Tilford tries to atone for her culpability in the gossip-mongering, Bainter conveys the proper shame. While sympathy for her character would be too strong, the remorse she exhibits does allow viewers to feel a certain amount of empathy. It's a shame that the young actress who plays Mary Tilford is not quite as convincing as the original troublemaker, Bonita Granville, in the earlier version. Instead, the best performance by the young cast is delivered by Veronica Cartwright as the manipulated Rosalie. Besides the viewer's sympathy for the two wronged women, Cartwright wrings some sympathy as well.

It was unfortunate for Garner, Hepburn, MacLaine, and the rest of the cast that *The Children's Hour* was not given its proper due upon its release. However, the film's significance as a touchstone in gay cinema has grown over the years, as evidenced by recent lists compiled by two prominent magazines, *Esquire* and *TimeOut London*, which cited *The Children's Hour* among their top fifty LGBTQ films. While *TimeOut* placed the film at the very bottom of its list,[9] *Esquire* ranked *The Children's Hour* at thirty-nine, in the company of contemporary films such as *The Kids Are All Right* (2010).[10]

THE GREAT ESCAPE

(1963)

★ ★ ★ ★

Director: John Sturges
Screenplay: James Clavell, W. R. Burnett, based the book by Paul Brickhill
Producer: John Sturges. *Director of Photography:* Daniel L. Fapp, ASC. *Music:*
     Elmer Bernstein. *Editor:* Ferris Webster. *Art Director:* Fernando
     Carrere. *Set Decorator:* Kurt Ripberger
Cast: Steve McQueen (Virgil Hilts), James Garner (Hendley), Richard
     Attenborough (Roger Bartlett), James Donald (Ramsey), Charles
     Bronson (Danny), Donald Pleasence (Blythe), James Coburn
     (Sedgwick), Hannes Messemer (Von Luger), David McCallum (Ashley
     Pitt), Gordon Jackson (MacDonald), Angus Lennie (Ives), John Leyton
     (Willie), Robert Graf (Werner)
Studio: United Artists; the Mirisch Company
Release Date: July 4, 1963
Specs: 172 minutes; color
Availability: DVD and Blu-ray (MGM)

SUMMARY

At a prisoner of war camp in Nazi Germany, the most active escapees have
been gathered together from camps around the country. Most of the prisoners arrive with a history of multiple escape attempts and are advised that

no attempts will be tolerated. But the officers are sworn to antagonize the enemy and to do so, they plot a massive operation, one that will allow 250 men to escape. To ensure success, the masterminds in charge of the operation call on the skills of each man—including a forger, a scrounger, and a tunnel king—to help achieve success.

BACKGROUND

Based on the real escape of seventy-six prisoners of war from Stalag Luft III in Sagan (Zagan) Poland, ninety miles southeast of Berlin, *The Great Escape* took liberties with a number of details to tell a compelling story that captures the bravery and resourcefulness of men during the war.

The Great Escape is based on the book of the same name by Paul Brickhill, a member of the Royal Australian Air Force who was "shot down over the Tunisian desert in 1943."[1] Soon after he was sent to Stalag Luft III in what is now a town in Poland. A few years after the war, Brickhill wrote about his experiences, and *The Great Escape* was published in 1950.

Director John Sturges had been trying to film the story as early as 1953, but it took nearly a decade to convince Hollywood executives to greenlight the project. Although hundreds of World War II films had been produced since the end of the war, very few focused on prisoner of war (POW) stories, a subgenre of the war film. Of these, the most notable were *Stalag 17* (1953), *The Colditz Story* (1955), and *The Bridge on the River Kwai* (1957). By the time Sturges was able to finally direct *The Great Escape*, he had helmed a few high-profile films, including *Escape from Fort Bravo* (1953), a POW film set during the Civil War starring *Stalag 17*'s William Holden; *Bad Day at Black Rock* (1955) with Spencer Tracy; and *The Magnificent Seven* in 1960.

Although another Australian POW, James Clavell—along with W. R. Burnett—was eventually credited with the screenplay, several others were brought in to adapt what turned out to be a tricky story. In *Escape Artist*, Sturges's biography, Glen Lovell writes,

> William Roberts, Walter Newman, Burnett, and Nelson Gidding, another former POW, each took a crack at adapting the book but wound up "inventing things," according to the director, because they thought Brickhill's story was too farfetched.[2]

Although the original breakout was conducted by officers of the Commonwealth, financing for the film depended on the star power of American actors. Bigger stars meant a bigger budget, so producer Walter Mirisch secured two actors who had first made names for themselves in television westerns, Garner in *Maverick*, of course, and McQueen in *Wanted: Dead or Alive*. The remaining cast was populated primarily by actors from the United Kingdom, including Richard Attenborough, David McCallum, and Donald Pleasance, who had also been a POW during the war. Two other notable exceptions to the primarily British cast were Charles Bronson, the son of Lithuanian immigrants, and James Coburn, a native of Nebraska, who plays an Australian in the film.

RECEPTION

Variety raved that "John Sturges has fashioned a motion picture that entertains, captivates, thrills and stirs" and singled out "some exceptional performances," including Steve McQueen, who makes "the most provocative single impression," and Richard Attenborough, who "is especially convincing in a stellar role." The publication also applauded "Elmer Bernstein's rich, expressive score."[3] In an otherwise negative review, Bosley Crowther called *The Great Escape* "surfacely engrossing" and Garner "silken and mysterious," but the critic summed up the film as "a strictly mechanical adventure with make-believe men."[4]

Released on July 4, 1963, no doubt to capitalize on patriotic fervor, the film debuted at number one at the box office. The film grossed more than $11.7 million,[5] placing it at number seventeen for the year, just behind two other Garner films, both with Doris Day: *The Thrill of It All* at number sixteen and *Move Over Darling* at fourteen.[6]

Despite the film's popularity and the favorable reviews, it did not get much attention during the awards season. Ferris Webster, who edited the film, received *The Great Escape*'s sole Oscar nomination but lost to *How the West Was Won*, the second shortest film at 164 minutes to be nominated in that category—all of them exceeding two and a half hours.[7] The film did receive a Golden Globe nomination for Best Motion Picture—Drama, but lost to *The Cardinal*, a ponderous film about a young priest. The screenplay received a Writers Guild of America nomination for Best Written American Drama, but lost to *Hud*, which was written by Harrier Frank Jr. and Irving Ravetch, future screenwriters of *Murphy's Romance*. The movie also was named one of the year's top ten films by the National Board of Review.

It's hard to believe that Elmer Bernstein's score did not receive even a nomination, especially since most of the other scores in contention—with the possible exception of *How the West Was Won*—are unmemorable.

COMMENTARY

According to *The Encyclopedia of Epic Films*, *The Great Escape* "was the last great film in the prisoner of war genre"[8] that had begun during the war itself, dating at least as far back as 1943. MGM's *The Cross of Lorraine*, a film about French POWs, starred Gene Kelly (in an early non–singing or dancing role), Jean-Pierre Aumont, Peter Lorre, and Hume Cronyn. More POW films sprung up after the war culminating in two epics, David Lean's *The Bridge on the River Kwai* and *The Great Escape*.

Feature films with extended running times were fairly common in the 1960s. While *Lawrence of Arabia* (1962), with a running time of 162 minutes, seemed perfectly reasonable, the Elizabeth Taylor fiasco *Cleopatra* the following year was rightly criticized for its excesses, including a three-hour-plus running time. *The Great Escape*, on the other hand, manages to remain thrilling for its nearly three-hour length. What helps sustain the movie over this time are the individual vignettes of the camp prisoners, both before and after the escape.

One noteworthy aspect of *The Great Escape* is that the film's nearly three-hour running time is not compromised by contriving to include female characters into the plot. While the filmmakers may have been tempted to insinuate a female character at some point—if only in a peripheral role—they did not succumb to such impulses. Even during scenes that take place outside the prison camp, there are no speaking roles for women in the film. The film follows several escapees whose paths veer in a variety of directions, some to the viewers' satisfaction and others to their heartbreak—but no budding romances are suggested.

Above all, *The Great Escape* is a magnificent ensemble film—a group of individuals working together in a nearly seamless effort to portray a group banding together to accomplish a dangerous mission. In an ensemble film, certain performances rise above, and in *The Great Escape*, Garner is among those standouts. Though Steve McQueen gets top billing and he's arguably the coolest member of the cast, it's Garner who delivers the most captivating (no pun intended) performance in the film. Garner's Korean War experiences may have informed his performance, since like his character Hendley, the actor was a scrounger during his service overseas.

In his memoir, Garner acknowledged, "I knew *Great Escape* was going to be good, I just didn't know how good. It had a little bit of everything: humor, pathos, and a wonderful sense of camaraderie among the fliers."[9]

That is not to say that Garner carries the film on his shoulders. As a true ensemble piece, the film benefits immensely from a cast that delivers fine portrayals all around. British veterans Richard Attenborough, Donald

Garner (left), James Coburn (right), and Donald Pleasence (middle) about to make their escape. *United Artists / Photofest © United Artists*

Pleasence, James Donald, and Gordon Jackson all deliver solid performances, though Angus Lennie as Ives is particularly memorable. Hannes Messemer as the camp Kommandeant Von Luger and Robert Graf as the prison guard Werner prove equally adept—and even draw a small measure of sympathy as men on the wrong side of history.

In other secondary roles, some actors give the finest performances of their careers, especially Charles Bronson as the tunnel king. Prior to *The Great Escape*, Bronson came to the public's attention in another period ensemble, Sturges's *The Magnificent Seven* in 1960, and he would also be called into action in another World War II ensemble thriller, Robert Aldrich's *The Dirty Dozen* in 1967. Ultimately, Bronson would achieve international stardom by headlining such action films as *Once upon a Time in the West* and *Death Wish*, but never is he more believable than as the claustrophobic Danny, who despite his fears, leads the digging of tunnels.

In addition to the acting, the film achieves its success in large part through a screenplay that is at varying times thrilling, humorous, and poignant. On one hand, the film—as with any motion picture based on real events—couldn't possibly depict every aspect of the events that took place. And as with every fact-based drama, the filmmakers necessarily had to compress events, create composite characters, and "artificially" heighten the tension of some scenes. On the other hand, some of the film's most effective moments come during quieter scenes that require no dramatic embellishment. As the film highlights the methods of each operation, the viewer becomes fascinated by the contributions of the various prisoners to help the escape effort. From tailoring German uniforms and forging traveling papers to collecting wood for the tunnel's infrastructure and devising a means to redistribute the tunneled dirt, the film honors the actual camp prisoners' ingenuity. While purists can argue that the film takes liberties with history by imposing American characters into the story or fabricating certain scenes, *The Great Escape*'s portrayal of the everyday mechanics of the operation are among the scenes that resonate most with viewers. Even decades later, it's hard not to marvel at the allied prisoners' efforts to thwart their German captors.

With films like *The Magnificent Seven*, John Sturges proved he was capable of handling action, but just as important to the film is the director's deft control of tense scenes in which the escapees face exposure, as well as lighthearted exchanges between characters, even between the prisoners and their captors. In such a film, a comic treatment would be inappropriate, but Sturges and the screenwriters rightly provide occasional moments of humor in the dramatic structure, particularly in the first third of the film, before the dramatics of the escape take center stage.

Complementing the film is one of the most memorable cinematic scores of the 1960s, composed by Silver Age great Elmer Bernstein. In a survey by the American Film Institute of the greatest film scores of all time, Bernstein's masterpiece, *The Magnificent Seven*, ranked eighth.[10] While his score for *The Great Escape* failed to make the AFI's top twenty-five, it does stand with *The Magnificent Seven* in the book *100 Greatest Films Scores*.[11] The film's title piece alone qualifies it for greatness, a rousing anthem that anticipates the tension throughout the film. Thirty years after the movie's release, the score was notably revived in a memorable episode of *The Simpsons*.[12]

No other conflict has been portrayed more often than World War II, which inspired hundreds of films. Notwithstanding the prolific output of films about wars throughout history, it isn't hyperbole to say that *The Great Escape* ranks as one of the greatest among the genre—and perhaps *the* greatest war film that never features a single battle scene.

7

THE THRILL OF IT ALL

(1963)

★ ★ ★

Director: Norman Jewison
Screenplay: Carl Reiner, based on a story by Larry Gelbart, Carl Reiner
Producers: Ross Hunter, Martin Melcher. *Director of Photography:* Russell
    Metty. *Music:* DeVol. *Editor:* Milton Carruth
Cast: Doris Day (Beverly Boyer), James Garner (Gerald Boyer), Arlene
    Francis (Mrs. Fraleigh), Edward Andrews (Gardiner Fraleigh), Elliot
    Reid (Mike Palmer), Reginald Owen (Tom Fraleigh), Zasu Pitts (Olivia),
    Carl Reiner (Actor)
Studio: Universal
Release Date: July 17, 1963
Specs: 108 minutes; color
Availability: DVD (Universal)

SUMMARY

Beverly Boyer is a contented housewife and mother of two small children
with her husband, Gerald, a New York obstetrician. After a dinner party
hosted by one of Gerald's patients, Beverly is recruited to become the
spokeswoman for Happy Soap, whose live commercials air during *The
Happy Hour Playhouse* television program. After a humiliating start, she
soon becomes a sensation for her every housewife persona. But as Beverly's

success and fame grow, she devotes less time to her husband and children, creating tension at home for the increasingly frustrated Gerald.

BACKGROUND

With the exception of star Doris Day, much of the cast and crew associated with *The Thrill of It All* earned their bona fides in television, so it's not surprising they tackled the medium with such relish.

Carl Reiner had made a name for himself as one of the stars of 1950s television, both as an actor and a writer. Reiner won two Emmys for Best Supporting Actor for the variety series *Caesar's Hour*, and achieved additional fame as the creator and head writer of *The Dick Van Dyke Show*. Larry Gelbart was also a writer for *Caesar's Hour*, earning several Emmy nominations during his tenure with the show, along with future comic legends Mel Brooks and Neil Simon.

While many directors who segue from television to film draw on their experience helming episodes of dramas and situation comedies, Norman Jewison's path took a slightly different route. Yes, he had directed for television, but rather than work on episodic programs, Jewison primarily produced variety shows and specials, featuring such stars as Perry Como, Danny Kaye, Harry Belafonte, and Judy Garland. While his first feature film, *40 Pounds of Trouble*, may have been a forgettable comedy, Jewison's work on the Tony Curtis production helped him develop and refine the skills needed to transition from the small screen to features. Within a few months of finishing *40 Pounds* he was applying those newly honed talents on *The Thrill of It All*.

According to Jewison, "Every picture has to have a raison d'être" and for the director's second film that reason to be was as "a satire of commercials."[1] Both the director and Carl Reiner were eager to "satirize the commercialization of our beloved medium of television," and Jewison felt "fortunate to work with such a gifted and generous man"[2] as Reiner. It was Jewison who advocated for Garner to play Day's husband. According to the director, the actor "was a master at looking exasperated, put upon, fed up,"[3] which is what was called for throughout the film.

Doris Day was among a rare group of performers, like Bing Crosby and Frank Sinatra before her, whose successful music career led to movie stardom. Before her first film, *Romance on the High Seas* in 1948, Day had sung on a half-dozen hits with a big band outfit, Les Brown and his Orchestra. Even as her profile in Hollywood rose, Day continued to record hits—many in conjunction with her movies, musicals and non-musicals alike.

By the late 1950s, the actress had shared the screen with Hollywood icons James Cagney, Clark Gable, and James Stewart. The new decade was no different, as she appeared with screen idol Rock Hudson, a frequent costar, and screen icon Cary Grant. But by then, Day herself had become a superstar, parlaying her wholesome image as a perpetual virgin into box office queen. By 1960, she was Hollywood's number one star, a rank she still held when she signed on to play James Garner's housewife in *The Thrill of It All*.

Familiar faces rounded out the cast, including Arlene Francis, who was known less as an actress and more as a television "personality"—primarily for her regular appearances on the celebrity panel game show, *What's My Line?* Her husband was played by character actor Edward Andrews, who seemed to appear in almost every comedy—film and television alike—of the decade. Andrews wasn't the filmmakers' first choice, however. Walter Matthau was offered the part, but he thought the role too minor for an actor of his stature. Rather than turn down the role, though, Matthau requested $100,000, an amount he knew would not be granted. Said Matthau, "If you are offered a weak part you ask for a hike in salary to compensate for it."[4] It was an odd comment, since Matthau had not quite established himself as a Hollywood name to be reckoned with, and at that time he was filming the dud *Ensign Pulver*, an anemic—and Jack Lemmon-less—sequel to *Mister Roberts*.

RECEPTION

In his *New York Times* review, Bosley Crowther heaped the majority of his praise on Doris Day and writer Carl Reiner. As Crowther remarked, the actress "is best at domestic comedy when it's got a real bounce and bite to it. And that's what this one has, thanks to Mr. Reiner and to Norman Jewison, who directed it." Although Crowther enjoyed the film, he also remarked, "I don't want to give you the impression that *The Thrill of It All* is a great film. I just want to tell you it is loaded with good, clean American laughs." As for Garner, the most the critic could muster was calling him "very wholesome and bland."[5]

Variety appreciated Reiner's screenplay, particularly his satirical takes on American institutions, but stated, "Ultimately, it is in the design and engineering of cumulative sight gags that *The Thrill of It All* excels."[6] The *BBC Times* called the film "an enjoyably wacky satire on the world of advertising, pairing Doris Day with the immensely likeable James Garner for the first time."[7]

At the box office, the film kept Day's streak of successes alive, grossing nearly $12 million and earning it a place among the top twenty films of 1963.[8]

COMMENTARY

Although Day was a huge box office star with a slew of hits to her credit, Garner proves her equal in this film. In his memoir and often in interviews, Garner claimed that he didn't act, so much as he reacted, but many of his fine performances over the years contradict this modest self-assessment. But if any film of Garner's career could corroborate such an assertion, *The Thrill of It All* would be a strong candidate. As director Norman Jewison attested, Garner could elicit even more laughs than the gag itself by punctuating it with his reaction—and he does so throughout the movie. It's the give-and-take of these sequences that comprise so many of the film's highlights.

Another key to the film's success is the genuine chemistry that Day and Garner generate. Many of Garner's comedies—and not a few dramas as well—rely on the actor's compatibility with his leading ladies. In *Thrill*, the actors are comic collaborators: Day plays her part by getting embroiled in an absurd situation, and then Garner cements the laughs by reacting to Day's predicaments.

Though the film could succeed on the performances of Day and Garner alone, there are other treats throughout. Some of the supporting performances are especially noteworthy, including that of Edward Andrews and Arlene Francis as a "fortyish" couple who are ecstatic about becoming first-time parents. Francis was fifty-five at the time of the filming, so a little suspension of belief is required, but the actress pulls it off, particularly in the opening sequences. And Andrews, who excelled at portraying frazzled characters, befuddled husbands, and obtuse bosses alike, fits the bill of the worrisome new father perfectly.

The most enjoyable supporting performance, though, comes from the film's screenwriter. In addition to fashioning the screenplay, Reiner made another contribution to the film, heralded in the opening credits: "Gowns by Jean Louis" and "Jewels by David Webb" are followed by "Cameos by Carl Reiner." Reiner outdoes both the gowns *and* jewels with comic gems of his own. These brief but very amusing vignettes demonstrate that in addition to being an inventive writer, Reiner was a captivating performer, too.

After the success of this film, Day and Garner were quickly reunited for another comedy, a remake of the Cary Grant–Irene Dunne semi-classic *My Favorite Wife*. In the remake, Day plays a wife who has been lost at sea

An exasperated Garner with Doris Day. *Universal Pictures / Photofest © Universal Pictures*

and presumed dead, but reappears on the day that Garner remarries. Unfortunately, lightning did not strike twice, and the Day-Garner version fails
to replicate the charm of the 1940 original. The box office results would
say otherwise, since *Move Over* performed slightly better than *Thrill*, but
creatively, it took a backseat to the earlier film, which may be why Day and
Garner did not make another film together.

8

THE WHEELER DEALERS

(1963)

★ ★ ½

Director: Arthur Hiller
Screenplay: George J. W. Goodman, Ira Wallach, based on the novel by
 Goodman
Producer: Martin Ransohoff. *Director of Photography:* Charles Lang, ASC. *Music:*
 DeVol. *Editor:* Tom McAdoo. *Art Director:* George W. Davis, Addison
 Hehr. *Set Decorator:* Henry Grace, Keogh Gleason
Cast: James Garner (Henry Tyroon), Lee Remick (Molly Thatcher), Phil
 Harris (Ray Jay Fox), Chill Wills (Jay Ray Spinelby), Jim Backus (Bullar
 Bear), Louis Nye (Stanislas), John Astin (Hector Vanson), Elliott
 Reid (Leonard), Pat Harrington (Buddy Zack), Joey Forman (Buster
 Yarrow), Patricia Crowley (Eloise Cott), Charles Watts (J. R. Martin),
 Howard McNear (Mr. Wilson), Marcel Hillaire (Giuseppe), Don
 Briggs (Len Flink), Vaughn Taylor (Thaddeus Whipple), Robert Strauss
 (Feinberg, taxi driver), John Marley (Achilles Dimitros), Peter Leeds
 (Arthur Watkins)
Studio: MGM/a Filmways Production
Release Date: November 14, 1963
Specs: 105 minutes; color
Availability: DVD (Warner Archive Collection)

SUMMARY

Henry Tyroon is a through-and-through Texas oil man—or is he? We know one thing for sure: no matter who he is, he loves making deals—whether it's in oil or oil paintings. When Henry needs money to drill even deeper to strike oil in his well in Texas, he heads to New York to hit up some familiar investors. Meanwhile, a stock analyst named Molly is one step away from being let go from her employer because of cost cutting. To avoid drawing unwanted attention for firing a woman without cause, her boss gives her an impossible task—manage their client Henry Tyroon.

BACKGROUND

The Wheeler Dealers is based on a novel by George J. W. Goodman, who achieved publishing success some authors only dream about—writing not only a best-selling book, but one that tops the best-seller charts for more than a year. However, it wasn't the fiction chart that Goodman conquered, but the nonfiction list. After modest success writing novels about the finance world—*The Bubble Makers* (1955), *A Time for Paris* (1957), and *The Wheeler Dealers* (1959)—Goodman turned to nonfiction works. His first, *The Money Game* (1968), was written under the pseudonym of Adam Smith and was an instant success. In 1984 Goodman parlayed his skill of conveying financial matters into palatable concepts by creating and hosting the series *Adam Smith's Money World*, which ran on PBS stations for several years. Before devoting himself to *The Money Game*, Goodman was hired to adapt *The Wheeler Dealers*, along with playwright novelist Ira Wallach, who had cowritten Garner's 1962 film *Boys' Night Out*.

As with many of Garner's directors, Arthur Hiller first cut his teeth directing for television, initially in his Canadian homeland, before moving to the States. And like Garner, Hiller paid many of his television dues by working on western programs, though *Maverick* was not among them. His first feature, *The Careless Years*, was released in 1957, but it would be another six years before he directed his next, a drama about Lipizzaner horses for Disney called *The Miracle of the White Stallions*. That same year, MGM produced Hiller's third feature, *The Wheeler Dealers*.

After the failure of *The Children's Hour*, an incendiary drama that no doubt irked conservative audiences, Garner returned to his comic roots in a role not unlike his earlier film *Cash McCall*. Unlike Garner, however, the film's leading lady, Lee Remick, had been building a stellar career in provocative dramas of her own, beginning with *A Face in the Crowd* (1957), in which she plays a teen who marries television con man Andy Griffith. This was followed by the controversial drama *Anatomy of a Murder* (1959), in which her character's husband is on trial for murdering the man she claims raped her. And in 1962, she took on her greatest challenge, playing alongside Jack Lemmon as a pair of struggling alcoholics in *Days of Wine and Roses*. The latter film earned the actress rave reviews as well as an Academy Award nomination. After playing in a string of heavy-duty dramas as well as thrillers like *Experiment in Terror*, *The Wheeler Dealers* was Remick's first true comedy, which she no doubt welcomed.

Though *Cash McCall* and *The Wheeler Dealers* are lighthearted tales of savvy businessmen who get tangled up in romance, the latter film appears less grounded in reality. This is evidenced in some part by the differences in the supporting casts. While *Cash McCall* boasted Oscar-winner Dean Jagger and other actors more likely to be found in dramas, such as E. G. Marshall, Nina Foch, and Otto Kruger, *The Wheeler Dealers* was populated with a virtual who's who of comic actors of the era: Chill Wills, Phil Harris, John Astin, Jim Backus, and Louis Nye.

RECEPTION

Bosley Crowther in the *New York Times* lamented that the screenplay didn't "jell and isn't droll," while "Arthur Hiller's direction is too slow for romantic comedy." However, the critic did find Garner "spry and briskly charming" in his role.[1] The *Cleveland Press* called the film a "pleasant, escapist, frothy affair" and praised Garner, saying the role of Tyroon was "tailor made for his talents" and that "he carries it off with a fine flourish."[2]

Garner received the film's only notable recognition, earning a Golden Globe nomination for Best Actor in a Comedy or Musical. That year the category was stacked with a host of comic heavyweights, including Cary Grant (*Charade*), Jonathan Winters (*It's a Mad, Mad, Mad, Mad World*), and Jack Lemmon (*Irma la Douce* and *Under the Yum Yum Tree*)—not to mention Frank Sinatra (*Come Blow Your Horn*) and Albert Finney (*Tom Jones*). Garner and the other illustrious nominees all lost to an actor unknown to most American viewers then and even more so now, Alberto Sordi. The Italian actor won for his performance as a businessman who travels to Sweden hoping to experience some sexual adventures in *Il Diavolo* (a.k.a. *To Bed or Not to Bed*).

Cigarette girl Shirley Bonne passes in front of a distressed Lee Remick in the restaurant that Garner has just bought. *MGM / Photofest © MGM*

The film did only modest business at the box office, easily the least successful of the four Garner releases of 1963, behind *Move Over, Darling*, *The Thrill of It All*, and *The Great Escape*.

COMMENTARY

Three years after playing Cash McCall, a corporate raider with a knack for making astute business deals, Garner was back at it in his second "financial romance." Of the four 1963 films the actor starred in, he thought most highly of two, *The Wheeler Dealers* and *Move Over, Darling*, but in retrospect, it was the two that he didn't cite that have better stood the test of time—*The Great Escape*, of course, and Garner's first pairing with Doris Day, *The Thrill of It All*. In Garner's memoir, his assessment of *Wheeler Dealers* must have mellowed since he didn't have much to say about the film, other than to mention that "for years, people came up to me and quoted lines from it."[3]

But that's not to take anything away from this movie. Like many comic films from the 1960s, *The Wheeler Dealers* plays its humor more broadly, often to ludicrous heights. Those moments of absurdity come chiefly through the antics of the supporting cast, most effectively by Louis Nye. The former alum of Steve Allen's variety show offers a droll performance as Stanislas, a man who exploits the art world by producing modern works at a relentless pace—just to make a financial killing. Garner's character recognizes a fellow player in Stanislas, someone who seizes opportunity to earn a buck—or a million of them—by capitalizing on the latest trend. And Tyroon, which so cleverly—or not—rhymes with "tycoon," is not above some outrageous behavior himself, from impulsively buying a taxicab for four days to purchasing a restaurant.

It seems that everyone in this film engages in suspect behavior for purposes of some sort of gain, primarily of the financial kind, and even the female lead is not immune to such shenanigans. None of the mischief is to be taken seriously, though—even the sexism of Remick's character, Molly, endures. For its time, the film at least offers some progressive notions and even makes a case against the boorish behavior of the men who don't take Molly seriously.

Despite its kinship with other contrived comedies of the 1960s, *The Wheeler Dealers* manages to charm and amuse—primarily because Garner's personable nature grounds the comedy amidst the broad comic strokes of the supporting players.

THE AMERICANIZATION OF EMILY

(1964)

★ ★ ★ ★

Director: Arthur Hiller
Screenplay: Paddy Chayefsky, based on the novel by William Bradford Huie
Producer: Martin Ransohoff. *Director of Photography:* Philip Lathrop, ASC.
   Music: Johnny Mandel. *Editor:* Tom McAdoo. *Art Directors:* George W.
   Davis, Hans Peters, Elliot Scott. *Set Decorator:* Henry Grace, Robert R.
   Benton. *Costume Designer:* Bill Thomas
Cast: James Garner (Lieutenant Commander Charles E. Madison), Julie
   Andrews (Emily Barham), Melvyn Douglas (Admiral William Jessup),
   James Coburn (Lieutenant Commander Paul "Bus" Cummings), Joyce
   Grenfell (Mrs. Barham), Edward Binns (Admiral Thomas Healy), Liz
   Fraser (Sheila), Keenan Wynn (Old Sailor), William Windom (Captain
   Harry Spaulding)
Studio: MGM
Release Date: October 27, 1964
Specs: 115 minutes; black and white
Availability: DVD and Blu-ray (Warner Home Video)

SUMMARY

The film takes place in war-time England, specifically beginning at midnight on May 4, 1944, at Hendon Airport. The opening crawl sets the scene:

In World War II, few men served their countries more ably than a small group of unheralded heroes known as "The Dog-Robbers."

A "Dog-Robber" is the personal attendant of a general or admiral and his job is to keep his general or admiral well-clothed, well-fed, and well-loved during the battle.

Every army and navy in the world has its "Dog-Robbers," but, needless to say, ours were the best.

Charles "Charlie" Madison, lieutenant commander in the US Navy, is one of these "dog-robbers"—a personal attendant to Admiral Jessup. Emily Barham is a motor pool driver assigned to Charlie. Having lost her father, brother, and husband to war, Emily is leery to fall in love with any man involved with combat.

As resourceful as any of his fellow dog-robbers, Charlie nonetheless is unable to avoid his greatest hurdle, one that will put him on the front line of danger. Because Admiral Jessup is concerned about the reputation of the US Navy, Charlie is ordered to film the invasion of Omaha Beach on D-day. His admiral demands, "The first dead man to land on Omaha Beach will be a sailor." After his initial resistance, Charlie finally agrees to take the trip to Omaha Beach—but only when he believes that the troops will ship off *before* he can board.

Garner and his grandest leading lady, Julie Andrews. *MGM / Photofest © MGM*

BACKGROUND

The Americanization of Emily is based on the 1959 novel of the same name by William Bradford Huie, a journalist and editor of the *American Mercury* magazine. Huie had served in the navy during World War II and participated in the D-day invasion, an experience he used for the setting of *Emily*, his third novel. Film and television producer Martin Ransohoff, whose first two movies—*Boys' Night Out* and *The Wheeler Dealers*—had starred Garner, was looking for a more prestigious film and bought the rights to Huie's novel. According to Shaun Considine, Paddy Chayefsky's biographer, "Five writers, including Huie, had worked on the script before Ransohoff spoke to Chayefsky,"[1] who until then had only written original screenplays. After reading the book, Chayefsky was intrigued but would only agree to take on the adaptation if he could change essential elements of the plot.

After the screenplay was well under way, three-time Academy Award–winning director William Wyler was attached to the project, along with actor William Holden. Both Holden and Wyler had worked on several war-related films, though the sensibilities and messages of those films are contrary to that of *Emily*. Holden had starred in *Stalag 17* (for which he won the Oscar), *The Bridge on the River Kwai*, and *Toward the Unknown*, Garner's film debut. Wyler had won two of his three Oscars for directing films related to the Second World War—*Mrs. Miniver* in 1942 and *The Best Years of Our Lives* in 1946. Both productions were earnest dramas, though not without some scenes of gentle humor. However, there was a wide gap between gentle humor and a scathing indictment of the military mind-set, and *Emily* represented a radical departure from Wyler's résumé of populist films.

Arthur Hiller, a veteran of episodic television, had completed only two feature films before he actively campaigned for the directing job. Said Hiller, "I was just bowled over by the script, and it was the first time—the only time—I kept at a producer to hire me"[2]

Julie Christie was first approached for the role of Emily, but she turned down Ransohoff. On the other hand, Julie Andrews, who was filming her first movie, *Mary Poppins*, was keen to take on a role that had more edge than that of the magical nanny. After reading Chayefsky's script, she was eager to play the female lead, and won the part after Ransohoff and Wyler viewed footage from the Disney film.

Garner signed on to play the part of Lieutenant Commander Bus Cummings, but according to the actor, Ransohoff asked if he would be interested in playing the lead if Holden pulled out. Garner enthusiastically agreed, noting, "I knew it was a hell of an actor's part. It was a different kind of role than I'd been doing, with a brilliant script."[3] Holden did indeed withdraw from the film. In his DVD commentary, director Hiller remembered, "James Garner was to play the James Coburn role, and we all thought, 'No, he should really be playing this leading role'—the very handsome, good-looking coward, so to speak, and so we moved him up to that."[4]

The role of Bus Cummings was given to Garner's *Great Escape* costar, Coburn. Melvyn Douglas took on the role of Admiral Jessup, Charlie's boss. A former 1930s and '40s leading man with such credits as *Ninotchka* and *Mr. Blandings Builds His Dream House*, Douglas developed into a reliable character actor and secured his first of two supporting actor Oscars—for *Hud*—six months before the release of *Emily*. Remaining cast members included Joyce Grenfell as Emily's mother, future Emmy winner William Windom (*My World and Welcome to It*) as one of Charlie's comrades, Steve Franken and Keenan Wynn[5] as drunken sailors, and in an uncredited role, another future Emmy winner, Diana Rigg.[6]

RECEPTION

Bosley Crowther of the *New York Times* appreciated *The Americanization of Emily*, calling it a "comedy that says more for basic pacifism than a fistful of intellectual tracts." In addition to calling Julie Andrews "irresistible," Crowther commended Garner for "his taut and stalwart perseverance in acting an unregenerate coward." Besides "the splendid performances" of Garner and Andrews—"his with an edge of crisp sarcasm, hers with a brush of sentiment"—Crowther also praises James Coburn, Edward Binns, and Melvyn Douglas, as well as the "deft" performances by Liz Fraser, Joyce Grenfell, and Keenan Wynn. Crowley called Paddy Chayefsky's screenplay "brilliantly adapted" from Huie's novel, lauding Chayefsky for "remarkably good writing with some slashing irreverence," and noted Hiller's "brisk" direction." According to the critic, *The Americanization of Emily* "is highly entertaining" and "makes a good case for pure romance."[7] The *Variety* critic offered the film faint praise, saying that it "is primarily interesting for the romance between Andrews and Garner." Apparently, the reviewer did not feel that Andrews's performance warranted mention at all, although other cast members were singled out, chiefly James Coburn, who is "outstanding particularly for his comedy scenes," along with supporting players Keenan Wynn and Joyce Grenfell, who "handle their roles well." As for Garner, he "generally delivers a satisfactory performance."[8]

Though not a blockbuster, *The Americanization of Emily* did reasonably well, earning $4 million at the box office. Compared to Andrews's other film of 1964, however, its box office take was a fraction. *Mary Poppins*, Andrews's film debut two months earlier, brought in more than $30 million, making it the third-highest-grossing film of the year, behind *Goldfinger* and the film that should have starred Andrews, *My Fair Lady*.

The film received two Academy Award nominations, for Best Art Direction-Set Decoration (Black and White) and Best Cinematography (Black and White). Andrews also received a BAFTA nomination for Best British Actress.

COMMENTARY

The release of *The Americanization of Emily* came nine months after the much more famous antiwar film of 1964, Stanley Kubrick's *Dr. Strangelove or: How I Learned to Stop Worrying and Love the Bomb*. Though both films can be appreciated for their irreverent humor, Kubrick's film is much more satirical, reflected in the three characters portrayed by Peter Sellers, particularly the absurd title role. *Emily*, on the other hand, plays much more as a black comedy, taking its shots at the military with a sting that is more potent because it takes aim in a much more realistic fashion. According to director Hiller, "I think about all the people who thought it was anti-American or antiwar, and it isn't. It's anti the glorification of war."[9]

Garner's chief concern was whether he could handle the wordy monologues, so that Cheyefsky's script could be properly expressed. This challenge proved to be one of the actor's particular on-screen skills, not just in *Emily* but other films as well. Indeed, throughout his career, Garner was always very respectful of the screenwriter's craft, so much so that he never ad-libbed. According to the actor's daughter, Gigi Garner, her father insisted on remaining faithful to the script and recited the written word verbatim. He allowed the writers to do their jobs, and he did his.[10]

In one of several memorable monologues delivered with the wit, sarcasm, and exasperation typical of a Garner role, his character declares,

I've dealt with Europeans all my life. I know all about us parvenus from the states, who come over here and race around your old cathedral towns with our cameras and Coca-Cola bottles, brawl in your pubs, paw your women, and act like we own the world. We overtip, we talk too loud, we think we can buy anything with a Hershey bar. I've had Germans and Italians tell me how politically ingenuous we are, and perhaps so. But we haven't managed a Hitler or a Mussolini yet. I've had Frenchmen call me a savage, because I only took half an hour for lunch. Hell, Miss Barham, the only reason the French take two hours for lunch is because the service in their restaurants is lousy. We crass Americans didn't introduce war into your little island. This war, Miss Barham, to which we Americans are so insensitive is the result of two thousand years of European greed, barbarism, superstition, and stupidity. Don't blame it on our Coca-Cola bottles. Europe was a going brothel long before we came to town.[11]

Garner delivers this scathing indictment so deftly, there's no hint that he may have suffered from a lack of confidence. If he had been unsure of himself, he certainly conquered such reservations.

Perhaps Garner plays Charlie so assuredly because the actor identified so thoroughly with his character. As Garner would later assert, "*Emily* is my favorite film that I've ever seen or been involved in, and Charlie Madison is my favorite character, probably because I share his views."[12]

In addition to Garner, *The Americanization of Emily* was also beloved by many others who worked on it, including the film's director, Arthur Hiller. Despite making several notable films that followed, such as the tearjerker *Love Story* (for which he received an Oscar nomination), *The Hospital* (his second collaboration with Chayefsky), and the hilarious *The In-Laws* (1979), Hiller cites *Emily* as "my favorite film and it's, I think, Marty Ransohoff's, James Garner's, James Coburn's, and Julie Andrews's favorite film."[13]

Garner had good cause to celebrate this work. It is certainly among his finest films, on par with his other outstanding war flick, *The Great Escape* from 1963. And though the prisoner of war classic with Steve McQueen is perhaps the best *film* of Garner's career, *Emily* features his finest feature film performance.

36 HOURS

(1964)

★ ★ ½

Director: George Seaton
Screenplay: George Seaton, based on "Beware of the Dog" by Roald Dahl
  and a story by Carl K. Hittleman, Luis H. Vance
Producer: William Perlberg. *Director of Photography:* Philip H. Lathrop, ASC.
  Music: Dimitri Tiomkin. *Editor:* Adrienne Fazan, ACE. *Art Directors:*
  George W. Davis, Edward Carfagno. *Set Decorators:* Henry Grace,
  Frank McKelvy. *Costume Designer:* Dorothy Jeakins
Cast: James Garner (Major Jefferson Pike), Eva Marie Saint (Anna Hedler),
  Rod Taylor (Major Walter Gerber), Werner Peters (Otto (Schack),
  John Banner (Ernst), Alan Napier (Colonel Peter MacLean), Ed Gilbert
  (Captain Abbott), Celia Lovsky (Elsa), Russell Thorson (General Allison)
Studio: MGM; made in cooperation with Cherokee Productions
Release Date: February 19, 1964
Specs: 115 minutes; black and white
Availability: DVD and Blu-ray (Warner Home Video)

SUMMARY

In early June of 1944, a major with insider knowledge about the preparations for the D-day attack on Normandy is drugged and kidnapped by Germans. He is sequestered to a "hospital" that has staged an elaborate scheme: dupe the American into thinking he has suffered from amnesia for several years, with the world war well behind him. Racing against the clock, the Germans hope the major will reveal details of the invasion—an attack that has *yet to happen*—before he catches on to their plan.

BACKGROUND

In 1964, James Garner took a bold step that few of his acting colleagues in Hollywood had ventured into: he founded his own production company. Though the practice has become fairly common over the past several decades—especially among A-listers like George Clooney, Brad Pitt, and Will Smith—it was a relatively rare occurrence in the 1960s. Burt Lancaster was one of the first actors to assume the role of producer, when he and Harold Hecht established Hecht-Norma Productions in 1948.[1] Their association evolved into various production companies under different names, including Hecht-Lancaster Productions, whose most prominent film was the Oscar-winning *Marty* (1955).

Honoring his Native American heritage, Garner named the new venture Cherokee Productions. Unlike Lancaster, who didn't always star in his productions, Garner appeared in each one of Cherokee's productions, which produced several of his films as well as his television shows *Nichols* and *The Rockford Files*. For the first film under the Cherokee banner, Garner chose a property with a setting that had served the actor well—World War II. According to biographer Raymond Strait, the actor "invested time and money in the picture with the hopes that it would produce handsome profits."[2]

The man hired to steer the film, George Seaton, had established a solid reputation as both a writer and director, and he brought both of those skills to bear in the making of *36 Hours*. Though not as esteemed as some of his contemporaries—perhaps because he wasn't very prolific—Seaton nonetheless was a "polished and professional" filmmaker "who occasionally rose well above his standard"[3] to write and direct such films as *Miracle on 34th Street* and *The Country Girl*, both of which earned him screenwriting Oscars.

There's no disputing who directed the film, but the writing credits for *36 Hours* are a bit murky. Seaton is credited with the screenplay. However, beloved children's book author Roald Dahl (*Charlie and the Chocolate Factory*, *The BFG*) is also cited in the credits, despite Dahl not having any direct participation with the film—in fact, not even knowing about the production until after the screenplay had been written. Dahl's wife, actress

Patricia Neal, who may have been under consideration for the female lead, had read the screenplay, which reminded her of one of her husband's short stories, "Beware of the Dog." Though Dahl's story focuses on a Royal Air Force pilot in occupied France, rather than an American in London, the main plots were too similar to ignore. Because there was no attribution to Dahl or his story, the writer felt he could squeeze some money from MGM, the studio financing the film. Advised to settle for a smaller payoff, Dahl held firm, primarily on behalf of his children, and he prevailed. As Dahl's biographer, Donald Sturrock, wrote, "MGM not only gave Dahl a credit as the originator of the story but a payment of $30,000 made directly into his children's trust account."[4]

Ultimately, the film credits read

Screen Play by George Seaton
Based on "Beware of the Dog"
by
Roald Dahl
And a Story by
Carl K. Hittleman and Luis H. Vance

But even this attribution bears some scrutiny. To capitalize on the release of the film, a paperback adaptation of the film was released by Popular Library in 1965. While the practice of issuing a "novelization" of a film is infrequent—it probably reached its peak in the 1970s and '80s when a number of science fiction films were produced with novel tie-ins written *after* the film—it's not unusual either. In the case of *36 Hours*, Hittleman is credited with writing the novel that is "Based on the Screen Play by George Seaton." However, neither Luis H. Vance, Dahl, or Dahl's story are referenced in the book's copyright page or on the cover. And even more curious: when the film was remade for cable television in 1989,[5] the screenplay was attributed to Stanley Greenberg, with a nod to Dahl, Hittleman, and Vance, but *no* mention of Seaton.

Garner spared no expense hiring other accomplished Hollywood veterans to bring the WWII story to the screen. The film's producer, William Perlberg, had worked with Seaton on several films dating back to 1940. Besides Seaton, other Oscar-winning talents behind the scenes included editor Adrienne Fazan (*Gigi*) and composer Dimitri Tiomkin, who had received four statues from the Academy of Motion Picture Arts and Sciences (including two for *High Noon*'s score and song). Both art directors on *36 Hours*, George W. Davis and Edward Carfagno, had experience working on period pieces and each had multiple Oscars to show for it.[6] Henry Grace

Eva Marie Saint and an "aged" Garner are both victims of Nazi treachery. *MGM / Photofest* © *MGM*

and Philip H. Lathrop, *Americanization of Emily* alum, were likely hired by Garner's company at the actor's insistence. Set decorator Grace and cinematographer Lathrop had both earned Oscar nominations for *Emily*, and their expertise added a level of quality to the new film.[7]

The other two leads were a pair of actors who both had played high-profile parts for the master of suspense, Alfred Hitchcock. For the part of the German doctor who leads the deception, the filmmakers picked Australian Rod Taylor, who was coming off one of the biggest hits of the prior year, Hitchcock's *The Birds*. Eva Marie Saint played the Jewish woman who is coerced into taking part in the masquerade. After winning a Best Supporting Actress Oscar for *On the Waterfront* ten years before, Saint had appeared in only a handful of films, most notably the 1959 Hitchcock thriller *North by Northwest* and *Exodus* in 1960 with Paul Newman.

The remaining roles were played by an international cast of Americans, Brits, and Europeans, including several German character actors, among them Werner Peters, Sig Ruman, and John Banner. The latter actor would soon gain fame on *Hogan's Heroes* as Sergeant Schultz, the befuddled prison guard who is constantly outwitted by the camp prisoners.

RECEPTION

Brendan Gill in the *New Yorker* found the film "so fresh and beguiling a thriller for much of its length" that he allowed himself to accept "again and again the most outrageous improbabilities" and was left wanting "for more."[8] The magazine later praised Garner, Saint, and Taylor for being "plausible in highly implausible roles."[9] However, Bosley Crowther, in the *New York Times*, could not get past such implausibility, asserting the film "has such a synthetic look . . . that the whole thing rings curiously false," despite director Seaton's "thorough and careful job." In praising Garner, Crowther notes his other recent WWII film stating, "Garner, who did very nicely as the Navy officer who finally got to Omaha Beach in *The Americanization of Emily*, does nicely as the fellow in this case, too."[10]

Variety called the film a "fanciful war drama" and singled out Rod Taylor in his "offbeat role of the German, playing it for sympathy and realistically," as well as Eva Marie Saint, who "delivers strongly as the nurse drafted by the Nazis." The reviewer gave a curious assessment of the film's star, however, declaring Garner as merely "okay" employing his "usual sound brand of histrionics"[11]—whatever that means.

COMMENTARY

While *36 Hours* was the first film for Cherokee Productions, it was the fifth—and final—picture Garner made with a WWII setting. Released on January 28, 1965, *36 Hours* followed *The Americanization of Emily* by a mere three months. As some critics noted, the film loses steam in the latter stages, but it still remains a unique thriller. While it may not be as consistently gripping as *The Great Escape* or as endearing as *Emily*, it remains a satisfying entertainment. And though the pacing of the story sometimes undermines the overall effectiveness of *36 Hours*, the trio of stars more than makes up for it, providing performances that make the improbable story somehow credible. Perhaps the only flaw that can be said about the actors is that Rod Taylor might not have been the best choice for the German doctor who masterminds the deception. As Mick Martin and Marsha Porter note, "Rod Taylor is so likeable as the doctor leading the ruse that you almost hope his plan succeeds."[12]

Garner, on the other hand, is perfectly cast in the lead, exhibiting the right amount of bewilderment and resourcefulness as the manipulated major. Garner excelled in gripping adventure stories, and this WWII thriller fits nicely into his wheelhouse.

Why? Because like many of his dramas, this film allows Garner to display his tough exterior and at the same time reveal an appealing vulnerability, a unique combination that was uncommon among leading men until the late 1950s/early '60s. Although Marlon Brando may have heralded the arrival of the new antihero, it wasn't until well into the 1960s that such figures began to truly populate American screens—and Brando's antihero differed from Garner's. The Brando male was an uncouth brute, while Garner personified the nascent hero beneath the hide of a coward. Little wonder that this version of the inadvertent hero, first developed by Garner in *Maverick* and then perfected in *The Rockford Files*, became an emblematic type for the actor.

Whether Garner played bewildered, befuddled, or cowardly characters, viewers were never deceived into thinking the role was anything less than capable. Circumstances may have unsettled his character, but he would ultimately prevail.

While the first two WWII films of Garner's career—1950s programmers *Darby's Rangers* and *Up Periscope*—could be characterized as simplistic adventure films indicative of the usual fodder of the decade, the same cannot be said of the actor's three WWII films of the 1960s. *The Great Escape*, *The Americanization of Emily*, and *36 Hours* comprise an unofficial trilogy for Garner that featured a much more sophisticated treatment of the war, each in its own way. *The Great Escape* managed to combine thrilling adventure with a humane tale of men risking their lives to achieve an objective far more important than simple survival. *The Americanization of Emily* was a hybrid as well—a blend of drama and satire that draws its own kind of blood—attacking the ludicrous machinations of war, even a "justifiable" one. While *36 Hours* might be the least successful of the three films, it nonetheless manages to be both a psychological thriller and a compelling man-on-the-run yarn that even Alfred Hitchcock might have appreciated.

GRAND PRIX

(1966)

★ ★ ★

Director: John Frankenheimer
Screenplay: Robert Alan Aurthur
Producer: Edward Lewis. *Director of Photography:* Lionel Lindon. *Music:* Maurice
    Jarre. *Supervising Editor:* Fredric Steinkamp. *Editors:* Henry Berman, Stu
    Linder, Frank Santillo. *Production Designer:* Richard Sylbert
Cast: James Garner (Pete Aron), Yves Montand (Jean-Paul Sarti), Eva Marie
    Saint (Louise Frederickson), Brian Bedford (Scott Stoddard), Toshiro
    Mifune (Izo Yamura), Jessica Walter (Pat Stoddard), Antonio Sabato
    (Nino Barlini)
Studio: MGM; a co-production of Joel Productions-JFP and Cherokee
    Productions
Release Date: December 21, 1966
Specs: 178 minutes; color
Availability: DVD and Blu-ray (Warner Archive Collection)

SUMMARY

A season in the life of Formula 1 racers. Pete Aron, a somewhat arrogant American, causes a devastating crash that leaves one of his rivals confined to a hospital. As Aron faces the consequences of his ruthless behavior on the track, he makes morally questionable decisions away from it. The personal lives of other drivers also come into focus as they compete in one Formula race after another, culminating in the final competition that takes a toll on several drivers.

BACKGROUND

John Frankenheimer was a prolific television director before amassing a string of successful features in the early 1960s. *Birdman of Alcatraz* (1962), the first of five films he made with Burt Lancaster, earned Frankenheimer a Directors Guild of America nomination and was followed by what is widely regarded as the director's greatest achievement, the cold war assassin thriller, *The Manchurian Candidate*. Another cold war film, *Seven Days in May*, followed in 1964, and then yet another Burt Lancaster film, the World War II thriller, *The Train*. Those black-and-white minor gems were followed by Frankenheimer's first color film and first epic, *Grand Prix*.

When Garner learned about Frankenheimer's plans to tell a story about Formula 1 racing, he pursued a part in the film. Steve McQueen, Garner's *Great Escape* costar, had initially signed on for the role of racer Pete Aron, but left the project because of conflicts with the film's producer. Against Frankenheimer's wishes, Garner was offered the role McQueen abandoned. Despite the resistance of Frankenheimer, who would often deride Garner in later interviews, the actor enjoyed the filming of *Grand Prix* more than any other project of his career. Said Garner, "For a guy who'd always loved cars and racing, it was a fantasy come true."[1]

Also signed on for the film was Garner's recent *36 Hours* costar Eva Marie Saint, who would provide the love interest to one of Aron's racing rivals, Sarti, played by French icon Yves Montand. To embody the international flavor of the competition, other key roles went to British stage actor Brian Bedford, Italian newcomer Antonio Sabato, and Japanese legend Toshiro Mifune. Unfortunately, Mifune's accent was too strong, so it was dubbed— a little too obviously—by voice actor Paul Frees.

In addition to actual races, several Formula 1 racing drivers figured in the cast and a few were even given small speaking parts. Among the drivers featured in the film were Bob Bondurant, three-time Formula 1 World Champion Jack Brabham, Jim Clark, and Lorenzo Bandini. Within two years of the film's release, the latter two drivers were killed on the track—Bandini at the Monaco Grand Prix, a mere six months after the release of the film, and Clark on April 7, 1968—Garner's fortieth birthday.

RECEPTION

Variety praised director Frankenheimer for creating "a sort of montage interplay of . . . the principals . . . that adroitly prevents the road running from overwhelming the personal drama."[2] While Bosley Crowther found the lead characters to be stereotypes and their relationships clichés, he applauded the "smashing and thundering compilation of racing footage shot superbly at the scenes of the big meets around the circuit, jazzed up with some great photographic trickery."[3] Crowther wasn't alone in finding more excitement in the racing sequences than interactions between the characters. Tony Mastroianni, writing for the *Cleveland Press*, found Garner "rugged and stoical," Brian Bedford "sensitive and stoical," and Yves Montand "disillusioned and stoical," ultimately advising viewers to "ignore the actors—the autos have the best parts."[4]

Grand Prix did very well at the box office, finishing in the top ten films of 1966 with a gross of more than $20 million.[5]

The film received three Academy Award nominations and won in all three categories: Best Film Editing, Best Sound, and Best Sound Effects.

Garner suiting up for another run around the track. *MGM / Photofest © MGM*

One assumes that none of those awards were bestowed upon the recipients for the dubbing of Japanese actor Toshiro Mifune's dialogue with Paul Frees, a distracting—if necessary—component of the film.

John Frankenheimer received a Directors Guild of America (DGA) nomination, which today often can translate into an Academy Award nomination. However, from 1952 through 1970, nominations under the Guild were much more prolific, when ten or more individuals would be recognized in a year;[6] the category was pared down to five nominees in 1971, the same number as Oscar contenders. Of the ten DGA nominees in 1967, four—Richard Brooks (*The Professionals*), Claude Lelouch (*A Man and a Woman*), Mike Nichols (*Who's Afraid of Virginia Woolf?*), and Fred Zinnemann (*A Man for All Seasons*)—would go on to receive Oscar nominations, with Zinnemann winning the top honor from the Guild and the Academy.[7]

The film also received two Golden Globe nominations, in absurd categories that thankfully no longer exist: Most Promising Newcomer—Male (Antonio Sabato), an award Garner himself received several years earlier for *Sayonara*, and Most Promising Newcomer—Female (Jessica Walter).[8] They lost to James Farentino (*The Pad and How to Use It*) and Camilla Sparv (*Dead Heat on a Merry-Go-Round*), respectively. What a shame.

COMMENTARY

Grand Prix was John Frankenheimer's first epic—whether it was his intention to make an epic or not. Like most epics, *Grand Prix* tells a much larger tale by focusing on the collective stories of individuals, of their romantic entanglements against the backdrop of exotic locales. While the number of characters in the film might not have matched that of recent blockbusters like *Dr. Zhivago* and *Khartoum*, *Grand Prix* had its own sense of spectacle.

Besides the concentration on a few characters, perhaps what also sets *Grand Prix* apart from other epics is its contemporary setting and its abbreviated timeline. Most epics feature stories sprawled out over years, if not decades. What also distinguishes this film from traditional epics is its fidelity to truth, courtesy of actual footage that captures scenes from the races as they occurred. Interwoven with the scripted roles are real racing car drivers who populate the film, providing it with a level of verisimilitude that a standard epic is incapable of conveying. Filmed among the real racing tournaments of Europe, *Grand Prix* immerses its viewers in a spectacle of immediacy. During the often-thrilling racing sequences, scenes of actors behind the wheel are seamlessly inserted into the action, making their participation in the races as believable as possible. Chief among those is Garner himself, who had trained for months to look and act like a racing competitor. If only more of the other actors had been so engaged in that aspect of filming, perhaps Frankenheimer would have reduced some of the more lifeless scenes that take place *out* of the vehicles.

The truth: *Grand Prix* is really two films in one. With its exciting racing sequences, the film is part thriller, providing dramatic conflict between the drivers on the tracks and occasionally away from the action. On the other hand, when the camera is not on the action, the interpersonal interludes play out like a Formula 1 soap opera, and such scenes drag the film down, making the viewer eager to return to the racing.

Off-track relationships of the principal figures, particularly the developing affair between driver Jean-Paul Sarti and magazine writer Louise Frederickson, unnecessarily bloat the film's running time. The leisurely pacing of their blooming romance plays out more like a melodrama than of two people falling in love, so that what should be engaging is instead a fairly tedious courtship. As a result, the viewer can't wait for the story to move elsewhere, either on to some other characters or preferably back to the action on the racecourse.

Despite its noticeable shortcomings—including an excessive running time of nearly three hours—*Grand Prix* has several things going for it, not the least of which is its dynamic racing sequences. These are emphasized with the unusual employment of split screens at opportune times. In addition to the energy generated by the racing scenes, the action becomes even more visceral as it plays out on three panels, heightening the tension.

For the first time in features, Garner plays a somewhat unsavory character. Pete Aron not only causes the accident that nearly kills another driver, Scott Stoddard, but he also takes up with Stoddard's wife, and his culpability adds an extra tension to the love triangle. When it comes to misbehaving in relationships, Pete is not alone, but his dubious decisions both on and off the track place him at a moral disadvantage compared to his fellow drivers.

Demonstrating morally questionable behavior makes Pete a less-than-honorable character, but Garner's portrayal of him provides one of the few highlights of the film, at least of those not set on the raceway. In Garner's five-decade career, the number of bad guys he played can be counted on one hand, and though Pete doesn't qualify as the film's "villain," his behavior does play against the Garner type—which the actor handles quite well. Pete isn't entirely unsympathetic—especially when he's forced to abandon driving for a less-than-adventurous role as a sportscaster—but for much of the film, he acts on less-than-honorable impulses.

With a flawed lead character, the film is able to undermine the viewer's allegiance to Garner's Pete—or at the very least instill doubt about the movie's outcome. Perhaps the film will subvert the Hollywood template of boy gets girl, boy wins race, boy becomes hero. By challenging that template, the film subtly suggests that the other contenders have just as much a chance to win as Pete, so a Hollywood ending is not assured. By focusing on a morally challenged lead, perhaps the film also implies that winning a race doesn't make you a hero; it just means you crossed the finish line first. And for some participants, merely surviving the race is a triumph in itself.

12

SUPPORT YOUR LOCAL SHERIFF!

(1969)

★ ★ ★

Director: Burt Kennedy
Screenplay: William Bowers
Producer: William Bowers. *Director of Photography:* Harry Stradling Jr. *Music:*
　　Jeff Alexander. *Editor:* George W. Brooks. *Art Director:* Leroy A.
　　Coleman. *Set Decorator:* Hugh Hunt
Cast: James Garner (Jason McCullough), Joan Hackett (Prudy Perkins),
　　Walter Brennan (Pa Danby), Harry Morgan (Mayor Olly Perkins),
　　Jack Elam (Jake), Bruce Dern (Joe Danby), Henry Jones (Henry
　　Jackson), Willis Bouchey (Tom Devery), Gene Evans (Tom Danby),
　　Dick Peabody (Luke Danby)
Studio: MGM (Cherokee Productions)
Release Date: March 26, 1969
Specs: 92 minutes; color
Availability: DVD (Warner Bros.)

SUMMARY

Jason McCullough arrives in the town of Calendar, Colorado, the site of
a recent gold rush, soon after the latest in a string of sheriffs has been
killed. Though intent on heading to Australia, Jason agrees to be the town's
interim sheriff as long as town officials allow him enough time to do some

gold prospecting of his own. The mayor's flighty—but also recently rich—daughter, Prudy, coyly shows interest in Jason. As the new sheriff, Jason quickly takes control of the town, first by arresting Joe Danby, for killing a man. This leads to a final confrontation with Pa Danby and his gang.

BACKGROUND

Following a few lackluster films—*Hour of the Gun, How Sweet It Is!*, and *The Pink Jungle*—Garner was ready for a hit, and the screenplay for "The Sheriff," as it was originally called, seemed a likely candidate. As with all of Garner's films since *36 Hours, Sheriff!* was coproduced by his company, Cherokee Productions.

When it came to westerns, screenwriter William Bowers and director Burt Kennedy were old hands at the genre. Bowers contributed to several westerns in the 1950s—earning Oscar nominations for screenplays to *The Gunfighter* (1950) and *The Sheepman* (1958)—and he was not a stranger to western spoofs. Indeed, his first credit on a western was his contribution to the 1947 Abbott and Costello film *The Wistful Widow of Wagon Gap*. Kennedy, in addition to helming episodes of television shows *The Virginian* and *Lawman*, directed several westerns of the 1960s including *The War Wagon*, *Welcome to Hard Times*, and the *Return of the Magnificent Seven*, the sequel to the 1960 classic. *Support Your Local Sheriff!* was the first collaboration between writer Bowers and director Kennedy, but would not be their last. Indeed, the two would work on several more productions including Bowers's final two credits—small-screen revivals of the popular Robert Conrad series: *The Wild Wild West Revisited* (1979) and *More Wild Wild West* (1980).[1]

Like Garner, the film's leading lady, Joan Hackett, earned her dues in television before breaking out on the big screen, notably in the adaptation of Mary McCarthy's novel *The Group* (1966), which earned the actress a BAFTA nomination for Best Foreign Actress. A year later she played opposite Charlton Heston in one of the more highly regarded westerns of the decade, *Will Penny* (1967), whose cast also included Bruce Dern, a veteran of TV westerns. Besides the overarching genre and Dern in a supporting role, however, *Will Penny* and *Sheriff!* could not have been more different.

RECEPTION

Variety called Garner "delightful as the stranger riding into town" who is "so perfect in his various abilities," which include "outthinking the Danbys (a superb quartet of villains)."[2] In an appreciation of Garner after his death, the *Hollywood Reporter*'s Stephen Dalton wrote, "Two of his most enjoyable and underrated starring roles were in the comedy westerns *Support Your Local Sheriff!* and *Skin Game*."[3] Vincent Canby in the *New York Times* was less enchanted, damning the film with something less than faint praise as "inoffensive and quiet, lacking one of those giggly laugh-tracks that can turn a mild bore into an unhinging nightmare."[4]

COMMENTARY

By the 1970s the western was beginning to ride into the sunset, as some of the biggest stars of the genre, including John Wayne and James Stewart, were showing their age. But in 1969, the genre did not appear to be slowing down. Indeed, nearly a third of the features to reach number one at the box office in 1969 were westerns, including the most successful film of the year, *Butch Cassidy and the Sundance Kid*, which spent eleven straight weeks at number one. Even *Support Your Local Sheriff!* managed to debut at number one, though like *The Wild Bunch*, which was released later in the year, it spent only one week atop the box office charts. When the film was released at the end of March, it was the second straight number one western to have an exclamation point in its title, following Elvis Presley's *Charro!*[5] The exclamation point must have been in style at the time, since those two films followed *Oliver!*, which had been riding high the year before.[6]

The comedy-western may have been around for decades, but it was still a fairly limited subgenre. Online polls listing the top films in this subgroup invariably include a Garner film or two—and even three. The website Flickchart places the big-screen *Maverick* at number eight, followed by *Support Your Local Sheriff!* at number fourteen and *Support Your Local Gunfighter* at fifteen.[7] A 2014 article about the top ten funniest comedy westerns features not one, but two Garner films—the 1994 *Maverick* at number ten and *Sheriff!* at eight.[8] Of course, both resources name *Blazing Saddles* as the greatest film in the hybrid genre.

Considering that Garner first came to prominence as the star of a western series, it's somewhat surprising that *Support Your Local Sheriff!* is only the third western feature the actor starred in after *Maverick* and the first that is more in tune with the tone of the lighthearted show. Perhaps Garner may have wanted to distance himself from the role/genre that brought him fame—if, at the very least, to show his range. Or perhaps it took nearly a decade for him to find a project that captured the sensibilities of the western genre that most suited him as an actor. Let's face it: the dryer westerns in Garner's career—including *Duel at Diablo*, *Hour of the Gun*, and especially *A Man Called Sledge*—are far less entertaining than *Support Your Local Sheriff!*, *Support Your Local Gunfighter*, *Skin Game*, and the feature film *Maverick*. In many ways, *Sheriff!* reminds viewers what they came to love about Garner in the first place, and it's not the dour, even grim, characters he plays in his other 1960s westerns.

If *The Great Escape* was Garner's most commercially successful film, *The Americanization of Emily* his personal favorite, and *Murphy's Romance* the film for which he received the most acclaim from his peers, then *Support Your Local Sheriff!* is possibly the film fans remember with the most affection—and it's not hard to reason why. In the film, he is genial, charming, and coolly assured—appealing characteristics that serve him well in his dramatic roles, but are even more attractive in the comedies. On occasion, Garner played mischievous con men or cowardly acting heroes who would eventually display their mettle, but in *Sheriff!* he resorts to neither such behavior. Jason McCullough is confident and clever and willing to take on the bad guys on his own terms. If he doesn't exactly embrace the absurdity of the situations that he confronts, he at least sees them for what they are and counters them with an equal amount of absurd behavior, or so it seems. And *absurd* is an apt term to describe the town he agrees to bring law and order to—at least until he books passage to Australia.

This is a film strewn with comic character actors, and it often runs the risk of becoming too farcical with the weight of so many people behaving irrationally. But the film also benefits from the inspired antics of several performers, chief among them Joan Hackett. Her histrionics throughout the film are balanced by Garner's cool demeanor and calming, sometimes bemused, presence. He not only keeps her and the townsfolk on an even keel, he manages to befuddle the Danby clan, which is terrorizing the good citizens of Calendar. Played by three-time Oscar winner Walter Brennan, the ever-exasperated Pa Danby can't understand how his sons haven't dispatched the new sheriff, just as they had done with the ones who came before McCullough.

If the film's twisted sense of humor can be encapsulated in one scene, that moment occurs in the jailhouse when Pa Danby threatens the new sheriff, waving a pistol in his face. The coolly indignant McCullough responds with a simple gesture—placing his index finger into the gun's barrel. This infuriates the Danby patriarch so fully he doesn't know how to respond, and leaves the jailhouse in a confounded huff.

Walter Brennan doesn't know how to handle Garner's gesture. *United Artists / Photofest* © *United Artists*

The film thrives on both Garner's behavior and his reaction to the buffoonery around him. He is never not in control of the situation, which in some ways is reminiscent of two earlier Garner films, *Cash McCall* and *The Wheeler Dealers*. The Garner character in all three films assesses the situation at hand and acts accordingly, so that he can supervise the chaos—as much to his advantage as possible. This is particularly true of *Sheriff!*, which helps make this such a fun film to watch.

That isn't quite the case with *Support Your Local Gunfighter*, the 1971 film some mistakenly regard as a sequel to *Sheriff!* Despite sharing the same star, the same director, and much of the supporting cast—not just Jack Elam, Harry Morgan, Henry Jones, and Kathleen Freeman, but bit players Walter Burke, William Bouchey, and Gene Evans—none of the actors plays the same character from the previous film.[9] And despite the similar title—and even farcical tone—this film doesn't quite measure up to *Sheriff!* What worked in the 1969 film—particularly the frantic behavior of the characters—comes across as too, too much this time. It's a shame, really, since *Gunfighter* features an addition to the cast who would seem well suited for the farce. The usually delightful Suzanne Pleshette, who would seem just about perfect a match for Garner, is forced to play a shrieking, unlikeable shrew, and it's nearly impossible to fathom what anyone would find appealing about her character. That's not to say the film doesn't have entertaining moments or that fans of Garner will be completely disappointed. But when comparing this film to others in the genre—or even to the actor's best—*Gunfighter* is difficult to support.

MARLOWE

(1969)

★★★ ½

Director: Paul Bogart
Screenplay: Stirling Silliphant, based on *The Little Sister* by Raymond Chandler
Producers: Gabriel Katzka, Sidney Beckerman. *Director of Photography:* William H.
   Daniels. *Music:* Peter Matz. *Editor:* Gene Ruggiero. *Art Directors:* George
   W. Davis, Addison Hehr. *Set Decorators:* Henry Grace, Hugh Hunt
Cast: James Garner (Philip Marlowe), Gayle Hunnicutt (Mavis Wald), Carroll
   O'Connor (Lieutenant Christy French), Rita Moreno (Dolores Gonzales),
   Sharon Farrell (Orfamay Quest), William Daniels (Mr. Crowell), H. M.
   Wynant (Sonny Steelgrave), Jackie Coogan (Grant W. Hicks), Kenneth
   Tobey (Sgt. Fred Beifus), Bruce Lee (Winslow Wong), Christopher Cary
   (Chuck), Corinne Camacho (Julie), Paul Stevens (Dr. Vincent Lagardie)
Studio: MGM; Katzka-Berne Productions, Inc., and Cherokee Productions
Release Date: October 29, 1969
Specs: 96 minutes; color
Availability: DVD (Warner Home Archive Collection)

SUMMARY

Private detective Philip Marlowe is working two cases: he is hired by a young woman, Orfamay Quest, to find her brother Orrin. He is also re-tained to find the person who is blackmailing actress Mavis Wald, star of the top-rated sitcom in the country. Mavis is romantically involved with gangster Sonny Steelgrave, and if their relationship is exposed, her career might implode. In the course of his investigations, Marlowe runs afoul of Steelgrave, his minions, and a killer who dispatches victims with an ice pick to the back of the neck. Straddling the worlds of entertainment and organized crime, Marlowe soon determines that the two cases may be intertwined.

BACKGROUND

Private investigator Philip Marlowe first appeared in the 1939 novel *The Big Sleep*, by Raymond Chandler, followed by six more novels through *Playback*, published in 1958, a year before the author's death.[1] Marlowe's first big-screen appearance occurred in the 1944 adaptation of *Farewell, My Lovely* entitled *Murder, My Sweet* starring Dick Powell, but perhaps his most iconic representation was in the Howard Hawks version of *The Big Sleep* in 1946, with Humphrey Bogart as the detective. On the small screen, the Marlowe character appeared in anthology segments (including *Robert Montgomery Presents* and *Climax!*) before headlining a short-lived television series, *Philip Marlowe*, that first aired in October 1959, seven months after Chandler's death. Garner's portrayal of Marlowe was the first big-screen appearance of the character that Chandler did not live to see, and based on the comments of some Chandler aficionados, the writer would not have been impressed.

The 1969 film is based on the fifth Marlowe novel, *The Little Sister*, which was published in 1949.[2] Stirling Silliphant, who had just won an Oscar and Golden Globe—as well as the Edgar Allan Poe award—for his adaptation of *In the Heat of the Night*, was hired to write the screenplay. Silliphant, whose credits also included several episodes of *Alfred Hitchcock Presents*, seemed particularly suited to adapt the mystery, since he was an admirer of Chandler; he had met the author on a few occasions and thought highly of *The Little Sister*.

In an effort to save on expenses, the producers opted to set the film in contemporary Los Angeles, rather than spend money on period sets from the 1940s. Updating the film meant crafting modern dialogue to suit the contemporary culture. It also allowed the filmmakers to change the medium in which Mavis Wald works, so she becomes a star of television rather than movies. But the screenwriter didn't want to entirely abandon the novel's 1940s origins. Scouting out locations for inspiration, Silliphant walked around the city looking for "places that [he] felt would remind one of the Forties and yet be the Sixties."[3]

Paul Bogart, an Emmy-winning veteran of episodic television, as well as live productions for the small screen, was hired for this, only his second feature.[4] Bogart disagreed with the decision to update the film and did his best to minimize a contemporary environment. On one of these points, he and Garner agreed, much to the frustration of Silliphant: the screenwriter wanted to portray Marlowe and his world in a much grittier and more vicious manner, but the director and star were reluctant to exhibit much violence in the film. While Silliphant's preference for textual fidelity was understandable, this particular challenge also inspired him to create one of the more memorable scenes in the film—Marlowe's second encounter with Winslow Wong, a henchman for gangster Sonny Steelgrave.

Garner hoped that Raquel Welch would be cast in the role of Mavis, but the actress "didn't like the part and turned it down,"[5] as did a few other actresses. Ultimately, the role went to Gayle Hunnicutt, a former model who had appeared in a few television episodes. Hunnicutt spent much of her subsequent career in television, albeit not with the same success as her character in *Marlowe*, an actress who headlines a number one program. Sharon Farrell, another actress with multiple television roles to her credit—before and after *Marlowe*—plays Orfamay.

A notable supporting role went to martial arts icon, Bruce Lee, in his first American feature—and first memorable role since playing Kato on *The Green Hornet* series a few years before. According to Garner, Lee shared with him "some martial arts moves between takes."[6]

Other key supporting roles went to future television stars, notably Carroll O'Connor of *All in the Family* fame and William Daniels of *St. Elsewhere*—not to be confused with the film's cinematographer, William H. Daniels. Along with Daniels, several other actors from the film would later appear in *The Rockford Files*, including Christopher Cary, Paul Stevens, Kenneth Tobey, H. M. Wynant, and Corinne Comacho, who played a recurring character in four episodes. Garner's most prominent costar from *Marlowe*, Academy Award–winner Rita Moreno (*West Side Story*), would appear in three episodes of *The Rockford Files*, receiving two Emmy nominations and winning the award in 1978.

RECEPTION

When it was released in late 1969, *Marlowe* received mostly mixed or negative reviews from several publications, including *Variety*, the *Chicago Sun-Times*, and the *New York Times*. The film was inevitably compared to the previous incarnations of Philip Marlowe, notably *The Big Sleep*. Some

Marlowe's rejection of a bribe from Winslow Wong (Bruce Lee) results in mayhem moments later. *MGM / Photofest © MGM*

critics were unimpressed with the updated setting and argued that Garner's performance was not right for the character or the movie. While Myles Standish in the *St. Louis Post-Dispatch* claimed that "Garner is no Humphrey Bogart (who is?)," the critic admitted that the actor "handles his role with ease and a charm we didn't suspect a movie private eye of having."[7]

Roger Greenspun, in the *New York Times*, acknowledged that other than his misgivings about Garner, "the cast is excellent and appropriate"and singles out Carroll O'Connor as "eloquent in the defense of tired principles."[8] *TimeOut London* called the film a "snappy and stylish update" that "is certainly watchable." Of the film's cast, "Garner's rumpled charm is engaging enough," and some fine supporting performances (particularly O'Connor) help to create an atmosphere of almost universal corruptability."[9]

COMMENTARY

So if not many critics were impressed with this film, why include it among Garner's essentials? Simple: most of the critics were wrong. Some lamented that the film does not capture the spirit or tone of the Chandler novels or that Garner is less cynical, less jaded, and less seedy than the Philip Marlowe who appears in the novels or in the earlier films. The unenviable task that most filmmakers—chiefly screenwriters and directors—face when adapting a novel, play, or even work of nonfiction to the screen is balancing fidelity to the source with creating a work that must stand on its own. And striking that balance is made even more difficult when tackling a body of work (in this case, the entire Chandler/Marlowe canon) that has engendered a following of purists—not simply the Chandler aficionados who grumble over liberties filmmakers take with the original book, but cinematic purists who cite previous films as litmus tests to compare against the new works. It appears that Garner's *Marlowe* comes up short in both of these comparisons, but in fact, it stands well on its own. No comparisons are necessary—or indeed, even apt.

While *Marlowe* may lack all of the noir-ish elements that viewers anticipated for a film based on a Raymond Chandler novel, the film nonetheless succeeds as an entertaining neo-noir. And though it may seem that the tone of the film relies almost entirely on Garner, who tempers the detective's cynicism with a sardonic sense of humor, in truth several hands help maintain the film's tenor.

Stirling Silliphant's screenplay straddles a fine line between wit and edginess, though one of the moments in the film features a contribution from Garner. In the actor's memoir, he recalls a restaurant scene where he tastes a sip of wine and declares it "impertinent" and "baroque." According to Garner, "Gore Vidal had just referenced my butt in his novel *Myra Breckenridge,* referring to it as 'impertinent' and 'baroque,'"[10] and the actor couldn't resist ascribing those adjectives to the wine.

Director Bogart maintains the tightrope of grit and grin throughout the film, and even composer Peter Matz seemed to understand the dual tone of the feature, providing a score that alternates between jaunty 1960s jazz and moody thriller.

All of the supporting players acquit themselves well, notably Bruce Lee. He plays a stylish enforcer who employs his martial arts skills to threaten Marlowe without actually laying a hand on him. Their second encounter is particularly enjoyable and concludes with a simple hand gesture that sums up the film's attitude—a mixture of menace and mirth.

Another significant feature of the film, particularly as it relates to Garner's career: his portrayal of Marlowe seems to presage the actor's antihero role on *The Rockford Files* some five years later. In fact, it's very likely that this version of Marlowe inspired *Rockford* cocreator Stephen J. Cannell, given that Marlowe's character traits are similar to those of Jim Rockford, and dialogue from the series echoed the tone of the 1969 film—not to mention both Marlowe and Rockford have a fondness for Oreos. If this comparison needs further corroboration, consider this: the name of the mobster in *Marlowe*, Sonny Steelgrave, is also the name of the mobster in the first season of another Cannell show, *Wise Guy*.[11]

Overall, the film bears repeated viewing, not simply to compare it to *The Rockford Files* but to appreciate how this neo-noir holds up over time, despite the groovy trappings of its 1960s setting. And of course, there are rewards to be had just by watching Garner interact with his capable costars, especially Moreno, O'Connor, Daniels, and Lee. And perhaps one other reason to watch this movie again and again: to determine how the final death in the film happens; despite multiple viewings, it's still not clear how the character's demise occurs.

SKIN GAME

(1971)

★ ★ ★ ½

Director: Paul Bogart
Screenplay: Pierre Marton (Peter Stone), based on a story by Richard Alan
    Simmons
Producer: Harry Keller. Director of Photography: Fred Koenekamp, ASC.
    Music: David Shire. Editor: Walter Thompson. Art Director: Herman
    Blumenthal. Set Decorator: James Payne
Cast: James Garner (Quincy Drew), Lou Gossett Jr. (Jason O'Rourke), Susan
    Clark (Ginger), Brenda Sykes (Naomi), Edward Asner (Plunkett), Andrew
    Duggan (Calloway), Henry Jones (Sam), Neva Patterson (Mrs. Claggart),
    Parley Baer (Mr. Claggart), George Tyne (Bonner), Royal Dano (John
    Brown), Pat O'Malley (William), Joel Fluellen (Abram), Napolean Whiting
    (Ned), Juanita Moore (Viney), Dort Clark (Pennypacker)
Studio: Warner Bros.; a Cherokee Production
Release Date: September 30, 1971
Specs: 102 minutes; color
Availability: DVD (Warner Archive Collection)

SUMMARY

A few years before the Civil War, a pair of con men wander from town to
town employing a unique scheme: Quincy Drew, a white man, and his best

buddy, Jason O'Rourke, a free black man from the North, pose as master and slave. Shortly after Quincy sells his friend to the highest bidder, Jason escapes, and the pair set off for the next town and the next swindle. Although they earn several hundreds of dollars for each con, Jason grows wary of tempting fate and the men agree on one more "sale" before putting the con to rest. Their travels take them to Kansas Territory and the town of Fair Shake, the site where their fortunes take several downturns. They quickly learn that they are not the only con artists in town and, worse still, that they have fooled one too many buyers.

BACKGROUND

Pierre Marton was a pseudonym for screenwriter Peter Stone, who wrote the screenplays for a couple of Cary Grant's final films, *Charade* and *Father Goose*, receiving an Oscar for the latter. Stone's original screenplay for *Skin Game* had been altered so much, though, that he asked his name be removed from the credits. It wasn't the first—nor would it be the last—time Stone had used the nom de plume.[1]

Paul Bogart, who had directed Garner in the underrated *Marlowe* a few years earlier, collaborated with him again on *Skin Game*. In between the two projects, Bogart had worked primarily in television, picking up an Emmy for the anthology series *CBS Playhouse*. The one feature he directed—*Halls of Anger*—had some similarities to *Skin Game*, since it tackled race relations as well, albeit in the contemporary setting of an integrated high school.

Besides the two leads, the supporting cast was filled by the familiar faces of character actors Royal Dano, Andrew Duggan, J. Pat O'Malley, and the seemingly ubiquitous Henry Jones. The actress who plays the object of Gossett's affection, Brenda Sykes, would soon appear in a number of blaxploitation films of the 1970s, including *Honky*, *Black Gunn*, and *Cleopatra Jones*. The minor role of Viney was played by Juanita Moore, an actress who was only the fourth African American woman to receive an Oscar nomination—hers for the 1959 remake of *Imitation of Life*.[2]

Another key member of the cast was Edward Asner, who had been working steadily in television for more than a decade before finally securing Hollywood gold in 1970. A year before *Skin Game*, Asner signed on to play newsman Lou Grant on *The Mary Tyler Moore Show*. But the legendary series was not assured of a second season, so perhaps Asner hedged his bets by taking on additional roles. In *Skin Game*, he plays a slave trader, and six years later he would play a similar role in the television miniseries *Roots*, in which he plays the captain of a slave trading ship. His performance earned him an Emmy for Best Supporting Actor, while the lead actor Emmy went to his *Skin Game* costar, Louis Gossett, also for *Roots*.

For the female lead, producers hired Canadian actress Susan Clark, whose most significant credit was the 1968 Clint Eastwood film *Coogan's Bluff*. Clark is probably best remembered for playing the white mother who adopts Emmanuel Lewis in the 1980s sitcom *Webster*.

The film's executive producer, Meta Rosenberg, had been James Garner's manager for several years and later served as a producer for several of his shows, including *Nichols* and *The Rockford Files*.

RECEPTION

Pauline Kael in the *New Yorker* called this "very enjoyable" film a "lighthearted and charming story of con artists in the Old South,"[3] while *Variety* declared, "Garner is at his best in years."[4] Citing *Skin Game*'s prescient view of race relations portrayed on film, film critic Bruce Fretts notes that the movie "prefigured at least five major pop-cultural landmarks,"[5] including the

A tense moment between Garner and Louis Gossett Jr. that undercuts the humor of *Skin Game*. *Warner Bros. Pictures / Photofest © Warner Bros. Pictures*

films *Blazing Saddles, 12 Years a Slave*, and *Django Unchained*, as well as the show *All in the Family* and the original miniseries, *Roots*.

Despite its favorable reviews, the movie failed to draw attention from the Academy of Motion Picture Arts and Sciences (Oscars) or the Hollywood Foreign Press (Golden Globes). However, the film did receive attention from the Image Awards, which had recently been established by the NAACP (National Association for the Advancement of Colored People). In its first two years, only winners were announced, but the year *Skin Game* qualified, nominees were also cited. The film received two nominations, for Outstanding Actor and Outstanding Actress: Louis Gossett and Susan Clark. Gossett and fellow nominees Bill Cosby, Richard Roundtree, Sidney Poitier, Moses Gunn, and Woody Strode lost to Donald Sutherland in *Klute*, while the award for Outstanding Actress went to Jane Fonda, also for *Klute*.

COMMENTARY

In the history of cinema—and television, for that matter—there is no actor more associated with the comic western than James Garner. Certainly the multiple iterations of his iconic hero, Maverick, account for the bulk of the genre: sixty episodes of the original series, two cameo appearances in the short-lived revival for ABC, eighteen more episodes in the 1982 reboot *Bret Maverick*, and of course, the blockbuster 1994 film starring Mel Gibson. In addition to these is the 1971 series *Nichols*, which lasted just one season (twenty-four episodes). Before any of these, Garner appeared in the lighthearted western *Shoot-Out in Medicine Bend* in 1957. And of course, there is the most popular feature of the actor's comic westerns, *Support Your Local Sheriff!* followed by the similarly toned—and titled, if not as successful—*Support Your Local Gunfighter* in 1971.

And then there is *Skin Game*, a curious film that traverses a fine line between comedy and drama. Though a lighthearted approach to the story runs throughout, the film can't help but turn somewhat somber when discussions of race take place, not to mention several scenes in which black men and women are sold. For Jason, playing the part of a slave is not the same as *being* one, and he is acutely aware of the dire circumstances of his fellow blacks, including a handful of recently secured tribal men from Africa.

And yet as a counter to this, the film also features an unusual relationship for two adults in that period: Garner and Gossett play characters who are not only best friends but equals. Either man would give up his life—or at the very least, his freedom—for the other, and the dynamic of their relationship is an ongoing highlight of the film. Another selling point is the chance to see Garner take on various personas, including men of faith, that allow him to sweet-talk one sucker after another out of his or her money or to extract some vital information.

Not only are Quincy and Jason equals in the film, but so are the men who play them. The chemistry between Garner and Gossett, even when they are squabbling, is unmistakable. One imagines that their characters have been together since they were pollywogs, so familiar they are with each other. Race may be a brutal reality neither can ignore, but it never divides their friendship. Garner is a delight in the film, but Gossett deserves equal praise for his performance. As one critic noted, Gossett delivers "a multilevel characterization that is very agile, very antic, and very right for a man who lives by turning his own peril into profit."[6]

Though *Skin Game* is certainly a must-see for fans of Garner and Gossett, viewers will also be rewarded by other performances, including those from major and minor players in the film. Susan Clark, amusing as a woman who may or may not be trusted, holds her own with the two leads. Among the supporting players, three in particular stand out. Henry Jones, who appears for a fourth time in a Garner movie, makes the most of a brief scene that is both humorous and gratifying. Royal Dano, in convincing makeup, appears as real-life abolitionist John Brown, but his sudden appearance is not necessarily helpful to Jason and his fellow slaves. And then there is the stunningly beautiful Brenda Sykes, who gives Jason a newfound purpose.

The screenplay for *Skin Game* ranks up there with some of the best in Garner's career. Sly, sometimes subtle, humor runs throughout the film, particularly in the banter between Quincy and Jason, but the film also makes more pointed barbs—especially about race. When a buyer hands $400 to Quincy with the assurance that "it's all there," Quincy nods at Jason and replies, "So is he, but you made me take his shirt off all the same." And though Jason and Quincy are equal partners and close friends, it's not lost on the black man that his fortunes can change at any moment, at the whim of any white man. Quincy's observation to Jason, "You're the color they're buying this year" may be uttered in ironic jest, but its raw sentiment undercuts the humor.

Many contemporary viewers will no doubt wince every time the N word is spoken during the film, but those same viewers can also take heart that all of the black characters come across far more favorably than the majority of the white ones. Indeed, the film seems to take great glee in portraying many of the white men as buffoons or despots—and seeing them suffer accordingly.

The film was remade in 1974 as a television pilot called *Sidekicks*. Though Garner was replaced by Larry Hagman in the role of Quincy, Louis Gossett reprised his role as Jason. The pilot never went to series, no doubt for the best. It's hard to imagine audiences embracing a program about a white man selling his black friend—week after week. That same year, the most successful comedy-western of all time, *Blazing Saddles*, debuted. It's not unlikely that Mel Brooks and/or one of his fellow screenwriters (which included Richard Pryor) might have been influenced by the story of a multiracial comedy set against the backdrop of the old west. One wonders if either film could be produced today, given the subject matter and—in the case of *Blazing Saddles*—its irreverent tone. On the other hand, Quentin Tarantino's *Django Unchained* seems inspired by one or both movies, and that 2012 film raked in more than $150 million and earned the director-screenwriter an Oscar for best screenplay—so who knows?

In a career noted for westerns, this little-known feature ranks as a hidden gem among Garner's films.

15

THEY ONLY KILL THEIR MASTERS

(1972)

★ ★ ½

Director: James Goldstone
Screenplay: Lane Slate
Producer: William Belasco. *Director of Photography:* Michel Hugo, ASC. *Music:*
    Peter Blotkin Jr. *Editor:* Edward A. Biery, ACE. *Art Director:* Lawrence
    G. Paull. *Set Decorator:* Philip Abramson
Cast: James Garner (Abel Marsh), Katharine Ross (Kate), Hal Holbrook
    (Dr. Watkins), Harry Guardino (Captain Streeter), June Allyson
    (Mrs. Watkins), Christopher Connelly (John), Tom Ewell (Walter),
    Peter Lawford (Campbell), Edmond O'Brien (George), Arthur
    O'Connell (Ernie), Ann Rutherford (Gloria)
Studio: MGM
Release Date: November 22, 1972
Specs: 97 minutes; color
Availability: DVD (Warner Bros.)

SUMMARY

Abel Marsh, police chief of small coastal California town, is probably a little too laid back, especially with his own police force. After returning from vacation in Los Angeles, Abel's first case concerns a woman who has been apparently mauled to death by her own dog, a Doberman pinscher named

Murphy. After Abel engages the help of a veterinarian's pretty nurse, he comes to believe that the canine may have been set up. Neat!

BACKGROUND

Before *They Only Kill Their Masters*, screenwriter Lane Slate had very few film or television credits to his name, the one standout a 1971 film that he wrote and directed, *Clay Pigeon*, starring Telly Savalas and Robert Vaughn. On the other hand, the film's director, James Goldstone, had helmed a number of projects dating back to the mid-1950s, including episodes of *The Outer Limits*, *The Fugitive*, *Voyage to the Bottom of the Sea*, and *Star Trek*. Goldstone's film career is of little note, though he did oversee one of Robert De Niro's earliest features, *The Gang That Couldn't Shoot Straight* (1971), just before this Garner film.

This movie was filmed while Garner was finishing up *Nichols*, his short-lived western on NBC, and was released in November of 1972, just a couple of months after *Nichols* concluded its network run in August. *They Only Kill Their Masters* was one of three features Garner would star in between *Nichols* and *The Rockford Files* (the others were two Disney movies with Vera Miles: *One Little Indian* and *The Castaway Cowboy*).

For Katharine Ross, an Oscar nominee for her performance in *Butch Cassidy and the Sundance Kid*, this film would be her second opportunity to work with Garner. Five years earlier she played a supporting role in the odd melodrama *Mister Buddwing*. Hal Holbrook, who could be counted on for fine performances in films and TV movies of the 1970s and '80s—often as authority figures, including presidents, both real (Abraham Lincoln and John Adams) and imaginary—plays a veterinarian. Rounding out the cast were June Allyson and Peter Lawford, frequent film costars of the 1940s and '50s, in curious—especially for Allyson—roles.

This was the first film Garner appeared in since *The Americanization of Emily* that was not produced by Cherokee Productions.

RECEPTION

Howard Thompson in the *New York Times* called *They Only Kill Their Masters* "the most original and likable whodunit I have seen in years," praising the "wisely amusing dialogue" as well as "exquisite sensibility" of both the screenplay and the film's direction. Thompson also favored the

Left to right: Ann Rutherford, Tom Ewell, Garner, and Katharine Ross—along with Murphy, the Doberman pinscher accused of killing his owner. *MGM / Photofest © MGM*

cast, particularly Katharine Ross, whom he calls "excellent" and June Allyson, "who does beautifully." As for the film's star, the critic notes, "Front and center is Garner in his most becoming performance, low-pedaling that blandness with just enough amusing bite."[1] On the other hand, Roger Ebert from the *Chicago Sun-Times* was not entertained, lamenting that Garner's charm is compromised because "neither the story nor the director gives him anywhere to go."[2] Apparently, Ebert disliked it so much, he felt no remorse for revealing spoilers in his review.

COMMENTARY

By the early 1970s, a curious trend in films about law enforcement had begun to take shape. Seemingly in response to the supposed looser morality of the swinging sixties, some films embraced a less tightly wound attitude, while others projected a resistant hostility to the new standards. In films as varied as *Bullitt* and *The French Connection*, iconoclastic lawmen took opposite sides: some were shown bucking the system to exact justice, while others demonstrated quirky demeanors, each apparently stretching the boundaries of acceptable behavior for "authority" figures. Underpinning most, if not, all of these characters, is a sense that each, in his own way, plays by his own set of rules. Some of these lawmen colored in between the lines, with occasional ventures outside the strict police code; others frequently sidestepped established protocols to get the job done.

On one end of the spectrum was Clint Eastwood's Harry Callahan, the San Francisco cop frustrated with by-the-book strictures that compel him to rile his superiors. For him, violence must be met with violence, which he metes out in such films as *Dirty Harry* and *Magnum Force*. Holding up the other end of justice's scale is Garner's Abel Marsh, whose laissez-faire attitude engenders loyalty from his staff and perhaps encourages suspects to let their guards down. Marsh's methods may be unorthodox, but they are less about antagonizing the powers that be and more about making sense of chaos.

Abel Marsh is tailor made for Garner. Filmed less than two years before the debut of *The Rockford Files*, *They Only Kill Their Masters* is one of two movies that anticipate the most iconic role of the actor's career. Along with Garner's interpretation of Philip Marlowe from a few years earlier, Abel Marsh serves as a template for Jim Rockford. Though Jim is not nearly as tough and cynical as Marlowe—and his Rockford is often at odds with law enforcement, unlike police chief Marsh—there are traits that all three men have in common. All three are resourceful, all three are charming, and all three have a sense of humor, though this last trait is conveyed in slightly different ways. Marlowe is wearily sardonic, Marsh is bemused, and Rockford is often whimsically sarcastic. No matter the differences, each exudes the Garner charisma. Each is a smartass in his own way—and that world-weary, wisecracking trait endears all three of them to viewers. Neat!

A few years after *They Only Kill Their Masters*, the character of Abel Marsh was resurrected in a television pilot for Andy Griffith, *The Girl in the Empty Grave*, that aired in September of 1977. Written and directed by *Masters'* screenwriter Lane Slate, the film was followed a few months later by a second "pilot," *Deadly Game*, but a series never materialized.

THE LONG SUMMER OF GEORGE ADAMS

(1982)

★ ★ ½

Director: Stuart Margolin
Teleplay: John Gay, based on the book *The Long Summer of George Adams* by
    Weldon Hill (William R. Scott)
Producer: Meta Rosenberg. *Director of Photography:* Andrew Jackson, ASC.
    Music: Murray MacLeod, Stuart Margolin, J. A. C. Redford. *Editor:*
    George Rohrs. *Art Director:* Ward Preston
Cast: James Garner (George Adams), Joan Hackett (Norma Adams), Alex
    Harvey (Ernie), Juanin Clay (Ann Sharp), David Graf (Olin Summers),
    Anjanette Comer (Mrs. Post), Barbara Lee Alexander (Joan)
Studio: Warner Bros. Television
First Aired: January 18, 1982 (CBS)
Specs: 93 minutes; color
Availability: DVD (Warner Home Archive Collection)

SUMMARY

Circa 1951, in the small town of Cushing, Oklahoma, George Adams, a
steam engine fitter for the railroad, faces unemployment as technology
threatens his livelihood. While his wife and two young boys visit a relative,
George contemplates his future, engages in some questionable behavior,
and gets himself in and out of trouble.

BACKGROUND

The Long Summer of George Adams was based on a novel by Weldon Hill, a pseudonym for William R. Scott, an Oklahoma-born author who wrote a handful of novels. The first of these—*Onionhead*—became a 1958 movie that starred Andy Griffith. Though *The Long Summer of George Adams* was written in the early 1950s, it took nearly three decades before Hollywood brought it to the screen. In fact, according to Garner biographer Raymond Strait, the actor had been trying to get the project produced for several years. The TV film was adapted by John Gay, whose prolific screenwriting credits included dozens of adaptations, including small-screen versions of *Captains Courageous*, *Les Misérables*, and *A Tale of Two Cities*.

The cast and crew of *George Adams* included some very familiar names—and faces—working with Garner. Behind the scenes, several *Rockford Files* alums were on hand, including Meta Rosenberg, a producer for the series, and Stuart Margolin, two-time Emmy winner for his portrayal of Angel Martin. Rosenberg and Margolin, respectively, produced and directed the film. Though known primarily as an actor, Margolin had directed several episodic shows before joining the cast of *The Rockford Files*, for which he also helmed two episodes. Margolin's involvement with *The Long Summer* was not limited to direction, however, since he also contributed to the film's score.

Also reuniting with Garner was Joan Hackett, his costar from *Support Your Local Sheriff!* thirteen years earlier. Between films, Hackett had made numerous appearances on television shows and made-for-TV movies. Perhaps her best films during that period were the 1973 thriller *The Last of Sheila*, cowritten by Broadway legend Stephen Sondheim and *Psycho* star Anthony Perkins, and the Neil Simon comedy *Only When I Laugh*, which earned Hackett an Oscar nomination for best supporting actress. For Hackett, *The Long Summer of George Adams* would be one of her last credits. She succumbed to cancer in October 1983, less than two years after the TV movie first aired.

In his memoir, Garner called *George Adams* a "delightful film," and his enthusiasm for the project stemmed from the opportunity to work again with Margolin and Hackett. Although he doesn't express it explicitly in his book, there must have been another lure for the actor—a rare chance to play a character who is born, bred, and living in Garner's home state of Oklahoma. Perhaps the role came with some bittersweet associations, though, since Adams is a man who faces his obsolescence—and perhaps his mortality. No doubt Garner, who lived through the Depression, could relate to such a character—even if the summer in question occurs in the 1950s. So while playing a protagonist from Oklahoma must have held special appeal to him, Garner might also have understandably considered how George's life differed so dramatically from his—and found some comfort in his ability to find a better life for himself than his on-screen character.

RECEPTION

Leonard Maltin called *The Long Summer of George Adams* a "lighthearted homespun period piece" that features "some lovely bits of Americana."[1] *People* magazine noted the film's "odd plot," but added that "Garner's wry style and an excellent supporting cast make this TV movie worthwhile."[2] The *Hollywood Reporter* declared that Margolin's "direction elicits a deeper shade of vulnerability from Garner than evidenced in previous roles."[3]

COMMENTARY

The Long Summer of George Adams is a film without edge. Even a moment potentially fraught with heightened tension—a bank robbery—plays out in scenes that are best described as low-key. Rather than a melodrama that exaggerates drama and tautness, *The Long Summer of George Adams* can be more aptly pronounced as a "mellow drama." To be sure, there are many moments that could be exploited for the raw emotions they might elicit, but that's not the aim of this film. Such scenes are rendered more subtly, in muted tones that might not always be what the viewer expects, but are conveyed consistently throughout the film. And in the middle of this subdued atmosphere is Garner's characterization of George, a role made more personal, more real by an actor who understood what made George the man he is—and what he might become if he is unable to find his purpose among the turmoil that occurs in the heat of an Oklahoman summer.

Make no mistake: *The Long Summer of George Adams* represented a new stage in James Garner's career. From the mid-1950s through the early 1980s, the actor's output was defined by one of two venues: episodic programs or feature films. By the time he filmed *George Adams*, television films had come of age and so, too, had Garner.

George Adams is a character that Garner had not really played before, a man who is beaten down by the burdens of life. An otherwise decent man of modest—at best—means, George struggles with the knowledge that his

Joan Hackett, Bobby Fite (front left), Garner, and Blake Tannery (front right) in one of Garner's most important television films. *NBC / Photofest © NBC*

livelihood may be coming to an end. With a wife and a family depending on him, George's uncertain future unsettles him, making him irritable and edgy. When his wife and sons leave for a few months, George spends the summer facing temptation and making moral choices that could compromise his family life.

It would be false to say that only Garner could play such a role, when in fact, he had never been challenged with the type of character he plays in this film. But it is a role the actor inhabits fully with a performance that is more nuanced than many of his previous roles. There is nothing sly or mischievous about his characterization, traits that were often on display in both Garner's best and worst films. His portrayal of George reveals a vulnerability that Garner rarely, if ever, tapped into in previous dramas, in part because those films did not feature an everyman at the center of the story—certainly not to the degree of George Adams. And George is a particular kind of everyman—a desperate figure who is not certain how to move forward in his life.

At the time *The Long Summer of George Adams* began filming, Garner was fifty-three years old, and though he seems slightly older than what the role calls for, there's no question George fits him. Older or not, Garner does what every good actor should do on behalf of his role: he breathes life into the character. Eliciting empathy for George, Garner does so not by relying on the easygoing charm that had characterized so many of his previous roles. Instead, he embraces George's flaws with an honesty that imbues his character with humanity, one that is as complicated as life itself.

For decades Garner had played characters that viewers idolized—particularly the ones who had an aversion for putting themselves in harm's way. Garner's fans always understood that underneath a character's professed cowardice, there lurked a man's man, someone who could take care of himself. Garner excelled at playing individuals who would eventually get past their apparent timidity to triumph over whatever obstacles confronted them.

George Adams breaks that mold. He lacks the wry humor of both Bret Maverick and Jim Rockford, and more significantly, he appears to lack the resourcefulness of those figures—a trait that would be more than welcome for a character facing real-world challenges. And though George Adams is prone to temptation, he's also inclined to give in to those temptations, regardless of the consequences. Playing flawed, humane characters who make questionable decisions and behave in ways that viewers had not associated with Garner heralded a new era for the actor. For this reason alone, George Adams is one of the most important roles of James Garner's career.

VICTOR/VICTORIA

(1982)

★ ★ ★ ½

Director: Blake Edwards
Screenplay: Blake Edwards, based on the screenplay for *Viktor und Viktoria*
    by Rheinhold Schünzel
Producers: Blake Edwards, Tony Adams. *Director of Photography:* Dick Bush,
    BSC. *Music:* Henry Mancini. *Lyrics:* Leslie Bricusse. *Editor:* Ralph E.
    Winters, ACE. *Production Designer:* Roger Maus. *Costume Designer:*
    Patricia Norris. *Choreographer:* Paddy Stone
Cast: Julie Andrews (Victoria Grant), James Garner (King Marchand), Robert
    Preston (Carroll "Toddy" Todd), Lesley Ann Warren (Norma Cassady),
    Alex Karras (Squash Bernstein), John Rhys-Davies (Andre Cassell)
Studio: MGM
Release Date: March 19, 1982
Specs: 133 minutes; color
Availability: DVD (Warner Archive Collection)

SUMMARY

In 1934 Paris, down-on-her-luck singer Victoria Grant auditions for a job
at a nightclub but does not get hired. A fellow struggling entertainer, a gay
performer named Toddy, befriends Victoria and convinces the desperate
woman to pretend to be a male drag queen. Soon after, her act becomes

the toast of gay Paree, and Victoria also draws the interest of a gangster from Chicago, who is confused by his feelings for the nightclub entertainer.

BACKGROUND

Blake Edwards came from a film and theatrical background, so it wasn't surprising that he would pursue a career in the performing arts. After achieving modest success as a film actor in the 1940s, Edwards turned to writing, and by the end of the decade had cowritten a few screenplays. By the mid-1950s he was writing *and* directing for both film and television, most memorably creating the series *Peter Gunn*. His first high-profile film, the Cary Grant submarine comedy *Operation Petticoat* (1959), was followed two years later by the 1961 adaptation of the Truman Capote novel *Breakfast at Tiffany's*. In 1963, Edwards cowrote and directed *The Pink Panther*, the first of many films featuring the bumbling French detective, Inspector Clouseau. In late 1969, Edwards married Julie Andrews and the following year, they collaborated on the 1970 musical *Darling Lili*. Edwards and Andrews would work together on more films—*The Tamarind Seed* (1974), *10* (1979), and *S.O.B.* (1981)—before producing their crowning achievement as a pair, a musical farce that would exploit each of their particular talents. In fact, Edwards adapted *Victor/Victoria* with his wife in mind for the leading role.

The story dates back to a 1933 German film, *Viktor und Viktoria*, written and directed by Rheinhold Schünzel. Like Edwards, Schünzel was a man of many talents who began his movie career as an actor but quickly took on writing and directing duties. The story has been remade several times since, first by Schünzel himself, when he codirected the French language version, *Georges et Georgette*, in 1934. A British remake, *First a Girl*, starring popular musical hall actress Jessie Matthews, followed a year later. In 1957, the film was remade in Germany, with the same name as the original.

Tapped to play the part of Victoria's gay accomplice was one of Andrews's costars from *S.O.B.*, Robert Preston, who had enjoyed wide acclaim, not to mention stardom, after assuming the title role in the stage and film versions of Meredith Willson's *The Music Man*.

For the film's leading man, Edwards secured fellow Oklahoma native Garner, Andrews's costar from nearly two decades before in *The Americanization of Emily*. The earlier film proved the two stars had chemistry, but the new film, with its conventional romantic entanglement, would test how well that chemistry held up.

The roles of Marchand's moll and henchman were played by two pros—Leslie Ann Warren, who had more than three dozen television and film credits, and Alex Karras, who had a . . . dozen seasons as defensive tackle for the Detroit Lions. Actually, even before his football career ended, Karras had picked up some parts, most notably in the Mel Brooks classic *Blazing Saddles*, so he was not unfamiliar with playing for laughs.

Another long-standing Edwards collaborator was the film's composer, Henry Mancini, whose work with the director dated back to the golden age of television. After scoring the memorable theme to *Peter Gunn*, Mancini composed the music for more than two dozen Edwards projects, including *Breakfast at Tiffany's* (1961), *Days of Wine and Roses* (1962), *The Pink Panther* (1963), and *10* (1979).

RECEPTION

Variety called the film "a sparkling, ultra-sophisticated entertainment" and credited Edwards for evoking two giants of film comedy—Billy Wilder (*Some Like It Hot*) and Ernst Lubitsch (*The Shop around the Corner*)—by creating a film of "sly wit and delightful sexual innuendo." According to the review, "everyone in the cast is given the chance to shine," including Garner, who "is quizzically sober as the story's straight man, in more ways than one," and Andrews, who "is able to reaffirm her musical talents." But the highest plaudits are reserved for the Music Man himself, as the review declares, "Most impressive of all is Preston, with a shimmering portrait of a slightly decadent 'old queen.'"[1]

Vincent Canby's endorsement of the film couldn't have been more effusive if the studio's publicity department had written it themselves. Writing for the *New York Times*, Canby directs readers to go "immediately" to see "a marvelous fable about mistaken identity, sexual roleplaying, love, innocence and sight gags." Of the three leads, he declares that Garner, Preston, and Andrews deliver "the performance of his and her career." Of Andrews, he raves, "She looks absolutely great and is at peak form both as a comedian and as a singer," while Garner "makes a splendid straight man for the others." Canby asserts that Preston's portrayal of Toddy "is the richest, wisest, most rambunctious performance he's given since his triumph in *The Music Man*." The supporting players are also celebrated, Warren as "enchantingly self-possessed" and Karras as a "fine comic actor."[2]

At the box office, *Victor/Victoria* earned a respectable $28 million, but the most successful film about cross-dressing that year—by far—was *Tootsie*, which starred Dustin Hoffman as an out of work actor who secures a soap opera part by playing a woman, a scenario not unlike *Victoria*.

The film received seven Oscar nominations, including three in the acting categories: Andrews received a nod from the Academy for best actress for the first time since *The Sound of Music* seventeen years earlier. It also brought Preston his first and only Oscar nomination. Leslie Ann Warren also was acknowledged for her supporting role as the ditzy mistress Norma. The film's only Oscar win was for the music, honoring composer Mancini and his longtime collaborator, Leslie Bricusse.

Andrews, Preston, and Warren also received Golden Globe nominations, though Preston's was in the Best Actor category, from which Garner was excluded. In a curious case of serendipity that year, the two winners in the lead acting Musical or Comedy categories won for playing in drag: Andrews for *Victoria* and Hoffman for *Tootsie*. Though he walked away empty-handed from the Oscars and Golden Globes, Preston was recognized by the National Board of Review, which awarded him Best Supporting Actor. And the Writers Guild of America named Edwards's screenplay the Best Comedy Adapted from Another Medium.

A bemused Garner tries to contain himself while Julie Andrews attempts to smoke a cigar. *MGM / Photofest © MGM*

COMMENTARY

Cross-dressing in film was nothing new in 1982. In fact, men dressing as women for the camera dates back to the early days of silent film, when comic genius Charlie Chaplin appeared in *A Busy Day* (1914). It seems that at least every decade since, one or more screen icons appeared in drag for comic effect, from Cary Grant in *I Was a Male War Bride* (1947) and Tony Curtis and Jack Lemmon in *Some Like It Hot* (1959) to Hoffman in *Tootsie* (1982) and Robin Williams in *Mrs. Doubtfire* (1993). In each, the characters they portrayed resorted to such extremes to achieve a certain end, survival not being the least of these. And while films featuring women dressing as men is not quite as common, there are plenty of examples, including Greta Garbo in *Queen Christina* (1933), Katharine Hepburn in *Sylvia Scarlett* (1935), Elizabeth Taylor in *National Velvet* (1944), Barbara Streisand in *Yentl* (1982), and Gwyneth Paltrow in *Shakespeare in Love* (1999).

And then there is *Victor/Victoria*, a unique twist on cross-dressing: a woman who pretends to be a man, who performs in drag. And even that particular twist wasn't entirely original, since the 1982 movie was based on the 1933 German film that had been remade at least two times before the Blake Edwards version.

In many ways, 1982 was a breakthrough year for films that depicted "alternative" lifestyles, although the second-highest-grossing film of the year, *Tootsie* (behind *E.T.*, an alternative life of a different kind) does not actually feature gay characters. Beyond the cross-dressing *Tootsie* and *Victoria*, another successful film that year, *The World According to Garp*, featured John Lithgow as a transsexual. Gay relationships also figured prominently in at least three other Hollywood features: *Deathtrap*, the film adaptation of Ira Levin's successful play, did moderately well at the box office. Less successful were two earnest dramas—*Making Love*, about a married man coming to terms with his desire for another man, and *Personal Best*, about two female athletes falling for each other. In addition to these was the reviled comedy *Partners*. While these latter films may not have made much of a financial impression individually, as part of a collective whole, they represented a progression of sorts for the LGBTQ community.

In some respects, *Victor/Victoria* can be compared to a film that arrived in theaters almost exactly ten years earlier, the Bob Fosse–directed *Cabaret*:[3] both are musicals set in 1930s Europe, both focus on cabaret performers, and in both films, the majority of the musical numbers are performed onstage, rather than in contrived moments of spontaneous singing.[4] Each film relies on a bravura performance by their central stars, Liza Minnelli as Sally Bowles in *Cabaret* and Andrews in *Victoria*. The films also depict more relaxed sexual standards. In *Cabaret*, one of the principal characters admits to a homosexual encounter, suggesting he is at the very least bisexual. In *Victor/Victoria*, not only is one of the principals gay—as well as a number of supporting characters—but Garner's character is forced to confront his sexual confusion after he is beguiled by "Victor."

There are, of course, differences, perhaps most tellingly the cultural climate in which the two stories occur. *Cabaret* takes place in 1931 Berlin, Germany, as Hitler ascends to power on the wave of fascism, while *Victor/Victoria* takes place in seemingly carefree Paris a few years later. These locations help establish the tone of each film, as a sense of melancholy and despair envelop the main characters in *Cabaret*, while *Victor/Victoria* represents an idealized city less concerned with world events. Ultimately, these are very different films, one a musical drama, the other a musical farce.

Perhaps the farcical elements are what drew Garner to the film in the first place, aside from the chance to work with Julie Andrews again. In his five-plus-decade career, James Garner avoided certain genres—namely, horror films and science fiction features—but until this point, he had not appeared in a musical either.[5] *Victor/Victoria* stands alone as Garner's only venture into the musical genre, though he doesn't sing in the film. The musical numbers are delivered chiefly by Andrews, allowing Garner to make his contributions as literally the film's straight man.

Ostensibly second fiddle to Preston as the film's male lead, Garner provides many of the film's most endearing moments. As Andrews wrote in her foreword for Garner's memoir, her husband, Blake Edwards, considered Garner "not only a good actor, he's a great *reactor*" and cites the scene in *Victor/ Victoria* when he believes that the woman he's drawn to is in reality a man.[6] And indeed, it's a priceless moment that Garner delivers with such convincing shock, it's a treat to watch.

The film also reignites the chemistry Garner and Andrews established in *The Americanization of Emily*. The two decades that lapsed between films does not diminish how well these two actors mesh on-screen. Their scenes together—before and after *Victor's* big reveal—highlight a coupling that Hollywood perhaps should have capitalized on more than twice during the peak of both stars' careers. Andrews and Garner would get a third opportunity to spark on-screen, but they would have to wait almost another seventeen years, as long as it took them to share the screen the second time.

HEARTSOUNDS

(1984)

★ ★ ★ ½

Director: Glenn Jordan
Teleplay: Fay Kanin, based on the book by Martha Weinman Lear
Producers: Fay Kanin, Fern Field. Executive Producer: Norman Lear. Director
    of Photography: Richard Ciupka. Music: Leonard Rosenman. Editor:
    John Wright. Production Designer: Ed Wittstein
Cast: Mary Tyler Moore (Martha Lear), James Garner (Harold Lear), Sam
    Wannamaker (Moe Silverman), Wendy Crewson (Judy), David
    Gardner (Barney Knapp), Carl Marotte (Michael)
Studio: AVCO Embassy
First Aired: September 30, 1984 (ABC)
Specs: 150 minutes; color
Availability: currently unavailable

SUMMARY

After twelve years of marriage, Dr. Harold Lear, a highly respected urologist, and his wife, Martha, face the biggest challenge of their lives together. While Martha is on a writing assignment in Paris, Harold has a heart attack, the first episode in a prolonged process that takes a toll on both him and Martha. For Harold, his evolution from doctor to patient is an eye-opening experience as his doctors treat him as a layman, rather than a colleague.

For Martha, she must stand by—sometimes helplessly—as her husband's health deteriorates.

BACKGROUND

In 1980 Martha Weinman Lear's book *Heartsounds: The Story of a Love and Loss* was published to critical acclaim and became a national best seller. The book chronicles five years in the life of Lear, a writer for the *New York Times*, and her husband, Harold, after he suffered a massive heart attack in 1973. Harold's cousin, producer and writer Norman Lear, who was behind several groundbreaking shows of the 1970s such as *All in the Family*, *Maude*, and *Good Times*, spearheaded the adaptation for AVCO Embassy, a studio he had recently acquired. According to Norman, the film was a "final hug" of his cousin Harold, the only member of his family who ever commiserated with him about their past.[1]

The screenplay was assigned to Fay Kanin, who had collaborated on screenplays with her husband, Oscar-winner Michael (*Woman of the Year*), before she took on solo projects for television in the 1970s. Kanin was particularly adept at writing films that centered on female protagonists, earning Emmys for writing and producing *Tell Me Where It Hurts* in 1974 and earning another nomination for the 1975 television film *Hustling*. Her most recent credit was *Friendly Fire* (1979), another nonfiction adaptation that starred Carol Burnett, taking on a dramatic role. *Fire* was nominated for seven Emmys, including nods to Burnett and Kanin, and took home four, notably Outstanding Drama or Comedy Special. A four-year gap between *Friendly Fire* and *Heartsounds* was attributed to Kanin being elected to the presidency of the Academy of Motion Picture Arts and Sciences, a position she held from 1979 to 1983. As with *Fire*, Kanin also coproduced *Heartsounds*.

Glenn Jordan, who had helmed several miniseries and made-for-television movies in the 1970s and '80s, directed the film, the first of several collaborations with Garner.

Mary Tyler Moore and James Garner had become famous playing light-hearted characters in episodic television, but both had also proven themselves capable in dramatic roles as well, particularly Moore. After her enormously successful sitcom ended in 1977, Moore played television journalist Betty Rollin in *First You Cry* (1978), an adaptation of Rollins's memoir about battling breast cancer. This performance was followed by Moore's role in *Ordinary People* as an icy mother who has lost one son in a boating

Two television legends, Mary Tyler Moore and Garner, in one of the highlights of their careers.
ABC / Photofest © ABC

accident and can't quite connect with her surviving son. Directed by Robert Redford, the film earned a slew of accolades, including four Oscars, one for Best Picture. Moore herself was nominated for Best Actress and won a Golden Globe for the film.

For both Garner and Moore, the film required them to portray real individuals, which likely presented the actors with different challenges than the characters they were used to playing. For Garner, especially, he hoped the film would show Hollywood that he was capable of tackling meatier material.

RECEPTION

John O'Connor of the *New York Times* was mostly complimentary of the adaptation, noting that the film is not nearly as critical of the medical community as Lear's book. Nonetheless, he contended that *Heartsounds* "packs something of the wallop of a powerful and unblinking documentary." In particular, O'Connor praised the two stars, noting, "With superb performances from Miss Moore and Mr. Garner, the highs as well as the lows of the couple's love story survive beautifully intact."[2] Alvin Marill declared that Tyler Moore—and Garner in particular—"demonstrated true grit" in this film that features a "persuasive script" by Fay Kanin.[3] According to Leonard Maltin, Garner and Moore "give the best performance of their careers" in this "justifiably acclaimed weeper."[4]

When it came time for awards in 1985, *Heartsounds* was one of many television films about topical and/or provocative subjects vying for honors. The television film was nominated for three Emmys including Outstanding Drama/Comedy Special, Outstanding Lead Actor in a Limited Series or a Special (Garner), and Outstanding Lead Actress in a Limited Series or a Special (Moore), though oddly Kanin's script was neglected. Both Moore and the production lost to *Do You Remember Love?*—another film about a mature couple coping with one spouse's health issue, in this case, the agonizing effects of Alzheimer's on Joanne Woodward's character. Also nominated in the lead actress category was Farrah Fawcett for *The Burning Bed*, a film about a battered wife who kills her abusive husband. Garner and Richard Kiley—the male lead of *Do You Remember Love?*—lost to Richard Crenna for a headline-making subject, *The Rape of Richard Beck*. Garner also received a Golden Globe Nomination for Best Actor in a Miniseries or TV Film, losing to Ted Danson for the incest drama *Something about Amelia*.

Most significantly, the film received a Peabody Award, which recognizes "excellence in a wide range of electronic media." In honoring the film, the Peabody organization called *Heartsounds* a "presentation of unusual compassion and emotional impact" and further commended the two stars, declaring, "Both Moore and Garner turn in captivating performances and take full advantage of a lean and emotionally powerful script."[5]

COMMENTARY

As the star of two incredibly successful—not to mention groundbreaking— comedy programs, *The Dick Van Dyke Show* and her eponymous series, Mary Tyler Moore was familiar to millions of viewers as a brilliant comedienne. Shortly after her series ended, Moore seemed intent on proving she had more to offer than the comedic skills for which she had become rightfully known. After portraying a real-life journalist who grapples with breast cancer, the actress dug even deeper in her role as a grief stricken, brittle mother in *Ordinary People*, a heart-wrenching film about despair and ultimately survival. Aside from the accolades Moore received, the performances confirmed that America's sweetheart was truly up to the challenge of more serious fare, and *Heartsounds* yet again displayed her versatility. For Moore, *Heartsounds* must have conjured up memories of *First You Cry* in that it required her to portray a real figure facing a medical crisis, albeit from a different perspective.

And though Garner had also played real figures in films—Colonel William Darby in *Darby's Rangers* and Wyatt Earp in *Hour of the Gun*—neither of those roles required the actor to delve into what were essentially one- and two-dimensional characters. *Heartsounds* presented an entirely different challenge, in both tone and portrayal. Playing Harold Lear demanded an emotional investment into the role, first by honoring the spirit of Lear, the man he portrays, and second, by effectively demonstrating the anguish of a person wracked by a debilitating disease.

On both accounts, Garner succeeds admirably. His performance even impressed the late doctor's wife, Martha, who was frequently on the set during filming and even appeared as an extra in one scene. While Garner and Moore exchanged their lines, Lear was struck by how close to home the moment felt, stating, "It was as if the whole thing was happening all over again."[6]

Consequently, it's not a stretch to say that *Heartsounds* represented a pivotal moment in Garner's career. While he had headlined two success-ful series and starred in nearly three dozen films, *Heartsounds* marked a breakthrough in the variety of roles he undertook. Garner demonstrated his dramatic range by playing a man facing his mortality, allowing the actor to display real vulnerability. Such a trait had not really been accessed much in the film and television roles of his already three-decade-plus career. As Garner himself admitted, "I think they may have begun to think about me differently after *Heartsounds*."[7]

Garner's transition from television star to a dramatic actor to be reckoned with really began two years before *Heartsounds*, with the television movie *The Long Summer of George Adams*. In both films, Garner plays against the charming, mischievous type he had long cultivated. While the 1982 previ-ous television film laid the groundwork for a new era in the actor's career, *Heartsounds* solidified this new phase, not just for him but for Hollywood and the actor's fans. It was a welcome evolution that not every actor is ca-pable of embracing.

Another aspect that can't be ignored is that Garner was also taking on more roles in which he shared the weight of films with other actresses and actors, rather than shouldering them alone. With a few notable exceptions, Garner had played the central figure in most films following his apprenticeship in the 1950s and his days on *Maverick*. In this new era, he seemed to hit his stride by playing one half of a "pair," whether portraying a confused suitor to Julie Andrews in *Victor/Victoria*, courting a younger Sally Field in *Murphy's Romance*, supporting James Woods in *Promise*, tolerating Joanne Woodward in *Breathing Lessons*, sparring with Jack Lemmon in *My Fellow Americans*, or administering to Gena Rowlands in *The Notebook*. Such roles allowed him to conduct a give-and-take with his costars, and their affinity for each other in these films is clear. Garner's instincts were right. He was in his midfifties when *Heartsounds* first aired, and the film signaled the beginning of more "matured" roles that were just as critical to the actor's legacy as the cowboy gambler or the private eye.

MURPHY'S ROMANCE

(1985)

★ ★ ★

Director: Martin Ritt
Screenplay: Harriet Frank Jr., Irving Ravetch, based on the novella by Max Schott
Producer: Laura Ziskin. *Director of Photography:* William A. Fraker. *Music:*
   Carole King. *Editor:* Sidney Levin. *Production Designer:* Joel Schiller.
   Costume Designer: Joe I. Tompkins
Cast: Sally Field (Emma Moriarty), James Garner (Murphy Jones), Brian
   Kerwin (Bobby Jack Moriarty), Corey Haim (Jake Moriarty), Dennis
   Burkley (Freeman Coverly), Georgann Johnson (Margaret), Dortha
   Duckworth (Bessie), Michael Prokopuk (Albert), Billy Ray Sharkey
   (Larry Le Beau), Charles Lane (Amos Abbott)
Studio: Columbia Pictures
Release Date: December 27, 1985
Specs: 108 minutes; color
Availability: DVD (Columbia Pictures)

SUMMARY

Emma Moriarty is a divorcee in her thirties looking for a new life for her and her young son, Jake. After leaving California, Emma and Jake move into a rundown ranch outside the town of Eunice, Arizona, where Emma hopes to find work as a horse trainer. While in town, she meets local pharmacist and drugstore owner Murphy Jones, a widower. As their friendship seems to be heading toward something more serious, Emma's irresponsible ex-husband, Bobby Jack, arrives on the scene, hoping to woo Emma back.

BACKGROUND

Murphy's Romance reunited Sally Field with Martin Ritt, the director of *Norma Rae*, for which Field won her first of two Academy Awards. Ritt was known for "making pictures long on character, depth, and social commitment, qualities that are tough to fake,"[1] and *Murphy's Romance* fit that description, albeit in a fairly lighthearted manner. The film also represented the seventh collaboration of Ritt with husband and wife screenwriters Irving Ravetch and Harriet Frank Jr., whose credits besides *Norma Rae* included *The Long Hot Summer, Hombre,* and *Hud*.[2] The film is an adaption of a novella by Max Schott, a writer and teacher.

After Field secured the rights to the novella for her production company, the actress and Ritt sought to secure Garner for the role of Murphy. However, Columbia Pictures had someone else in mind. According to Garner,

> The studio wanted Marlon Brando for the part of Murphy Jones. Marty and Sally loved Marlon, but they thought he just wasn't right for it. The studio was adamant, but Sally and Marty went to bat for me.[3]

With Garner in place, the other principal roles—that of Emma's ex-husband and son—went to Brian Kerwin and Corey Haim, respectively. Like the two leads, Kerwin had substantial television credits—either as a regular in short-lived series or in guest roles and made-for-television films—but *Murphy* was only his fourth feature. Thirteen-year-old Haim had appeared in a Canadian kids show, *The Edison Twins,* but almost as many features as Kerwin, among them *Firstborn* as Teri Garr's youngest son and in Stephen King's *Silver Bullet* (with Gary Busey). On the other end of the film experience spectrum was Charles Lane, a prolific character actor whose career began in 1930, just two years after Garner was born. At the time of filming *Murphy's Romance,* Lane's résumé numbered more than two hundred television credits and even more film credits, among them several Frank Capra classics, including *It's a Wonderful Life.*

Grammy Award–winning singer-songwriter Carole King was hired to compose the film's score, perform the songs (with David Sanborn), and even appear in the film—but spotting her character is a challenge.

RECEPTION

Although *Murphy's Romance* was not a critical darling (Vincent Canby of the *New York Times* reserved all his praise for the set of the film's drugstore), it did receive some good notices, and Garner earned some of the best reviews of his career. In *The Chicago Sun-Times*, Roger Ebert wrote that Garner played Murphy "in more or less his usual acting style, but he has been given such quietly off-beat dialogue by the screenwriters, Harriet Frank Jr. and Irving Ravetch, that he comes across as a true original." Ebert reiterated his admiration for the film's screenplay, particularly the ending, which he called "one of the most carefully and lovingly written passages in any recent movie."[4] Leonard Maltin called the film a "charming easy-going comedy . . . with Garner in a standout performance."[5]

The film did reasonably well at the box office, ultimately earning nearly $31 million, placing it just inside the top thirty films released in 1985 (though most of its revenue was generated in 1986, when it was given a wide release).[6]

Of course, the film is notable for securing Garner his first and only Oscar nomination. The film also received an Oscar nomination for William Fraker's cinematography. Garner lost the Best Actor award to William Hurt

Of all her costars, Sally Field said Garner delivered the best on-screen kisses. *Columbia Pictures / Photofest © Columbia Pictures*

for *Kiss of the Spider Woman*, and Fraker lost to that year's winner for Best Picture, *Out of Africa*. Both Garner and Field received Golden Globe nominations as well, in the lead acting Comedy or Musical categories. They lost to another pair of romantic partners, albeit a much more twisted duo—Jack Nicholson and Kathleen Turner in *Prizzi's Honor*. With all due respect to Nicholson, Garner should have won.

COMMENTARY

Although most critics didn't swoon over the film when it was released, this gentle comedy has retained its appeal over the years, which is not an easy feat for films of the 1980s.

When Field and director Ritt pushed for Garner to play Murphy over Marlon Brando, they were right, of course. Despite Brando's revered acting skills, it's hard to picture Garner's *Sayonara* costar in the role of Murphy. Garner and Field play off each other with a sense of ease that seems to come naturally to the pair. In fact, Field has publicly said on more than one occasion that Garner delivered the best kiss she's ever had on-screen (perhaps even better than what she has received off camera). In an appearance on Bravo television's *Watch What Happens Live*, Field was asked by a viewer who was the worst kisser in her career. Struggling for an answer, the actress offered an alternative response: "Best without a doubt is James Garner. I could close my eyes and go there." When host Andy Cohen prodded her to reveal how good a kisser her new film's costar—thirty-four years her junior—was, Field replied, "He was pretty darn good, but you know he wasn't Jimmy Garner."[7]

Hollywood has been guilty of producing some May–December romances that stretch credibility. For decades, the studios have often paired starlets with aging leading men they assumed could still produce virile box office numbers—but those films rarely acknowledged the differences between the leading man and woman, or at best downplayed the issue by shrinking the on-screen age gap, so that it didn't appear quite as alarming.

Such was not the case for this movie. In fact, the filmmakers undertook a different approach regarding Garner and Field's characters, whose age difference is very much at the forefront of their minds. When *Murphy's Romance* finished filming, Garner was fifty-seven,[8] nineteen years older than his costar, but in the film, the filmmakers stretched the truth—in the opposite direction—spreading the characters' ages by twenty-seven years.[9]

Despite the leads' age difference, the film is credible because Field and Garner looked so comfortable together. Said Garner, "It's a cliché, but we had great chemistry on the screen."[10] Indeed, they did. Field and Garner fit perfectly, not only into their roles but as a couple tentatively leaning toward each other, not quite sure if they should. Murphy addresses the sexual tension of their burgeoning relationship late in the film, when he declares,

> "You want advice? Write Dear Abby. You've got problems? Take them to your local minister. Your head isn't on straight? The mental health clinic is in the phone book. I'm not a lifeguard. I don't put up bail and I'm not your damn Dutch uncle."

Murphy spins her around on the stool to face him and kisses her, then lifts her off the stool and walks her to the door. "Now if you don't know how things are, you're not as smart as I thought you were."[11]

Clearly, the only thing keeping the two apart from each other is the age difference, and it's an obstacle of little substance, so the story introduces something more conventional to impede their romance: Emma's ex-husband. The contrivance is both momentary and insubstantial, since the filmmakers—and the audience—know the film isn't called *Murphy's Romance* for nothing.

Murphy's Romance was among Garner's favorites of his films, for more than one reason. In his memoir, the actor stated that he enjoyed the film "as much for the people I worked with as the film itself."[12] It might not be a great film, but after more than thirty years, it retains its charms, and it remains one of the finer examples of what made Garner one of the more admired actors in Hollywood.

PROMISE

(1986)

★ ★ ★ ½

Director: Glenn Jordan
Teleplay: Richard Friedenberg; story by Kenneth Blackwell and Tennyson Flowers, and Richard Friedenberg
Producer: Glenn Jordan. *Director of Photography:* Gayne Rescher. *Music:* David Shire. *Editor:* Paul Rubell. *Production Designer:* Fred Harpman
Cast: James Garner (Bob Beuhler), James Woods (D. J. Beuhler), Piper Laurie (Annie Gilbert), Peter Michael Goetz (Stuart), Michael Alldredge (Gibb), Alan Rosenberg (Dr. Pressman), Mary Marsh (Mrs. Post), Barbara Lee Alexander (Joan)
Studio: Hallmark Hall of Fame (Garner-Duchow Productions)
First Aired: December 14, 1986 (CBS)
Specs: 97 minutes; color
Availability: DVD (Warner Archive Collection)

SUMMARY

Bob Beuhler, a real estate agent in White River, Oregon, returns to his family home after his mother passes away. With both parents now deceased, Bob feels obligated to fulfill a vow he made to his mother when he was a young man—to care for D. J., his younger, schizophrenic brother. Bob's apprehension is well founded when the two brothers are under one roof again, and D. J.'s behavior becomes increasingly unsettling. Meanwhile, Bob's high school sweetheart, Annie, also comes back in the picture and she does her best to support the two siblings.

BACKGROUND

Before it was a cable television channel that aired schmaltzy Christmas movies (and eventually reruns of mystery shows from the 1970s and '80s like *Columbo*, *The Rockford Files*, and *Murder, She Wrote*), the Hallmark Hall of Fame name had been synonymous with quality programming. Sponsored by Hallmark greeting cards, the show began as a weekly anthology program in the first half of the 1950s, starting with "Amahl and the Night Visitors" in 1951. By the autumn of 1955, weekly programming had been abandoned in lieu of specials that were sporadically broadcast for the next half century. Many of those specials were highly regarded by critics and earned multiple awards, including Emmys for dramatic programs of the year, beginning with *Macbeth* in 1961.

Promise was the first of four Hall of Fame ventures for Garner. With several successful films and two iconic television characters behind him, the actor started to take on more challenges, both on-screen and behind the camera. In addition to acting in *Promise*, Garner was also a producer on the film with Peter Duchow, a former agent, and the team worked in collaboration with Hallmark.

Costarring with Garner were three-time Academy Award–nominee Piper Laurie, as an old love interest who wants to rekindle the flame, and James Woods, as Garner's schizophrenic younger brother, D. J. This was the first (and only) time Garner and Laurie appeared on-screen together, but the two Jims had crossed paths more than a decade before. Woods, in fact, appeared in the first episode of *The Rockford Files*, playing a quirky murder suspect in "The Kirkoff Case."

The teleplay by Richard Friedenberg was based on a script titled "Watercolors," that Garner had bought several years before filming began. According to the actor, he showed it to his *Murphy's Romance* director, Martin Ritt, who emphatically declared that the story could not work as a feature. But this did not dissuade the actor from pursuing the project, since he felt "the best writing is in television."[1]

Behind the camera, director Glenn Jordan, who had helmed *Heartsounds* two years earlier, reteamed with Garner, a collaboration that would continue in the 1990s.

Promise Emmy winners James Woods (Best Actor) and Garner (as producer of Outstanding Drama/Comedy Special). *Hallmark Productions / Photofest © Hallmark Productions*

RECEPTION

The *New York Times* raved about the film, declaring, "A television movie has finally done it—tackled a disease for which there is no cure, no comforting bromides, and, therefore, no opportunity for easy uplift." The review commends Garner who "come[s] through powerfully as he delves into a character very different from those in his familiar repertory," but also praises Woods who "is thoroughly riveting as he flits through a staggering range of emotions, sometimes in a single scene." Summing up, the reviewer notes that "together, Mr. Garner and Mr. Woods bring to *Promise* their own special brand of inspiration. It is far more effective than the standard formula variety."[2]

Leonard Maltin gave an "Above Average" to this "beautifully written drama of love and responsibility."[3] Michael Sragow in the *New Yorker* said the film "is the pinnacle of its clinical-psychology genre, dramatically, emotionally, and in its scrupulous unwillingness to let any character off the hook." Sragow also called James Woods "brilliant" as he "lets the audience see beyond this man's funky surface and into his afflicted soul."[4]

According to Hallmark, *Promise* was "the most honored dramatic special in television history,"[5] a lofty, perhaps hyperbolic boast. Nonetheless, the film was nominated for seven Emmys, including acting nods to Garner, Woods, and Laurie, as well as Best Cinematography. Garner lost to his costar Woods, but as coproducer of the film, he shared the Emmy for Outstanding Drama/Comedy Special. In addition to Drama Special and Lead Actor, the film also won Emmys for writing and directing, and Laurie earned an Outstanding Supporting Actress Emmy. In addition to its five Emmys, the film won two Golden Globes for Best Miniseries or Motion Picture Made for Television and Woods as Best Performance by an Actor. Garner and Laurie were also nominated. Laurie lost to screen legend Olivia DeHavilland for *Anastasia: The Mystery of Anna*.

The film was also recognized by the Peabody Awards, which honors excellence in broadcasting. Citing the film, the organization stated,

> For a sensitive, exceptional production which does immense credit to both those who perform as well as to Producer/Director Glenn Jordan and Producer/Author Richard Friedenberg, a Peabody Award to *Promise*.[6]

It was the second such distinction bestowed upon a Garner production, following *Heartsounds* two years earlier.

COMMENTARY

Garner knew that the role he would undertake—an irresponsible, irritable bachelor whose self-serving impulses contrasted with the mostly likable characters that viewers had come to expect of him—was a risk worth taking. Easygoing types had been Garner's specialty, but Bob Beuhler presented a different challenge: turning an amiable everyman into a bitter, sometimes angry figure who is forced to face real responsibility for the first time in his life. Of the character Garner assumed, "People will hate me." But he also admitted, "That doesn't bother me."[7] The actor also acknowledged that his decision to take on such roles had changed over time. Said Garner, "I couldn't have played the character five years earlier. I'd have thought he was too unsympathetic."[8]

Taking on a difficult subject like schizophrenia is one thing, but executing a critically acclaimed depiction of the disease required both sensitivity and restraint. That restraint was especially needed for the film's final act. Television films—and features for that matter—often fall prey to the happy ending curse, offering a resolution, no matter how improbable, to appease viewers. What *Promise* provides is something else entirely. D. J. does not miraculously recover from his illness, nor does Bob become a self-sacrificing saint. While Garner's character makes emotional progress during the film, he does not transform into his brother's savior. Rather, he comes to realize that he is incapable of offering the best care for his brother and doesn't fool himself into thinking otherwise. It's an awareness that is both selfish and self-less at the same time. He grieves for his brother's illness, while also coming to terms with his own limitations, which cause him even more regret.

While the evolution of Bob's character is gradual and by no means complete, the role itself represented the latest development of Garner as an actor. Recognizing that his growth as an actor meant tackling roles different from those that had made him a star, Garner gamely pursued those opportunities. As Garner admitted, he needed to "make that transition from the leading man to more character roles, and still stay in sort of a leading man capacity."[9] That realization had manifested first in *The Long Summer of George Adams* in 1982, followed by *Heartsounds* in 1984, and now *Promise*. The earlier films allowed Garner to play a flawed everyman and a doctor facing his mortality, in each capturing a vulnerability that made them all the more real.

Promise is also noteworthy for the actor in a different capacity, that of producer. Ever since *36 Hours* in 1964, Garner had worked behind the scenes on many of his films, after forming his own production company. The films and shows produced under the Cherokee Productions banner aimed no more than to entertain audiences and lacked any true social meaning. In his new partnership, Garner was able to produce films that entertained, of course, but also offered something of more substance.

Producing purposeful films required hiring men and women who were capable of delivering quality work, behind the scenes and in front of the camera. To that end, Garner and company secured the services of exceptional talent, in particular director Glenn Jordan and two acting heavyweights, James Woods and Piper Laurie. *Promise* delivers because of these individuals and their commitment to telling a compelling and, one could argue, necessary story.

While the film would earn Woods the first of two Emmys, the opportunity to work with Garner offered a greater reward. Reflecting on the film, Woods once revealed, "People ask me, 'What's the favorite thing you've ever done in your life?' and I always say *Promise* because it was a perfect part for me and a perfect experience with Jim."[10]

For Woods—and no doubt Garner—winning awards was beside the point. This was true of *Promise* and perhaps even more so for their next collaboration when they addressed the insidious disease of alcoholism.

21

MY NAME IS BILL W.

(1989)

★★ ½

Director: Daniel Petrie
Teleplay: William G. Borchert
Producer: Daniel Petrie. *Director of Photography:* Neal Roach. *Music:* Laurence
    Rosenthal. *Editors:* Paul Rubell and John Wright. *Production Designer:*
    Fred Harpman
Cast: James Woods (Bill Wilson), JoBeth Williams (Lois Wilson), James
    Garner (Dr. Robert Holbrook Smith), Gary Sinise (Ebby Thatcher),
    George Coe (Frank Shaw), Robert Harper (Dr. Jeremy Partlin), Ray
    Reinhardt (Dr. Silkworth), Fritz Weaver (Dr. Burnham)
Studio: Hallmark Hall of Fame (Garner-Duchow Productions)
First Aired: April 30, 1989 (CBS)
Specs: 99 minutes; color
Availability: DVD (Warner Archive Collection)

SUMMARY

After struggling with alcoholism for years, successful businessman William
Wilson seeks to combat his addiction. With the support of his wife, Lois,
and the wisdom of fellow alcoholic "Dr. Bob" Smith, Wilson is determined
to conquer the disease. Wilson and Smith find that sharing their struggles—rather than hiding them because of shame and embarrassment—is

the path to redemption, and they embark on a mission to share their message with others.

BACKGROUND

William Wilson was born in 1895 and suffered a fairly chaotic childhood, including parents who abandoned him at a very young age, leaving him and his sister in the care of their grandparents. After enlisting to serve in the First World War, Wilson was "offered his first drink, a Bronx cocktail," which took away "his sense of inferiority."[1] It also led to two decades of alcohol abuse, which he attempted to combat in a spiral of successes, that were ultimately followed by failure. Finally, in 1934 a fellow alcoholic, Ebby Thatcher, who had managed to stay sober for several weeks, inspired Wilson to embark on a new means of treating his illness. But Wilson's resolve to beat the bottle continued to be undermined until he met Dr. Bob Smith, and the two cofounded the first chapter of Alcoholics Anonymous. Wilson did not take another drink and remained sober until his death in 1971.

Though he himself was not an alcoholic, Garner could relate to the pull of addiction—for the actor, it was cigarettes—and he saw in Wilson's life an opportunity to tell a story that could have a profound impact, much like his earlier film, *Promise*. While Garner's Cherokee Productions was dormant, the actor worked again with Peter Duchow, a partnership that produced *Promise*. Hallmark Hall of Fame had sponsored the Emmy-winning film, and Garner-Duchow Productions again worked with the esteemed company on this second prestige project.

One of the first orders of business was finding the right actor to manifest both the intensity of William Wilson during his manic episodes as well as the vulnerable man when he hits bottom, again and again. Duchow and Garner recruited the actor's *Promise* costar, James Woods, to take on the part of William Wilson. Perhaps because of the film's subject matter, Garner the producer knew that the story of Bill W. might not have drawn viewers by its subject matter alone, so he enlisted Garner the *actor* to play a role, but not the lead. The core of the film's story occurs in the 1920s and '30s, culminating in Wilson's commitment to sobriety, after he had just turned thirty-nine. Garner was sixty at the time of filming and would have been too old for the part, particular during Wilson's early years. But he was just about the same age of Dr. Bob Smith, when Wilson and Smith met in 1934, so the decision to portray Smith was a sensible one.

JoBeth Williams, who had appeared in two prominent films of the early 1980s—as the mother of a family terrorized in *Poltergeist* (1982) and as one of a circle of friends who reunite for their college buddy's funeral in *The Big Chill* (1983)—was cast as Lois, Wilson's devoted and desperate wife. For the role of Wilson's drinking buddy, the filmmakers hired Gary Sinise, a young actor who had cofounded the famed Steppenwolf Theatre Company.

The screenplay by William Borchert "was based upon material gathered from personal interviews and in-depth research" the writer had conducted.[2] The film was helmed by Daniel Petrie, an accomplished director whose credits included dozens of television shows, several feature films, and a handful of prominent television movies, highlighted by the 1976 dramatic special *Eleanor and Franklin* and its sequel, *Eleanor and Franklin: The White House Years*, both of which earned Emmys for the director.

RECEPTION

Most of the reviews for the film focused on James Woods and deservedly so. As John O'Connor wrote in the *New York Times*, "The burden of the film rests on the performance of Mr. Woods and, once again, he proves to be one of the most riveting actors of this generation." Calling the film "a powerful dramatization" of Alcoholics Anonymous's early history, O'Connor further noted that Woods's "television collaborations with Mr. Garner have served him well."[3] While *Los Angeles Times* critic Howard Rosenberg praised both the leads, calling JoBeth Williams "sterling" and Woods "utterly convincing in this drunk's-eye-view of the world from the bottoms up," he questioned the pacing of the film. Rosenberg felt the deliberate and lengthy lead-up to Wilson's ultimate triumph over alcohol sabotaged the film's overall effect with its rushed conclusion—a not unreasonable observation. Leonard Maltin praised both Woods's acting and the film's "strong script,"[4] while Mick Martin and Marsha Porter said the "impressive" film was highlighted by "outstanding performances by a fine cast."[5]

COMMENTARY

Like *Promise*, *My Name Is Bill W.* had a purpose beyond that of entertainment. The former film held a spotlight on the very real challenges that schizophrenia presents not only to those who suffer from the disease but also to those who are called upon to care for the afflicted. *Promise* accomplished

James Woods and Garner tackle another difficult issue in their second film together. *Warner Bros. Pictures / Photofest © Warner Bros. Pictures*

its mission and captured the heartbreak that families face trying to care for loved ones. In doing so, the film earned acclaim from mental health groups for its handling of the subject, in particular the film's lack of melodrama but also its avoidance of a simplistic resolution. And like other productions that successfully tackle difficult topics, the film received Emmys—a handful in fact—including Outstanding Drama/Comedy Special. Perhaps more significantly, *Promise* was cited by the Peabody Foundation—which honors works of distinction in the media—for being a "sensitive, exceptional production."[6]

The key difference between *Promise* and *My Name Is Bill W.* is in the rendering of the characters. While *Promise* presented a fictional account of brothers who face the trials of a mental illness, *My Name Is Bill W.* dramatizes the lives of real people and re-creates actual events. Much like *Heartsounds* from several years earlier, Garner and his fellow filmmakers were tasked with balancing the dramatic license required of a television film with an obligation to portray real individuals as faithfully as possible. For the most part, the film successfully straddles these two goals. The film suffers slightly from disease-of-the-week conventions, but otherwise manages to tell Wilson's story in a credible—if sometimes melodramatic—manner.

For the first time in more than thirty years, Garner undertook a supporting role, his first since attaining leading man status in the wake of his breakout role of Bret Maverick. Playing an important figure in *Bill W.* made sense, not only for Garner the actor, but for Garner the producer, who knew his presence would likely draw more viewers. Smith played a pivotal role in the development of Alcoholics Anonymous, and it made sense for his part to be played by an actor of Garner's stature. But because Smith did not appear until very late in Wilson's sobrietal breakthrough, the filmmakers no doubt didn't want to wait until the final act for Garner to appear. The screenplay solves this by introducing Smith in a scene that sets up the story in flashback. The film opens in 1950, framing the story by placing Bill and Lois Wilson at Smith's deathbed, and then retracing the steps leading to Bill's road to recovery. This framing device assures some viewers that this is indeed a James Garner movie even if the central figure of the film is portrayed by James Woods.

In many ways, the 1980s was James Garner's most creatively productive and personally rewarding decade in the actor's fifty-plus-year career. From the airing of the final episode of *The Rockford Files* in January of 1980 to the broadcast of *My Name is Bill W.* on April 30, 1989, Garner asserted his reputation as an actor (not to mention producer) of quality work, both on television and in feature films. Of course, like every actor of any stature, the peaks were compromised by the occasional valleys, such as the weak

The Fan and absurd *Tank*. And even working on feature films with three acclaimed directors—Robert Altman, Blake Edwards, and Martin Ritt—during that decade produced a set of admittedly mixed results. But between the lows of Altman's *HealtH* in 1980 and Edwards's *Sunset* in 1988, there was also the high of *Victor/Victoria* in 1982 and, of course, the Oscar-nominated performance in Ritt's *Murphy's Romance* in 1986.

On the small screen, the highs profoundly dwarfed the lows. On the one hand, Garner was no doubt thrilled to reassume the role that put him on the map, the charming schemer Bret Maverick in the series of the same name. On the other hand, the revival didn't gain traction, and was canceled before it could even last a full season, producing only eighteen episodes. Nonetheless, that short stint still earned Garner Emmy and Golden Globe nominations for lead actor.[7] More significantly, the actor starred in four highly acclaimed television films. After *The Long Summer of George Adams*, *Heartsounds*, and *Promise*, Garner ended the decade on a high note with *My Name Is Bill W.* Besides the accolades and the awards bestowed upon the film, *My Name Is Bill W.* was one of the most significant productions of Garner's career, a fact he acknowledged in his memoir. According to Garner, "Of all the things I've ever done as an actor or a producer, I think *My Name Is Bill W.* has had the greatest impact."[8]

22

DECORATION DAY

(1990)

★ ★ ★ ½

Director: Robert Markowitz
Teleplay: Robert W. Lenski, based on the novella by John William Corrington
Producer: Anne Hopkins. *Director of Photography:* Neal Roach. *Music:* Patrick
   Williams. *Editor:* Harvey Rosenstock. *Production Designer:* Donald Light
   Harris
Cast: James Garner (Albert Sidney Finch), Judith Ivey (Terry Novis), Ruby Dee
   (Rowena), Bill Cobbs (Gee Penniwell), Laurence Fishburne (Michael
   Waring), Jo Anderson (Loreen Wendell), Norm Skaggs (Billy Wendell)
Studio: Hallmark Hall of Fame
First Aired: December 2, 1990 (NBC)
Specs: 100 minutes; color
Availability: DVD (Artisan Home Entertainment)

SUMMARY

Retired Judge Albert Sidney Finch is a widower whose wife passed away
a few years ago. He wants nothing more than to be left alone and allowed
to fish in peace. But his godson Billy asks Finch to intervene on behalf
of the judge's childhood friend, a black man named Gee Penniwell. The
Department of Defense wants to award Gee the Congressional Medal of
Honor for his service during World War II in which he took out "a bunch

of Germans" by himself. But Gee wants nothing to do with the honor, and his refusal to accept the award stirs up questions about racism. When Albert becomes involved, buried frictions resurface, and Finch must learn to mend fences while helping out his estranged friend.

BACKGROUND

The 166th Hallmark Hall of Fame production was the third for Garner, who was pleased to be working with them again. Garner appreciated their support of the project, because "they give you everything you need to make a great picture" and "they have faith in the integrity of the material."[1]

Decoration Day began as a novella by John Corrington, a highly regarded poet, short story writer, screenwriter, and novelist. For executive producer Marian Rees, the complex novella addressed universal concerns about crises in "relationships, which we all have, and how in dealing with them rather than avoiding them, there is the possibility of change."[2]

Robert Lenski, who adapted the novella to the small screen, had previously penned a number of episodes for successful miniseries such as *Chiefs* as well as private eye television shows of the 1970s, including *Mannix*, *Barnaby Jones*, and *Cannon*, though none for *The Rockford Files*.

In addition to working with Hallmark again, Garner had another compelling reason to take on the project. Before he had received the script, Garner learned that Corrington had written the novella with him in mind. According to Garner, "I had goose-bumps when the script arrived at the house."[3] The actor identified with his character, noting, "Like him, I don't like to see wrongs done. And when I do see wrong, I like to try and right it."[4]

For the other principal actors who worked on the film, the experience was nothing less than rewarding. Judith Ivey was drawn to the film, which allowed her to play a woman who harbors an unexpected secret. Said Ivey,

> You thought she was one person when it starts and then there's this twist, and the script was so well-written that I had no idea that that was going to be the twist—or that there even was a twist. I really like that in characters—when they surprise us.[5]

Norm Skaggs, who plays Garner's godson in the film, lauded the film's "integrity and purpose," which gave him the sense that "the film needs to be made."[6]

Bill Cobbs reiterated that sentiment, stating that he was pleased to be in a production "that talked about African Americans in World War II, and their contribution to that war, because there haven't been a lot of scripts dealing with this subject."[7] Acclaimed actress and civil rights activist Ruby Dee plays Rowena, the judge's "housekeeper, friend, and conscience." The actress understood the dynamics of her character, a black woman in 1970s Georgia, and how she related to the judge: "He has no secrets from her. It's not his obligation to know Rowena and her life and care about it, but her life has to be his life."[8]

RECEPTION

Leonard Maltin called *Decoration Day* a "top-notch drama" that was "sensitively adapted."[9] John O'Connor in the *New York Times* agreed, noting that the film, "proceeds without fireworks, taking its time and carefully revealing its gentle insights into memory, friendship, race relations and the simple fact that time passes and things change."[10] In addition to citing the "deliberate thoughtfulness" of director Markowitz and "an impeccable supporting cast," O'Connor calls particular attention to Garner's performance. Comparing him to Hollywood legends Jimmy Stewart and Gary Cooper, O'Connor remarks that Garner instills "what could have been a fairly pedestrian role with remarkable weight and insight."[11]

When it first aired, *Decoration Day* was the highest rated special of the week (November 26–December 2, 1990), and the seventh highest rated program overall, following episodes of *Cheers*, *60 Minutes*, *A Different World*, *Roseanne*, *The Cosby Show*, and *Murder, She Wrote*. According to the A. C. Nielsen ratings, the program reached an audience of more than twenty-six million viewers.[12]

Garner's third Hallmark Hall of Fame special was also the third in row that earned him an Emmy nomination for Outstanding Lead Actor in a Miniseries or a Special. The program was nominated for five other awards, including Outstanding Drama/Comedy Special and Miniseries, and Outstanding Directing in a Miniseries or a Special. The film's only Emmy winner was Ruby Dee, who plays Rowena, the judge's housekeeper and friend. For Dee, who had been nominated four times prior to *Decoration Day*, dating back to 1964, this was her first and only Emmy win.

The film also received two Golden Globe nominations—and won both—for Best Miniseries or Motion Picture Made for Television, and

Emmy winner Ruby Dee and Garner. *NBC / Photofest © NBC*

Garner for Best Performance by an Actor in a Miniseries or Motion Picture Made for Television.

COMMENTARY

Just as he had concluded the 1980s, Garner began the new decade on a
high note. *Decoration Day* was the first of several prestigious television
films the actor headlined in the 1990s. Although the decade would be
sprinkled with some lows for Garner—an unfortunate cameo in an Eddie
Murphy film and a failed television series, *Man of the People*—there were
also highlights, in particular the revivals of his two most popular television
characters, Bret Maverick on the big screen and Jim Rockford in a series
of TV movie specials.

But perhaps this film tops them all. Garner's performance in *Decoration
Day* solidified his role as one of the few leading men who could carry a film
with an understated performance. In keeping with the film's deliberate
and minimalist tone, there's nothing flashy or consciously dramatic about

Garner's portrayal of Judge Finch. In this beautifully rendered film, Garner delivers one of his best performances, on par with *The Americanization of Emily* and *Murphy's Romance*. It's a portrayal that is matched by an outstanding cast, notably Ruby Dee, Bill Cobbs, and Judith Ivey. But they are not alone. In smaller, but no less satisfying roles, Laurence Fishburne, Norm Skaggs, and in particular, Jo Anderson, convey a humanity that does justice to the quiet but powerful screenplay. With Garner leading the way, all of the actors embody the film's themes—forgiveness and acceptance—that make watching *Decoration Day* a rich viewing experience.

BARBARIANS AT THE GATE

(1993)

★ ★ ★

Director: Glenn Jordan
Teleplay: Larry Gelbart, based on the book *Barbarians at the Gate: The Fall of RJR Nabisco* by Bryan Burrough, John Helyar
Producer: Ray Stark. *Directors of Photography:* Tom Del Ruth ASC, Nic Knowland, ASC. *Music:* Richard Gibbs. *Editor:* Patrick Kennedy. *Production Designer:* Linda Pearl. *Art Director:* Michael Armani. *Set Decorators:* Jan Bergstrom, Karen O'Hara
Cast: James Garner (F. Ross Johnson), Jonathan Pryce (Henry Kravis), Peter Reigert (Peter Cohen), Joanna Cassidy (Linda Robinson), Fred Dalton Thompson (Jim Robinson), Leilani Sarelle (Laurie Johnson), Matt Clark (Edward Horrigan Jr.), Jeffrey DeMunn (H. John Greeniaus), David Rasche (Ted Forstmann), Ron Canada (Vernon Jordan)
Studio: HBO Films
First Aired: March 20, 1993 (HBO)
Specs: 102 minutes; color
Availability: DVD (HBO)

SUMMARY

In 1989, F. Ross Johnson, the CEO of R. J. R. Nabisco, puts plans in motion to engineer the largest corporate buyout in history. With the financial backing of Shearson Lehman, an investment banking firm, and American Express—and drawing on decades of slick salesmanship—Johnson hopes to conduct the transaction expediently. His plans are thwarted, however, when Wall Street tycoon Henry Kravis of Kohlberg Kravis Roberts & Co. enters the race, and the result is a battle of wills between the two men. As the stakes get higher and higher, the morals sink lower, as everyone involved—from the board of Nabisco to other possible investors—seek to add to their already considerable wealth.

BACKGROUND

Published in late 1989, *Barbarians at the Gate* chronicles the multi-billion-dollar buyout of R. J. R. Nabisco—up to that time the biggest such transaction in history. The book, which was written by two journalists for the *Wall Street Journal*—Bryan Burrough and John Helyar—reached number one on the *New York Times* hardcover best-seller list in March of 1990 and remained on the list for nearly forty weeks.

Acclaimed screenwriter Larry Gelbart was hired to adapt the book. Gelbart had first made a name for himself in the 1950s, writing for such shows as *Caesar's Hour*. After a few screenplays—as well as collaborating with Carl Reiner on the story for *The Thrill of It All*—Gelbart helped adapt the 1970 film *M*A*S*H* into the highly acclaimed, long-running series. Screenplays for later features included *Oh, God!* and *Tootsie*, both of which earned Gelbart Oscar nominations.

For Gelbart, there were two significant challenges to adapting the non-fiction work: he had to "peel away the layers of names and complexity to get to the central story" and "make a rather dry financial story entertaining."[1] Rather than dramatizing the events in a sober, by-the-numbers manner, Gelbart opted for a humorous take, deciding early on to translate the details of the financial maneuverings as a "bedroom farce—substituting money for sex, people getting paid instead of laid."[2] By approaching the subject as a satire, the filmmakers could also take liberties with the characterization and antics of certain individuals without fear of litigation.

Produced by Ray Stark (*The Way We Were*, *Steel Magnolias*), the film was originally planned for the big screen, but the switch to HBO appealed to the producer, especially regarding finances. "I usually pay an actor what we made this whole picture for," admitted Stark of the film that cost a "mere" $7 million to make.[3] There is no record of what Garner received for the film, but for what he brought to the production, he no doubt made a fraction of what Johnson earned after the buyout—an estimated $30 million. Glenn Jordan, who had collaborated twice with Garner on two of the actor's most distinguished television productions, *Heartsounds* and *Promise*, joined him again on this production.

Welsh actor Jonathan Pryce, who had a successful stage career, most notably in the London production of *Miss Saigon*, and who first came to widespread attention in Terry Gilliam's *Brazil*, plays Oklahoma-born Kravis. The rest of the cast included Peter Reigert, whose first notable role was in the film *Animal House*; Joanna Cassidy; and Fred Dalton Thompson— former attorney and future senator—as the head of American Express.

RECEPTION

In his review for *Variety*, Tony Scott called the film "a droll flight, with James Garner assertively setting the pace" and cited Gelbart's "sharp, ingenious teleplay." Scott summed up his appraisal:

> As a telefilm, *Barbarians* fascinates; as social commentary, it excels. Making an intricate business exercise both entertaining and engrossing takes lots of doing; it's handily accomplished here.[4]

Leonard Maltin called *Barbarians* a "dynamite seriocomedy" and Garner "ideal" in his role as Johnson.[5] While the *New York Times* critic enjoyed the film overall and praised the strong cast, he also had slight reservations about the casting of Garner, whose "energetic performance is perhaps a touch too winning, making Mr. Johnson such a helluva guy." Despite any reservations, the review ends with the affirmative recommendation: "Don't miss it."[6]

In his aptly titled review "Who Knew Greed Could Be So Fun?" for the *Los Angeles Times*, Howard Rosenberg declared, "You can't imagine a more deliciously entertaining movie about the $25-billion leveraged buyout of R.J.R. Nabisco Co." The review singled out Larry Gelbart, who "is as acutely clever and witty as ever," calling *Barbarians* a "'hoot' of a film."[7]

In addition to the glowing reviews, the film received a slew of Emmy nominations—nine in all—including one for Garner as Outstanding Lead Actor in a Miniseries or a Special, and two supporting actor nods to Jonathan Pryce and Peter Reigert. Glenn Jordan and Larry Gelbart were nominated for Outstanding Directing and Outstanding Writing, respectively. Ultimately, the film won just a single Emmy, but it was *the* award—for Outstanding Made for Television Movie, shared with *Stalin*, another HBO

Garner as F. Ross Johnson. *Columbia Pictures Television / Photofest © Columbia Pictures Television*

movie. The rare tie was a double distinction, since it was the first time any HBO production had won the coveted award. In fact, it led to a string of HBO winners in that category through 1999.[8]

Other awards included three Golden Globe nominations, of which the program won two: Best Miniseries or Motion Picture Made for Television, and Garner for Best Performance by an Actor in a Miniseries or Motion Picture Made for Television. Gelbart's screenplay also received a Writers Guild of America award in the Adapted Long Form category (again, tying another production, this time *Silent Cries*, a film about women surviving in a prisoner of war camp during World War II). The Television Critics Association named it Program of the Year,[9] although they chose a television series, *I'll Fly Away*, over it for Outstanding Achievement in Drama.[10]

COMMENTARY

The Nabisco buyout capped a decade of Reagan-era greed, with inside traders like Michael Milliken and Ivan Boesky grabbing the headlines for their illegal actions—which the film references. Sadly, it would not be the end of such corporate machinations, as the country would learn, from the Enron scandal of the early 2000s to the housing market bust a few years later.

By the time this film was produced, Garner had portrayed a litany of scheming—but likable—characters, including Cash McCall in the eponymous film and Henry Tyroon in *The Wheeler Dealers*. Aiming mostly for laughs, those films poked fun at the business world through the prism of fictional connivers, but taking on F. Ross Johnson presented a darker challenge for Garner—portraying not only a real person but one whose ostentatious lifestyle and underhanded maneuverings might not appeal to audiences in the same way as those conventional comedies had.

To Garner, Johnson did not represent the typical bad guy. The actor regarded the tycoon as more of a "salesman who got in over his head."[11] That assessment may be too kind, but many actors who take on villainous roles often look for the good in the characters they portray. The same could be said for Garner, but he was also embodying the greed as glib ethos that permeates Gelbart's script. Garner's Cash McCall of thirty years prior had evolved over the decades into a brazen showman whose heart has been replaced by junk bonds. While the audience might not be able to stomach Johnson's behavior, that doesn't prevent us from savoring Garner's performance, which he tackles with apparent glee.

BREATHING LESSONS

(1994)

★ ★ ★

Director: John Erman
Teleplay: Robert W. Lenski, based on the novel by Anne Tyler
Producer: John Erman. *Director of Photography:* Gayne Rescher, ASC. *Music:* John
     Kander. *Editor:* John W. Wheeler, ACE. *Production Designer:* James Hulsey
Cast: James Garner (Ira Moran), Joanne Woodward (Maggie Moran), Kathryn
     Erbe (Fiona), Joyce Van Patten (Serena), Eileen Heckart (Mabel), Paul
     Winfield (Daniel Otis), Tim Guinee (Jesse), Jean Louisa Kelly (Daisy),
     Stephi Lineburg (Leroy), Henry Jones (Sam Moran)
Studio: Hallmark Hall of Fame
First Aired: February 6, 1994 (CBS)
Specs: 97 minutes; color
Availability: DVD (Hallmark Hall of Fame)

SUMMARY

A Saturday in the life of Ira and Maggie Moran, a Baltimore couple of modest means who have been married for almost thirty years. They have two children, a son Jesse, who has never amounted to much, and a daughter Daisy, who will be leaving for college the next day. Ira and Maggie begin their day preparing to leave for a funeral—the husband of Maggie's best friend, Serena. Their long day ends after a minor car accident, a peculiar memorial service, a misunderstanding with Serena, an encounter with an elderly man on the road, and a hopeful reunion with Jesse's ex-wife, Fiona, and their oddly named granddaughter, Leroy.

BACKGROUND

Breathing Lessons marked the fourth and final time Garner appeared in a Hallmark Hall of Fame special, following the highly acclaimed films *Promise*, *My Name Is Bill W.*, and *Decoration Day*. The film was adapted from a novel by Anne Tyler, who set many of her fictional works in Baltimore, Maryland, the author's home since the mid-1960s. Of Tyler's more than fifteen novels, only a third of them have been adapted to the screen. *Breathing Lessons* followed the feature film adaptation of *The Accidental Tourist*, which starred William Hurt, Kathleen Turner, and Geena Davis in her Oscar-winning performance.

Published in 1988, *Breathing Lessons*, received rave reviews from *Publisher's Weekly*, the *Washington Post*, the *Baltimore Sun*, the *Wall Street Journal*, and other esteemed publications. The accolades culminated the following year when Tyler's novel was awarded the Pulitzer Prize for fiction. Robert Lenski, who wrote the Emmy-nominated screenplay for Garner's previous Hall of Fame film *Decoration Day*, also adapted *Breathing Lessons*.[1]

Director John Erman was a television veteran, whose small-screen credits dated back to the early 1960s, working on such shows as *My Favorite Martian*, *That Girl*, and *The Ghost and Mrs. Muir*. By the end of the 1970s, he had transitioned to television movies, most notably *Who Will Love My Children?*—for which he won an Emmy in 1983—and one of the first productions that tackled the subject of AIDs, *An Early Frost*, in 1985.

The film's score represented a rare television venture for composer John Kander, who had made a name for himself on Broadway as a multiple Tony Award winner for such musicals as *Woman of the Year*, *Kiss of the Spider Woman*, and the brilliant *Cabaret*.

This was the first and only on-screen pairing for Garner and Joanne Woodward, and according to the actor, they "hit it off right away."[2] Additional cast members included Kathryn Erbe (who would go on to star as Detective Eames in *Law and Order: Criminal Intent*) as their former daughter-in-law, Oscar-nominee Paul Winfield (*Sounder*), and Academy Award–winner Eileen Heckart in a brief—almost throwaway—appearance as a waitress. In another small role, character actor Henry Jones played

Garner's father. For Jones, this was the sixth and final time he would share the screen with Garner, dating back nearly forty years to *The Girl He Left Behind* in 1956.

RECEPTION

As with the previous Hallmark Hall of Fame specials associated with Garner, *Breathing Lessons* was a critical success. Leonard Maltin called the film a "wry, nicely paced road movie,"[3] and the *New York Times* noted that the "deliciously on-target performances by Joanne Woodward and James Garner" make their "almost eccentric relationship thoroughly appealing."[4] Another pair of critics declared that "Joanne Woodward steals the show" as a "whimsical, meddling woman who tries to make things right but usually makes matters worse," and they also cite Garner's performance as "excellent."[5] Pondering the fictional couple's future, John O'Connor in the *New York Times* surmised that "Ms. Woodward and Mr. Garner will leave you convinced they'll stick it out."[6] Writing for *Variety*, Roberta Bernstein called *Breathing Lessons* "an antidote" to violent made-for-television movies, praising Lenski's adaptation of the novel, in particular "the homey flavor and realistic dialogue." The critic also cited the contributions of director John Erman, production designer James Hulsey, and cinematographer Gayne Rescher. Of the two leads, she writes, "Their easy chemistry makes believable the longtime union."[7] *VideoHound's Golden Movie Retriever* reiterated the success of the pairing, noting that the "drama rests easily on the capable shoulders of the veteran performers."[8]

The film was acknowledged by the Emmys with nominations for Outstanding Made for Television Movie and Robert Lenski's screenplay, as well as Garner and Woodward for their performances. No one walked away with Emmy statues—the film lost to the AIDS drama *And the Band Played On*, Garner lost to Hume Cronyn for *To Dance with the White Dog*, and Woodward lost to Kirstie Alley for *David's Mother*, which also won best writing. However, Woodward did receive both the Golden Globe and the Screen Actors Guild award for her performance. Garner received a Globe nomination but was not acknowledged for his role in *Breathing Lessons* by the Screen Actors Guild that year—instead SAG recognized him for the return of his beloved Rockford character in *The Rockford Files: I Still Love L.A.* (he lost to Raul Julia, who received a posthumous win for *The Burning Season: The Chico Mendes Story*).

Garner and Joanne Woodward, who won both a Golden Globe and a Screen Actors Guild award for her performance in *Breathing Lessons*. *Hallmark Productions / Photofest © Hallmark Productions*

COMMENTARY

True to its source material's tone, *Breathing Lessons* is a quiet film about a long-married couple whose interplay, including more than a few moments of bickering, belies a long affection the husband and wife have for each other. Maggie is the eternal optimist who often feels compelled to take action when the natural course of events run counter to her desires. Ira is alternately bemused and bedeviled by his wife's sometimes impulsive behavior. By focusing not on the highs and lows of married life over the decades but on a few emblematic days in their lives, the film encapsulates in two hours the dynamics of this endearing couple.

In order to establish this familiarity, the film needed two actors who could not only embody each role but also convincingly convey a life shared over decades, two halves complementing each other. So, ultimately, the key to the film's success is the lead actors' believable portrayals of Ira and Maggie. According to Garner, "Playing Ira wasn't a stretch, because I understand him and I like him."[9] Even more important is the credibility of Garner and Woodward's interactions as a husband and wife who know each other only too well. While each has opportunities to exasperate the other, they also express true affection, not to mention intimacy.

The casting of Garner and Woodward as a comfortable—if not always comforting—pair was inspired. Asked if he saw himself and his wife in the fictional couple, Garner replied, "I was trying not to think about that during the picture. But I don't think Joanne or I could help but relate to our respective spouses."[10] Throughout the film, Woodward, as the daffy but loving Maggie, elicits confounded responses from Garner's Ira. The exasperated looks that Garner had perfected in comedies of the 1960s have mellowed into a quieter form of comic bewilderment. His reactions might not have been quite as amusing as the earlier films, but they seem more real in this film. *Breathing Lessons* is the kind of film that rarely makes it to the small screen, much less the large one. It's a character study of a marriage in twilight as two individuals know full well that they are meant for each other, no matter how aggravated they might get. This warm, somewhat off-kilter coupling has stood the test of time, and the pair will likely remain mutually devoted until their dying days. And viewers of a certain age can easily see echoes of their own relationships in this duo—an affirmation of choices that somehow, some way, ultimately proved to be the right ones.

MAVERICK

(1994)

★ ★ ★

Director: Richard Donner
Screenplay: William Goldman, based on the television series *Maverick* created
    by Roy Huggins
Producers: Bruce Davey, Richard Donner. *Director of Photography:* Vilmos
    Zsigmond, ASC. *Music:* Randy Newman. *Editor:* Stuart Baird, ACE.
    Production Designer: Tom Sanders. *Art Director:* Daniel Dorrance.
    Costume Designer: April Ferry
Cast: Mel Gibson (Bret Maverick), Jodie Foster (Annabelle Bransford), James
    Garner (Zane Cooper), Graham Greene (Joseph), Alfred Molina (Angel),
    James Coburn (Commodore), Geoffrey Lewis (Matthew Wicker), Paul L.
    Smith (Archduke), Max Perlich (Johnny Hardin)
Studio: Warner Bros.
Release Date: May 20, 1994
Specs: 121 minutes; color
Availability: DVD (Warner Home Video)

SUMMARY

In early September 1875, Bret Maverick is intent on joining a high-stakes
riverboat poker tournament, not merely for the payoff but to prove himself
among other skilled card players. He is four days of travel time away and

$3,000 short of the $25,000 buy-in. As he makes his way to St. Louis, he encounters Annabelle Bransford, a female con artist, and Zane Cooper, a lawman. Opportunities to secure his final $3,000 come and go, and he encounters several obstacles, both accidental and intentional, that threaten to derail his ambition.

BACKGROUND

The original *Maverick* series was conceived and produced by Roy Huggins, who had previously worked on *Cheyenne*, a western starring Clint Walker. Richard Bare, who directed the first episode of *Cheyenne*, was responsible for Garner's first on-screen appearance. In 1955 the director met Garner (then Jim Bumgarner) in a Hollywood bar and tapped him for the role of a lieutenant in the Union Army in *Cheyenne*'s first episode. Within two years of that appearance, Garner was given the lead in a new series. *Maverick* was the perfect vehicle for Garner, showcasing his sardonic humor in a program that broke the mold of television westerns.

Maverick became an instant success and quickly bolted up the Nielsen ratings charts, making a star of Garner in the process. Although the show ran for five seasons until 1962, Garner left in 1960 following a dispute with Warner Bros., the owner of the show. And despite appearing in just under half of the show's 124 episodes, Garner would forever be identified with the character of Bret Maverick, an association he would cherish for the rest of his life.

By the early 1990s, the trend of adapting successful television shows to the big screen was no longer a "fresh" concept. Before *Maverick*, at least a dozen feature films based on successful series had been produced already, including *Dragnet*, *Dennis the Menace*, *The Beverly Hillbillies*, and *The Addams Family*, not to mention the *Star Trek* films dating back to 1979. The most successful of these—commercially and critically—had been *The Fugitive* starring Harrison Ford as a wrongly accused doctor on the run. A revival of the 1960s classic series created by Roy Huggins and starring David Janssen, *The Fugitive* feature not only scored big at the box office— earning $183 million domestically in 1993—it also received seven Academy Award nominations, including one for Best Picture, a feat no other big-screen adaptation has achieved.[1] In fact, most movie versions of television shows have been dismal failures, if not commercially, at least creatively.

But the big-screen *Maverick* had one advantage over other TV shows-turned-movies in that a two-time Academy Award–winning screenwriter,

William Goldman, had been hired to adapt the film. Goldman, one of a handful of individuals to win Oscars for an original screenplay (*Butch Cassidy and the Sundance Kid*) and an adaptation (*All the President's Men*), was offered the screenwriting job by Mel Gibson and his producing partner Bruce Davey. Goldman signed on for a number of reasons, including his affection for the original series but also the belief that the project fit his skills. Goldman also admitted that he took the job primarily because he believed "it would be easy."[2] He watched the original series with an eye toward an episode that featured "too much plot"—so that the screenwriter could open it up for a feature length film. However, Goldman soon realized that his approach had a significant flaw. Although the shows had plenty "of charm, most of it supplied by Garner," the episodes had "almost no plot at all."[3] For Goldman, the task would require his skills as both an adaptor—mainly drawing on the traits of the lead character—and an originator, since he was unable to draw on true source material from the series.

Richard Donner, who had first worked with Gibson on *Lethal Weapon* and its sequels, took on the directing job. Donner's background included directing several episodes of 1950s westerns—*Wanted: Dead or Alive*, *The Rifleman*, *Have Gun—Will Travel*—but none for *Maverick*.

Gibson, who had enjoyed watching the series as a child, bought the rights to the Maverick character for his Icon Productions. The New York–born actor had played in a variety of films, both in his adopted country of Australia, as well as in Hollywood blockbusters like *Lethal Weapon*. However, *Maverick* would be his first—and to date, only—western. Regardless of the setting, the wry nature of Bret Maverick seemed to suit the actor's skill sets. Said Gibson of the series, "I was five or six and I really liked it. I liked the theme song, you know, the tall dark stranger and all that stuff."[4]

For Jodie Foster, appearing in the film offered her a change of pace from recent roles in somber films like *The Accused* and *The Silence of the Lambs*, for which she had won Academy Awards. Said Foster, "I was really interested in doing a comedy that was light-hearted and witty."[5] The film would also reunite her with Garner, who had appeared with her in the 1973 Disney film *One Little Indian*.

For Garner, this movie would allow him the opportunity to come full circle, as part of a property that had meant so much to his career. Although it's difficult to know what trajectory Garner's career might have taken if he hadn't been assigned the original series, the show was certainly a significant milestone for the actor and made him a star. Even after Garner fought to be released from his contract in 1960, he never lost his affection for the character that would help define him for many viewers.

The 1994 film was not the first resurrection of Bret Maverick, nor even the second. By the time cameras began rolling on the Gibson version, Garner had already appeared as the character three times after leaving the show in 1960. A 1978 TV pilot, *The New Maverick*, starred Garner and Jack Kelly, and introduced cousin Ben (Charles Frank). Garner also appeared in the first episode of the 1979 series, *Young Maverick*. A couple of years later, Garner headlined a new series, *Bret Maverick*, which also featured an episode with Bart Maverick, once again portrayed by Jack Kelly from the original series.[6] Although the revival lasted for only eighteen episodes, it did manage to earn Garner Emmy and Golden Globe nominations for lead actor. Aside from these attempts to resuscitate the character, "Garner had been approached to make *Maverick* features in the past, none appealed to him" like the Gibson film.[7]

And yet, according to Garner, he almost did not play the character of Marshal Zane Cooper because Garner's friend Paul Newman had been first approached about the part. Fortunately, Newman turned the role down, leaving Garner to step in. It's hard to imagine the filmmakers even thinking of any other actor for such a pivotal role in the movie.

RECEPTION

Maverick debuted to a number of positive reviews, including one from Roger Ebert of the *Chicago Sun-Times* who called the film "the first light-hearted, laugh-oriented family Western in a long time, and one of the nice things about it is, it doesn't feel the need to justify its existence."[8]

Caryn James in the *New York Times* more or less raved about the film: "Fast, funny, full of straight-ahead action and tongue-in-cheek jokes, *Maverick* is *Lethal Weapon* meets *Butch Cassidy and the Sundance Kid*." James also had superlatives for the three leads, saying, "The stars are wildly comfortable in roles that seem shaped for them." She calls Garner

> the father of all Mavericks and the master of the wry, slow take. He also brings to his character a lot of Jim Rockford's dryness. And while his presence adds a warm and generous touch to the movie, as the story develops it becomes clear that his role is not just ceremonial. More than a stable counterpoint to the reckless Maverick, his Coop becomes central to the plot in a couple of unpredictable ways.[9]

David Sterritt in the *Christian Science Monitor* noted that "apart from the clever casting . . . it's cleverly crafted, and you can't help enjoying it even

Jodie Foster (left) cringes while Mel Gibson and Garner shoot it out. *Warner Bros. Pictures /
Photofest © Warner Bros. Pictures*

when you know it's manipulating you as brazenly as a poker dealer with
tricky fingers and a well-stacked deck."[10] While there were some negative
reviews, in general they focused on the film's lack of originality, which may
be true, but also beside the point for a movie inspired by a television show.

Audiences embraced the film when it debuted in theaters Memorial Day
weekend of 1994. Its box office draw of more than $17 million "was the big-
gest debut for any film so far"[11] that year. By the end of 1994, it had raked in
just over $100 million domestically and another $82 million worldwide, making it the fifteenth-highest-grossing film of the year (twelfth in the United
States). It is also among the ten-highest-grossing westerns of all time, along
with Academy Award–winners *Dances with Wolves* and *Unforgiven*.[12]

COMMENTARY

There are so many reasons to enjoy this film, not the least of which are the
engaging performances of the three leads and their on-screen interplay.
If viewers were primarily drawn to the film by Gibson's star power, they
surely were left satisfied with his take on a role made famous by another
actor. Gibson's version of Bret does not diminish what Garner had created

decades earlier. If Garner's Bret was more of a genial antihero, then Gibson's Bret might more aptly be characterized as a rogue, and it's as just such a character that Gibson proved he was capable of playing.[13]

There's a spirit of fun that Garner embodies in his role as a marshal that doesn't quite fit the behavior of a by-the-book lawman of the West. And the marshal doesn't seem too inclined to put himself in danger, not unlike Bret.

Foster, playing against type, also displays a faux coquettishness that she delivers with unexpected ease. But the supporting cast—particularly Graham Greene and Alfred Molina as Maverick's Native American ally and nemesis, respectively—also contribute significantly to the film's enjoyment.

Besides the engaging story line, the winning performances, and the opportunity to see Garner shine in his final *Maverick* vehicle, the film offers yet another delight: a game of spot the cameo. Movie cameos were nothing new, of course, but the filmmakers pulled out all the stops for *Maverick*. There are so many cameos, in fact, that they can be arranged by fairly distinct categories.

First, there is the Donner party: friends (and even family) from the director's earlier films who pop up in amusing vignettes. Margot Kidder, who played Lois Lane to Christopher Reeve's Superman, appears as a frontierswoman a little too desperate for a husband. Danny Glover, Gibson's police officer pal from the *Lethal Weapon* series, works the other side of the law as a bank robber, quoting his exasperated Murtaugh character with the familiar phrase, "I'm too old for this shit." Additional actors from Donner films include Michael Paul Chan and Corey Feldman from *The Goonies*.

Even the film's cinematographer, Academy Award–winner Vilmos Zsigmond (*Close Encounters of the Third Kind*), and the director's wife—and a producer in her own right—Lauren Shuler-Donner get screen time, the latter playing a bathhouse maid.

The final sequence on the riverboat features cameos by a slew of performers from country music: Clint Black, Carlene Carter, Janis Gill, Vince Gill, Hal Ketchum, Waylon Jennings, Kathy Mattea, and Reba McEntire.

And then there's the James Garner alumni—actors and actresses who had appeared in his shows: Bert Remsen (*Maverick*); Dennis Fimple (*The Rockford Files*); Art Le Fleur, Geoffrey Lewis, and Dub Taylor (*Bret Maverick*); and actor and writer Leo Gordon, who appeared in a handful of *Maverick* episodes as well as *The Rockford Files* nearly twenty years later. Garner's older brother, Jack, can also be seen in the film. Beginning with the short-lived series *Nichols*, Jack appeared in dozens of Jim's shows and movies, including twenty-six episodes of *The Rockford Files* and all eighteen episodes of *Bret Maverick*.

And then there's a cameo that must have been unintended, by actor Dan Hedaya. Perhaps best known for the Coen brothers first feature, *Blood Simple*, as well as his role as Nick Tortelli, the ex-husband of Carla (Rhea Perlman) on the show *Cheers*, Hedaya appears very briefly at the end of the film and doesn't deliver any lines. And yet he gets eighth billing in the opening credits and tenth billing in the closing credits. It's probable that Hedaya's scenes were left on the cutting room floor, as were those of Academy Award–winning actress Linda Hunt, whose scenes were *entirely* cut from the film, much to lament of screenwriter Goldman.

But easily, the most fun for fans of the western genre was spotting all of the actors from vintage series of the 1950s and '60s: Paul Brinegar (*Rawhide*), Henry Darrow (*The High Chapparal*), Robert Fuller and Doug McClure (*The Virginian*), Read Morgan (*The Deputy*), William Smith (*Laredo*), and Will Hutchins (*Sugarfoot*). Special mention must be made of Denver Pyle, a western series stalwart who showed up in *The Adventures of Kit Carson*; *Bonanza*; *Gunsmoke*; *Have Gun—Will Travel*—to name a few—and yes, even *Maverick*, though after Garner departed the series.[14]

By featuring all of these actors, it's clear the filmmakers wanted not only to pay homage to Garner and his iconic role but to honor a genre that had more or less evaporated from the screens, both large and small, by the time of *Maverick*'s release. The success of the film, however, did not herald a boom in westerns features. Well into the twenty-first century, such films remain few and far between.

26

MY FELLOW AMERICANS

(1996)

★ ★ ★

Director: Peter Segal
Screenplay: E. Jack Kaplan and Richard Chapman, and Peter Tolan; story by
   E. Jack Kaplan, Richard Chapman
Producer: Jon Peters. *Director of Photography:* Julio Macat. *Music:* William Ross.
   Editor: William Kerr. *Production Designer:* James Bissell
Cast: Jack Lemmon (President Russell P. Kramer), James Garner (President
   Matthew Douglas), Dan Aykroyd (President William Haney), Everett
   McGill (Colonel Paul Tanner), Bradley Whitford (Carl Witnaur), Wilford
   Brimley (Joe Hollis), John Heard (Vice President Ted Matthews), Lauren
   Bacall (Margaret Kramer), James Rebhorn (Reynolds), Sela Ward (Kaye
   Griffin), Conchata Ferrell (Truck Driver), Michael Peña (Illegal alien)
Studio: Warner Bros.
Release Date: December 20, 1996
Specs: 101 minutes; color
Availability: DVD (Warner Bros. Home Video)

SUMMARY

Two former presidents from opposite parties uncover a conspiracy that implicates the current president. On the run from assassins, Presidents Kramer and Douglas must put aside their political differences and personal animosities to secure the evidence that will expose a scandal and save their lives. Traveling by various means from Washington, DC, to a presidential library in Ohio, they encounter an array of former constituents who remind them of why they pursued political careers in the first place.

BACKGROUND

One of Hollywood's most successful actors, Jack Lemmon was perhaps James Garner's most accomplished costar, Marlon Brando notwithstanding. Like Brando, Lemmon was nominated for eight Academy Awards, and like Brando, Lemmon won two Oscars. And though many have regarded Brando as America's greatest actor, he was no match to Lemmon's comedic skills. On the other hand, Lemmon was comfortable in both dramatic and comic films and easily segued between both throughout his career. Brilliant in such heavyweight films as *Days of Wine and Roses*, *The China Syndrome*, and *Missing*, Lemmon was perhaps even more effective in two of the greatest comedies every produced, *The Apartment* and *Some Like It Hot*, classics written and directed by cinema great Billy Wilder.

One of Lemmon's great traits in comedies was his ability to play off a fellow actor. His most frequent on-screen foil was Walter Matthau. Their first—and possibly best—pairing was *The Fortune Cookie* in 1966. By the time they wrapped their final on-screen outing, *The Odd Couple II* in 1998, the pair had costarred in ten films over a span of thirty years.[1] *My Fellow Americans* was slated to be the pair's follow up to *Grumpier Old Men*, their third film in a row, following a TV movie *The Grass Harp* and the surprise hit *Grumpy Old Men* in 1993. However, Matthau had to pull out of filming *Americans*, presumably for health reasons.

The screenplay was written by a trio who seemed destined to write a buddy film. Richard Chapman's most significant credit was as a writer and producer for the 1980s series *Simon and Simon*, featuring a pair of brother detectives. E. Jack Kaplan also wrote an episode for *Simon and Simon*, as well as a TV movie featuring another 1980s detective pair, *Hart to Hart*. And Peter Segal created a short-lived sitcom called *Buddies*. Peter Tolan had more substantial television credits, penning episodes for acclaimed series *Murphy Brown* and *The Larry Sanders Show*.

However, Peter Segal's directing credits did not bode well for the film. After a trio of television specials with comedian Tom Arnold, Tolan helmed his first feature, *Naked Gun 33 1/3: The Final Insult* (1993), the third—and easily worst—film in a series starring Leslie Nielson as inept police lieuten-

Garner spars with Jack Lemmon. *Warner Bros. Pictures* / *Photofest* © *Warner Bros. Pictures*

ant Frank Drebbin. This was followed by *Tommy Boy*, the first leading role for Chris Farley, a *Saturday Night Live* regular, along with fellow *SNL* player David Spade. The film's sophomoric humor suggested both actors were better suited to the small screen, in particular Farley, whose broad antics wore thin outside the parameters of sketch comedy.

One of the original *SNL* cast members, Dan Aykroyd, was tapped to play the current president, while John Heard took on the role of vice president. The role of former first lady Margaret Kramer went to Hollywood icon Lauren Bacall, in a rather small part, while other cast members included character actors Wilford Brimley (so memorable as Lemmon's coworker in *The China Syndrome*), James Rebhorn, and Conchata Ferrell. In a curious bit of prescient casting, Bradley Whitford plays a White House chief of staff, which would anticipate his work for another fictional president on television's *The West Wing* a few years later.

RECEPTION

Stephen Holden, writing for the *New York Times*, called *My Fellow Americans* a "funny, farcical spoof of Presidential mediocrity, greed and arrogance." According to Holden, Garner and Lemmon act with "an exhilarating comic gusto" and "are such pros that they carry the movie smoothly over its dull patches."[2] The *Washington Post* noted that the "script is well stocked with snappy put-down humor"[3] while Roger Ebert, who found the film otherwise unconvincing still enjoyed how "the movie skewers the human weaknesses of the two old Presidents."[4] For the *Hollywood Reporter*, Stephen Dalton wrote that Garner was a replacement for Walter Matthau, "and it is a testament to Garner's comedic skills that this veteran duo summons up an equally irascible, irresistible screen chemistry."[5]

Todd McCarthy of *Variety* found the film "broadly comic and with an extreme reliance on unexpected vulgarities," called the screenplay "hokey through and through," and declared the direction "will win awards only for obviousness." On the other hand, he remarked that "the ever-reliable Lemmon and Garner prove as audience-friendly as old easy chairs." He also admitted, "The shameless laughs flow off the prefab assembly line with sufficient regularity to please audiences with a taste for comfortable tradition spiced with a bit of contempo naughtiness."[6]

Released on Friday, December 20, *My Fellow Americans* debuted at the number two spot, coincidentally behind another comedy about a pair of males traversing the United States: *Beavis and Butthead Do America*. The Garner-Lemmon film would earn only a third of the revenue generated by the animated morons, bringing in an estimated $22 million compared to the $63 million earned by the MTV idiots during their respective runs. *My Fellow Americans* ultimately ranked number seventy-one of feature films released in 1996.[7]

COMMENTARY

James Garner once remarked, "I'm not going to make you fall down and laugh. I don't do comedy. I do humor."[8] And for the bulk of his career, that comment held true. But he made that statement in 1981, a few years before the Blake Edwards's farce, *Victor/Victoria*, which had its fair share of genuine laughs—many of which relied on Garner—and another outright comedy, *My Fellow Americans*.

If Garner was brought in to replace Walter Matthau, the film and viewers benefited. To be perfectly candid, the Matthau–Lemmon matchings had become stale by the mid-1990s, and pitting a fresh comic adversary in the form of Garner against Lemmon couldn't help but invigorate the film—and that's exactly what Garner does. The result is a very funny movie about two former leaders of the free world on the run. Jack Lemmon plays former president Russell Kramer, who is not only a fiscal conservative but on a very personal level, a cheapskate. His political adversary, Matt Douglas, is a womanizer, very much in the vein of President Bill Clinton, who was serving his first term when the film was released in theaters. And like Clinton, Douglas comes across as having a far superior intellect to his Republican adversary, who seems to be a cross between Dan Quayle and Ronald Reagan.

While acknowledging that they need each other to stay alive, neither man is capable of squelching their barbs. Their constant snipes against each other provide the core of the film's humor, and despite their mismatched affiliations, Garner and Lemmon display an edgy rapport. The two pros know not only how to zing each other but also are adept at getting stung in such a way that maintains laughs throughout the film. Intentional or not, the majority of the barbs strike the conservative Kramer, while the worst that can be said about Douglas is that he is a serial philanderer—certainly a serious personal flaw, but not indicative of political corruptness (not to mention, homicidal intent) that characterizes several of the Republicans in the film.

The film ultimately shows that it does have a heart, or at least suggests that the two ex-presidents do. By the movie's end, the two acknowledge the concerns of the men and women who voted for them—which suggests that they are not as self-absorbed as the majority of the film's ninety-minute running time spends convincing us otherwise.

One quibble with the film is the essentially thankless role assigned to screen legend Lauren Bacall, who plays Lemmon's wife. It's possible the filmmakers wanted someone of Bacall's stature to make a credible spouse for Lemmon, but the truth is, the part didn't need a known name—much less an icon—to fill the role since the character's screen time is minimal, and Bacall is not given an opportunity to shine in her brief scenes.

Garner himself was not very fond of the film or the director, and to be honest, the two stars are asked to carry several of the weaker scenes, making the most of less than stellar dialogue. But even a formulaic buddy movie can work, especially with two comic veterans.

ONE SPECIAL NIGHT

(1999)

★ ★ ½

Director: Roger Young
Teleplay: Nancey Silvers, based on the play *A Winter Visitor* by Jan Hartman
Producer: Mark Bacino. *Director of Photography:* Guy Dufaux. *Music:* Richard Bellis.
 Editor: Benjamin A. Weissman, ACE. *Production Designer:* Anne Pritchard
Cast: James Garner (Robert Woodward), Julie Andrews (Catherine
  Howard), Patricia Charbonneau (Lori Campbell), Stacy Grant (Jaclyn
  Woodward), Stewart Bick (Jeff Campbell), Daniel Magder (Michael)
Studio: Green-Epstein Productions
First Aired: November 29, 1999 (CBS)
Specs: 92 minutes; color
Availability: DVD (MTI Home Video)

SUMMARY

On Thanksgiving Day, Robert Woodward's children drop him off at a hospice where his wife is being treated for Alzheimer's. Elsewhere in the hospice, Catherine Howard, a widow, is reminiscing in her deceased husband's old room. With some misgivings, Catherine offers Robert a ride home during a winter storm. While driving in the treacherous conditions they crash and find refuge in a cabin. As they spend the evening together, they get past their fractious bickering and find common ground.

BACKGROUND

One Special Night was first a play called *A Winter Visitor* written by Jan Hartman, who had won two daytime Emmys for his work on a pair of ABC network's Afterschool Specials. Nancey Silvers adapted the play for the small screen, and Roger Young, a veteran of television shows and made-for-TV movies, directed.

Thirty-five years after their first movie, *The Americanization of Emily*, and seventeen years after *Victor/Victoria*, James Garner and Julie Andrews reunited, for this, their final screen pairing. For the two actors, the decision to make the movie was based on two factors: the script and the opportunity to work together again, the latter probably proving too irresistible. Andrews and Garner shared a mutual admiration, but also a genuine affection, for each other.

"The premise of the script is just charming," said Andrews, whose costar concurred, noting that "the script was very good for the two of us."[1] Even more important, said Andrews, "What I liked most of all was there was a chance to work with James Garner again." She admitted that she may not have "realized that together we had a chemistry," but that she "loved working with him." She also confessed, "It's hard not to realize it—he's such a delicious looking guy and he's so sweet to work with."[2]

Garner was just as effusive: "Anybody who's been around Julie for ten minutes falls in love with her."[3]

Despite the stars' eagerness to work together, there were challenges. Filming took place in January 1999 in Montreal, Canada, both outdoors and at night, where the temperatures were often below freezing. But according to director Young, Andrews and Garner "are wonderful people. They're very professional, prepared. The crew loves them, I love them. They're the best."[4]

RECEPTION

John Leonard in *New York* magazine found merit in the two leads as well as the screenplay and direction. Said Leonard of the film's narrative, "Nancey Silvers and Roger Young deliver, as screenwriter and director. They get us to the clinch we need. And if there isn't a tear in our eye when we finally arrive, we should probably give up on ourselves." But his strongest advice to viewers: "Skip this at your own peril."[5] For *TV Guide*, Robert Pardi wrote, "This character-driven holiday drama is light on plot but heavy on honest sentiment and wintry romance." Pardi summed up the film aptly: "Unlike

Garner and Julie Andrews reunited for the final time. *CBS / Photofest © CBS*

the treacle-sprinkled seasonal entries that regularly emerge during the holiday season, director Roger Young's engaging adaptation of Jan Hartman's play doesn't overdo the heartstring tugging." He also gives proper due to Andrews and Garner, citing their "stellar chemistry, which goes a long way."[6]

COMMENTARY

When it came to finding someone to write a foreword to Garner's memoir, it was little surprise that Julie Andrews was asked to do the honors. Andrews and Garner starred in three films together, and of them, the first two represented significant milestones in both of their careers. The first, of course, was *The Americanization of Emily*, which Garner considers the peak of his screen work. The second, *Victor/Victoria*, earned Andrews a Golden Globe award, as well as an Oscar nomination. It also was Garner's first major box office success after his *Rockford Files* days.

If the third movie they made together does not hold up as well as the first two, it still remains a sweet coda to the pair's films. The lapse of time between each production allows viewers to see them in three distinct ages—first as a fairly young couple (Andrews was twenty-nine and Garner thirty-six when *Emily* was released), then as seasoned professionals (Andrews and Garner were forty-seven and fifty-four, respectively, when *Victor/Victoria* hit the screen), and finally as a matured couple (sixty-four and seventy-one when *One Special Night* first aired). In each film, the pair face obstacles—albeit very distinct ones—before finding each other.

To be sure, there is nothing particularly unique about this film, other than the stars themselves. The screenplay is adequate and doesn't force either of its leads to rise above the material, which is certainly in both actors' wheelhouses. The no-frills direction is appropriate for the story, the screenplay, and the actors. If the film suffers from any deficiencies, it's during the moments when the story and camera veer away from the two principals. Scenes focused on other family members are, at the least, unnecessary and at best distracting, since the viewer wants to see Garner and/or Andrews, preferably together, whether sparring with each other, commiserating about their heartaches, or tentatively leaning toward romance.

In all three of their screen pairings, Garner and Andrews's characters at first antagonize each other before they finally can't resist each other—and it's the tense undertone that gives their exchanges a slightly edgy dynamic and makes them so engaging as a couple. It served them well in their first film, and that romantic tension is no less palpable in the twilight of their careers.

What makes *One Special Night* essential is that—after thirty-five years—Garner and Andrews still have *it*: the on-screen chemistry that makes their pairing so believable. While the film itself has the feel of a latter-day Hallmark movie—that is, a romance earmarked for the Hallmark channel, rather than the acclaimed, Emmy-winning specials the company sponsored for decades—it also rises above such fare. The majority of the credit belongs to the experienced leads who are supported by a script that doesn't aim to do much more than bring two grieving strangers together. It's simple without being overly sentimental, allowing Garner and Andrews to showcase the genuine charm that made them stars and the affinity that brought them together for a final time.

THE NOTEBOOK

(2004)

★ ★ ★

Director: Nick Cassavetes
Screenplay: Jeremy Leven; adaptation by Jan Sardi, based on the novel by
    Nicholas Sparks
Producer: Mark Johnson, Lynn Harris. *Director of Photography:* Robert Fraisse.
    Music: Aaron Zigman. *Editor:* Alan Heim, ACE. *Production Designer:*
    Sarah Knowles. *Art Director:* Scott Ritenour. *Set Designers:* Mark E.
    Garner, Geoffrey S. Grimsman. *Costume Designer:* Karyn Wagner
Cast: Ryan Gosling (Noah Calhoun), Rachel McAdams (Allie Hamilton), James
    Garner (Duke), Gena Rowlands (Allie Calhoun), James Marsden (Lon
    Hammond), Kevin Connolly (Fin), David Thornton (John Hamilton),
    Jamie Anne Brown (Martha Shaw), Heather Wahlquist (Sara Tuffington),
    Sam Shepard (Frank Calhoun), Joan Allen (Anne Hamilton)
Studio: New Line Cinema
Release Date: June 25, 2004
Specs: 124 minutes; color
Availability: DVD (New Line Video)

SUMMARY

In the present day, at a nursing home facility: Duke, a man in his seventies,
reads from a journal to fellow resident, Allie, who suffers from Alzheimer's

disease. The story Duke reads to her is about the tangled romance between Noah Calhoun and Allison that took place in North Carolina before, during, and after the Second World War. The impetuous, free-spirited, and poor Noah pursues the more chaste and proper Allison, who comes from a wealthy family. Their romance is complicated by the appearance of Lon Hammond, an earnest soldier who offers Allison a comfortable life after the war. This settled, wholesome scenario is endorsed by Allison's mother, Anne Hamilton, whose perspective on the matter is tinged by her own experiences.

BACKGROUND

The Notebook is based on the first published novel by Nicholas Sparks, who carved a career out of writing melodramatic romances that have sold in the millions. The author of several best sellers such as *Message in a Bottle*, *A Walk to Remember*, *Nights in Rodanthe*, *Dear John*, and *Safe Haven*—all of which have been adapted to the big screen—Sparks knows what formula appeals to his readers and he delivers it—again and again. As such, his plots are ideal for mass audiences, if not for inspired moviemaking.

The film was directed by Nick Cassavetes, whose parents—actor, writer, and director John Cassavetes and actress Gena Rowlands—were accomplished Hollywood veterans. John first made his mark as an actor, appearing in such films as *Rosemary's Baby* and *The Dirty Dozen* (for which he received an Oscar nomination as Best Supporting Actor), but he made an even greater mark in cinema as the writer and director of highly acclaimed independent films from the 1960s and 1970s. The senior Cassavetes received Oscar nominations for best screenplay for *Faces* in 1969 and best director for *A Woman under the Influence* in 1975.[1] The latter film also gained Rowlands her first Oscar nomination for best actress, and she received a second nomination in that category a few years later for her husband's film, *Gloria*. Seven years after John Cassavetes died in 1989, Nick directed his first feature film, *Unhook the Stars*, which included his mother among the cast.

The Notebook would be the second collaboration between Rowlands and her son (but not their last). When Garner was sent the script, he couldn't tell if it was intended to be produced for television or the big screen. Ultimately, he accepted the part because he believed in the film's overarching theme of everlasting love. To embody the earlier phase of that theme, producers selected two young Canadian actors, Ryan Gosling

Garner reads to an attentive but confused Gena Rowlands. *New Line Cinema / Photofest © New Line Cinema*

and Rachel McAdams, to play the North Carolinian lovers. Gosling and McAdams were just beginning to make names for themselves in Hollywood. Gosling, once a member of the 1990s Mickey Mouse Club, had recently played a teenage killer in the Sandra Bullock police procedural *Murder by Numbers,* and his performance was by far the best element about the otherwise anemic thriller. McAdams, with significantly fewer credits than her costar, would draw attention as one of the title *Mean Girls* in the Tina Fey–written comedy. The love triangle was completed by James Marsden, who had already appeared in the first two *X-Men* features by the time filming began on *The Notebook.* No Southerners were used in the making of the movie.

RECEPTION

Roger Ebert, who gave the film three and a half stars and called *The Notebook* "a sentimental fantasy" and a good "tearjerker," praised all four leads. About Rowlands and Garner he wrote, "They are completely at ease in their roles, never striving for effect, never wanting us to be sure we get the message. Garner is an actor so confident and sure that he makes the difficult look easy, and loses credit for his skill."[2] For the *Hollywood Reporter*, Stephen Dalton said of Garner, "The old heavyweight of American screen masculinity turned in a grand autumnal performance."[3]

Stephen Holden of the *New York Times* was less kind, remarking, "Mr. Garner and Ms. Rowlands are wonderful actors, but Mr. Garner, in particular, plays 'old' with a hammy avuncularity that sugarcoats his character with a glaze of nostalgia. His performance reinforces the impression that in Hollywood, old age is even more difficult to depict with real honesty than young love." As for the film overall, Holden declares, *"The Notebook* is a high-toned cinematic greeting card. It insists on true, mystical, eternal love, till death do us part, and won't have it any other way."[4]

Desson Thomson of the *Washington Post* acknowledged that the film "may be one hundred percent sap, but its spirit is anything but cloying, thanks to persuasive performances, most notably from Rachel McAdams."[5] Anne Hornaday, also of the *Post*, called the film "a confection syrupy enough to satisfy nearly every cinematic sweet tooth." She also points out one of the film's most glaring faults—that "McAdams and Gosling don't for a minute call to mind 1940s."[6]

At the box office, the film grossed $81 million, placing it at thirty-two among the top films of 2004—not bad for a cinema overcrowded with fantasy films and animated features.[7] Among nongenre dramas for that year, *The Notebook* came in fourth, behind *The Passion of the Christ*, *Troy*, and *The Aviator*.[8]

As for awards, the film received several acknowledgements, though almost all of them were silly designations from MTV (Best Kiss) and other marginal associations. Not to be taken too seriously, the Teen Choice Awards nonetheless nominated the film for nine awards in 2005, and the film won eight of them, including Best Drama, Date Movie, Actor, Actress, Love Scene, Movie Chemistry, and Movie Liplock (really?). The only award the film failed to win that year was Movie Dance Scene, which instead went to Jon Heder in *Napoleon Dynamite*. Oddly enough, though Ryan Gosling also won Movie Breakout Performance—Male, Rachel McAdams wasn't even nominated. Why? She and the film had already been nominated in that category (and Best Summer Movie) the year before. We repeat: these awards are not to be taken seriously.

In fact, the only true nomination of note came from the Screen Actors Guild, which cited Garner in the category of Outstanding Performance by a Male Actor in a Supporting Role. Though he lost to Morgan Freeman for *Million Dollar Baby*, Garner did receive SAG's Lifetime Achievement Award that year.

COMMENTARY

There's no getting past the fact that this is a manipulative soap opera centered on the lives of beautiful people trying to find happiness while the world is in chaos. Though no one could confuse this film for the ultimate romance, *Casablanca*, there are some similarities: both are love triangles set against the backdrop of World War II, and in each the female protagonist must choose between two noble men. And that's where the comparisons should stop. *The Notebook* is no *Casablanca*. Ryan Gosling is no Humphrey Bogart, and Rachel McAdams is no Ingrid Bergman. Maybe, just maybe, one could make a case that Conrad Veidt is no James Marsden, but that's about as far as it goes. Truth be told, *The Notebook* really doesn't measure up against most romantic dramas, since it's hard not to catch oneself from realizing how calculated the story is. While it may not have been intended for the small screen, it could fit easily in the Hallmark channel's programming schedule among other schmaltz.

So why is this film among Garner's essentials? For a film so steeped in sentiment, the answer is obvious: sentimentality. Though the actor worked on a handful of projects after *The Notebook* was released in 2004, no other credit resonated as much as this film during the actor's last years. It's also the last work for which Garner was recognized by his peers. And it's a film that the actor held dear, calling it a "magnificent love story."[9]

As for Garner's performance, sentimental or not, it's a genuine depiction of a deeply devoted man facing the heartbreaking decline of a loved one. His scenes with Rowlands alone make the film worth seeing. Some might argue that the flashbacks that revolve around beautiful people in their twenties with anachronistic haircuts comprise the heart of the film, but it's really the acting veterans who steal the show. Their story is the heartbreaking coda of love that lasts for decades, and Garner delivers the film's message of eternal devotion with bittersweet honesty.

PART II

TELEVISION SERIES

29

MAVERICK

(1957–1960)

While the film western has long been out of favor, it was once one of the most popular genres in cinema, dating back to the silent era. In 1957, there were westerns aplenty, both on the silver screen and in living rooms across the country. In addition to literally dozens of B westerns, other movies in the genre released that year included *3:10 to Yuma*, *The Big Land*, *Decision at Sundown*, *Drango*, *Forty Guns*, *Night Passage*, *The Oklahoman*, *The Tall T*, *The Tin Star*, and the most successful western of 1957, *Gunfight at the O.K. Corral*. On television, the 1956–1957 fall schedule included *Broken Arrow*, *The Life and Legend of Wyatt Earp*, *The Lone Ranger*, *The Adventures of Jim Bowie*, *Dick Powell's Zane Grey Theater*, and *Gunsmoke*. And of course, *Cheyenne*, the show in which James Garner made his screen debut. Although *Gunsmoke* was the only western in the 1956–1957 top ten (at number seven), the following season reflected a dramatic shift in America's viewing habits—and confirmed that the genre's popularity had spread to the small screen. *Gunsmoke* not only ascended to the number one position—where it stayed for three more seasons—but was joined in the top ten by *Tales of Wells Fargo*, *Have Gun—Will Travel*, *The Life and Legend of Wyatt Earp*, and *The Restless Gun*. Other popular programs that season were *Cheyenne*, *Zane Grey Theater*, *Wagon Train*, *Sugarfoot*, and *Zorro*.

So did America need another western in the fall of 1957? Probably not. But *Maverick* would prove to be more than just another western.

Publicity still of Garner in *Maverick*. ABC / *Photofest* © ABC

The series was the brainchild of Roy Huggins, a writer who had sold his first novel to Hollywood in the late 1940s and soon after began writing screenplays, including one of the last great noirs of the 1950s, *Pushover*. Although Huggins also dabbled in feature film directing—helming a western called *Hangman's Knot*, in 1952, from his screenplay—he found his true calling on the small screen. As a writer and producer, he worked on two anthology series, *Conflict* and *Warner Bros. Presents*, which included rotating episodes of the western *Cheyenne*. Indeed, Huggins contributed the story to the seventh episode of the first season, "Decision," which was Garner's second screen credit, after debuting on *Cheyenne*'s premiere episode.

In the first two years of his career, James Garner worked in both film and television, frequently portraying military figures, either in contemporary settings or in westerns. Although Garner demonstrated an aptitude for dramatic roles, one performance suggested he had something more to offer. Yes, Sergeant John Maitland was an army man, and yes, *Shoot-Out at Medicine Bend* was a western, and yes, it was a drama. But interspersed with typical moments of dramatic gravity, the screenplay called for some lighthearted banter and moments of levity that loosened the narrative's grim grasp. Though the film's star, Randolph Scott, was a western stalwart, he was no stranger to light comic roles, such as his supporting role in the Cary Grant comedy *My Favorite Wife*. And fellow costar, Gordon Jones, seemed to wear a perpetual smile on his face in a plethora of roles. But for Garner, playing John Maitland afforded him a new opportunity to shine in a type of role that offered something different. And while it's an overstatement to say that his performance in *Shoot-Out* made Garner's career, it's not hyperbole to say that this was the true start of things to come, a first-time opportunity for audiences and Hollywood folk alike to see what this young man had to offer. If John Maitland isn't quite Bret Maverick, he's the closest kin to Bret that Garner yet had the chance to play.

How fortuitous that Warner Bros. was looking for an actor to inhabit the role of a new, almost antihero. According to Garner, Warners tried out every actor in Hollywood, but the studio only had to look as far as its backlot.

When audiences were first introduced to Bret Maverick, they quickly realized he did not fit the stereotypic western hero. First of all, he wasn't a cowboy. Nor was he a lawman. For a genre that typified an earthy ruggedness, Bret Maverick's appearance ran contrary to the western hero. He was a bit of a dandy—a sharply dressed, neatly groomed gentleman who looked much more at ease fanning a deck of cards than facing down a villain on a dusty main street. Bret Maverick didn't look for trouble—he would even sidestep it if he could—but when confronted with injustice, he was only too eager to reverse it, in his own inimitable style.

In a treatment for *Maverick* that he submitted to Warner Bros., Roy Huggins wrote that the two Maverick brothers

> were raised in Texas by the father, a retired Mississippi gambler from whom they learned every trick of the gambler's trade and something more: a hatred for cheaters and a respect for honesty in gambling.[1]

In a template that served for many of the episodes in the series, "a dishonest person or crook tries to use Maverick for an illegitimate purpose only to be outwitted and see justice done in the end."[2] Occasionally, an episode would resort to standard western fare.

Unlike most western heroes, Maverick did not ride his own horse. He traveled from town to town—sometimes by horse, but just as likely by train or stagecoach—in search of a high-stakes game of poker. Although his pockets may have been empty, he always had a $1,000 bill pinned inside his jacket, ready in case of emergency. And in the first episode, he uses that bill to both comic and conning effect. It was a signature ploy that demonstrated the wiliness of Bret Maverick throughout Garner's run on the series.

Besides his sharp attire, his $1,000 bill, and his aptitude for poker, Bret was also known for recalling his father's sage advice—declaring either, "As my pappy used to say . . ." or "As my old pappy used to say . . ."—often to avoid a confrontation.

And one other trait that summed up Bret Maverick: he was a sucker for the ladies, most of whom were as eager to con Bret as they were to woo him. Has anyone in the history of episodic westerns ever been duped by pretty women as much as Bret Maverick? Perhaps only one: his brother Bart.

The first seven episodes were devoted to Bret, but beginning with episode 8, "Hostage," brother Bart was introduced. For the remainder of the first season, as well as seasons 2 and 3, the series would air an episode featuring one brother or the other with occasional episodes that featured the pair together. It was not until the third season that the episodes would alternate the brothers' adventures on a weekly basis—with an occasional pairing sprinkled throughout—until the final three episodes, which featured only Bret.

In addition to the brothers, a handful of recurring characters popped up on the series, though their appearances were intermittent at best. Big Mike McComb, played by Leo Gordon, appears in seven episodes.[3] Dandy Jim Buckley, played by Efrem Zimbalist Jr., appears in five episodes, though his appearance in episode 21 of the first season, "Trail West to Fury," seems wholly unnecessary.

And then there was Samantha Crawford, a woman who vexed both brothers in four episodes, beginning with one of the series' most memorable, "According to Hoyle," in season 1. However, Samantha was just one of many deceptive women who plagued the Maverick brothers. Encountering duplicitous females was just as likely for the brothers as facing down con men. Sometimes the women resorted to deceit for benign—or at least seminoble—reasons, but more often than not, their motives were pure larceny.

In addition to the recurring characters, many actors returned to the series again and again, but in different roles, and frequently fatal ones. The height of this absurdity may have been in the first episodes of the second season. In that season's inaugural episode, actor Richard Reeves plays a character who gets killed—only to reappear in the very next episode playing a different character who endures the same fate. Nonetheless the actor would return to the series three more times.[4] And then there was Gerald Mohr, who appeared in six different roles on seven episodes. Although his turn as a casino owner in "Escape to Tampico" was perhaps his finest contribution to the series, his most memorable role was that of Doc Holliday in two episodes. In addition to Holliday, the Maverick brothers encounter several other "real-life" figures of the Wild West, most notably in the third season episode "Full House" in which Bret squares off against Jesse James, Belle Starr, and Billy the Kid, among others.

As for Garner, he appeared in less than half of the show's 124 episodes. Although the series ran for five seasons—from the fall of 1957 through the early spring of 1962—Garner left the show in the spring of 1960. In a salary dispute with Warner Bros., Garner sued the studio to be released from his contract, allowing him to pursue a movie career. But the studio took comfort in the knowledge that one Maverick brother remained—and other Mavericks would follow.

Bret's last solo appearance takes place in the third season finale, though Garner would return for one more episode in the fourth season ("The Maverick Line"), a story that features both brothers. By then, the series had welcomed another member of the Maverick family, cousin Beau, played by Roger Moore.

In the end, Garner acted in fifty-two episodes: thirty-seven of them featuring Bret in solo adventures and another fifteen with Jack Kelly as Bart—although in a handful of these, Bart appears almost tangentially, popping up in a scene or two. In Bart's first "solo" adventure, Bret appears in the first and final scenes of the episode. Midway through the first season, beginning with episode 13 ("The Naked Gallows"), Garner introduces a few of Bart's stories, and Kelly returns the favor in episode 25. However, this gimmick was abandoned in the second season.

One popular feature of the series did not arrive until the beginning of the second season: lyrics to the show's theme song, sung during the closing credits. Although the jaunty theme is well remembered by Maverick aficionados, the verses were not sung with any regularity until the third season.

When it debuted in the fall of 1957, Maverick made an immediate impact. Programmed against popular variety shows featuring Ed Sullivan, Jack Benny, and Steve Allen, the series succeeded against competition thought to be too fierce. But Bret and Bart not only survived; they thrived. In its first year, the show received three Emmy nominations, including Best Dramatic Series with Continuing Characters and Best New Program Series of the Year. In the former category, it lost to fellow western *Gunsmoke* and in the latter, to *The Seven Lively Arts*, a short-lived anthology program. By the following season, it was a top ten hit and earned double the Emmy nominations from the previous year—including one for Garner as Best Actor in a Leading Role (Continuing Character) in a Dramatic Series.[5] The program won only one Emmy, Best Western Series, beating out rivals *Gunsmoke*, *Have Gun—Will Travel*, *The Rifleman*, and *Wagon Train*. In Garner's final season, the show failed to earn any awards, but it did finish in the top twenty. Although the series never earned any Emmy nods for its writing, it did receive a Writers Guild of America nomination for the episode "The Quick and the Dead" written by Douglas Heyes, who contributed to many of the most memorable episodes from the first two seasons.[6]

With the November 10, 1960, episode, Garner rode off into the black-and-white sunset and would not assume the Bret Maverick persona for another eighteen years. But nothing breeds success like success, and where else but Hollywood does success get bled dry.

In 1978, a television movie (Garner's first) was produced as a pilot for a new series featuring a younger Maverick. *The New Maverick* starred Garner and Jack Kelly, who were joined by Charles Frank as Ben, the son of Beau. The lackluster TV movie did generate a new series, *Young Maverick*. The short-lived spin-off reunited Frank with his real-life wife, Susan Blanchard, from the film, and also featured John Dehner, an actor who had made such a memorable impression in the "Shady Deal at Sunny Acres" episode of the original series. Garner even offered a token appearance in the premiere episode, but the series came and went in less than half a season.

And yet, Garner still wasn't finished with Bret. Within a few years of the failed series, the actor and his now *second* most famous role returned to television. *Bret Maverick* debuted in late December of 1981. Unfortunately, some of the elements that had made the original series such a success were in short supply for the second revival. Garner and his charm were intact, of course, but the show's premise was not nearly as engaging as the original. Instead of traveling from town to town in search of poker gold, Bret decides to settle down in the town of Sweetwater somewhere in the Arizona territory. Gone also was the show's hummable theme song, replaced by a new one sung by series costar Ed Bruce. More than anything else, the show lacked the writing wit of the original series, and within a few months, the series was canceled as well. Nevertheless, Garner did receive both Emmy and Golden Globe nominations for his role.

And of course, Garner was still not yet done with Bret, but more than a decade would pass before he would be back in the *Maverick* saddle again. The feature film of *Maverick*, starring Mel Gibson, would provide Garner a triumphant farewell to his beloved character. It was this final incarnation that finally did justice to a character that first appeared nearly thirty years earlier.

But it was the original series and the original Bret that first brought James Garner to the wide attention of audiences all over the country, if not the world. And it is the episodes of that series that are celebrated here. Note that with a few exceptions, episodes featuring *only* Bart are not rated here.

SEASON 1

E1: "War of the Silver Kings" (September 22, 1957) ★ ★ ★ ★: Bret Maverick rides into a town where the local silver baron not only cheats at cards but also is willing to have a man killed for crossing him. An essential to watch because (1) it's the premiere episode that introduces Bret Maverick, and (2) this is James Garner's first starring role. The episode also features Leo Gordon as Big Mike McComb, an engaging supporting character who appears a few more times in the series.

E2: "Point Blank" (September 29, 1957) ★ ★ ★: Bret is hired as a casino spotter and encounters his first treacherous female—one who is setting him up to be murdered.

E3: "According to Hoyle" (October 6, 1957) ★ ★ ★½: Bret meets his poker-playing match in the form of female gambler Samantha Crawford (Diane Brewster). Elements of this episode—as well as "Diamond in the Rough" (episode 18, featuring Bart)—no doubt inspired William Goldman's screenplay for the 1994 film *Maverick*, in particular the character of Annabelle Bransford (Jodie Foster).[7]

E4: "Ghost Rider" (October 13, 1957) ★ ★ ★: After the young man who robs Bret is killed, Maverick becomes suspicious of the man's fiancée—and the town undertaker.

E5: "The Long Road" (October 20, 1957) ★ ★ ★: After a dying man confesses to Bret that he is responsible for a killing, Maverick embarks on a mission to save the wrongfully convicted prisoner from execution.

E6: "Stage West" (October 27, 1957) ★ ★ ★: In an isolated tavern, Bret comes to the aid of a young widow whose claim to gold is jeopardized by a conniving man and his two sons.

E7: "Relic of Fort Tejon" (November 3, 1957) ★ ★ ★: Bret "wins" a camel in a card game. The first—though not the last—time Garner rides a camel in the Old West; he does so again in the 1974 Disney film *One Little Indian*.

E8: "Hostage" (November 10, 1957) ★ ★½: Brothers Bret and Bart Maverick intervene when a young woman stages her own abduction, not realizing the man she loves doesn't intend to share the ransom money. Average episode introduces Jack Kelly as Bart.

E9: "Stampede" (November 17, 1957) ★ ★½: Bret and his acquaintance Dandy Jim Buckley take on a crooked gambler, but Dandy Jim is not to be trusted either. Literally or metaphorically speaking, the title of this episode makes no sense.

E10: "The Jeweled Gun" (November 24, 1957) ★ ★: The first "solo" Bart story. At the beginning of the episode, Bret appears very briefly as the brothers split off and then reappears in the final scene.

E11: "The Wrecker" (December 1, 1957) ★ ★: The Maverick brothers pay an exorbitant amount of money for a broken-down wreck, and Bart investigates why it was so expensive. Though Garner appears throughout the episode, his role is secondary to Jack Kelly in this pedestrian adaptation of a Robert Louis Stevenson story.

E12: "The Quick and the Dead" (December 8, 1957) ★ ★ ★: Doc Holliday seeks retribution against Bret, not realizing he has targeted the wrong man.

E13: "The Naked Gallows" (December 15, 1957): Bart story. Garner, dressed as Bret, introduces and narrates a story featuring Bart. This is the first episode in which Garner does not receive episode credit, despite his participation.

E14: "Comstock Conspiracy" (December 29, 1957) ★ ★ ★: Bret thinks he has killed a man, but no one believes him, especially when the "corpse" turns up alive. Fun episode that presages *The Rockford Files* in its title and some plot elements.

E15: "The Third Rider" (January 5, 1958): Bart story.

E16: "Rage for Vengeance" (January 12, 1958) ★ ★½: A widow who is traveling with $200,000 in cash—or is she?—hires Bret to be her bodyguard. A quirky episode with a few twists.

E17: "Rope of Cards" (January 19, 1958) ★ ★ ★½: Bret serves on a jury, and like the plot of *12 Angry Men* that was released in theaters April 1957, there is one holdout. Bret uses cards and percentages to make a case for acquittal. Another fun, quirky episode.

E18: "Diamond in the Rough" (January 26, 1958): Bart story.

E19: "Day of Reckoning" (February 2, 1958) ★ ★ ★: A town is besieged by a gang after a marshal accidentally kills a man who accuses Bret of cheating. Atypical episode in the series that lacks a lighthearted tone—until the very end, which seems out of place for such a serious story line.

E20: "The Savage Hills" (February 9, 1958): Bart story that also features Samantha Crawford (Diane Brewster).

E21: "Trail West to Fury" (February 16, 1958) ★ ★½: Bret and Bart are hired as trail bosses by a woman whose schemes are not as nefarious as they seem.

E22: "The Burning Sky" (February 23, 1958): Bart story introduced by Garner.

E23: "The Seventh Hand" (March 2, 1958) ★ ★ ★: Samantha Crawford entices Bret into in a private poker game, which is then robbed.

E24: "Plunder of Paradise" (March 9, 1958): The first Bart story not introduced by Garner also features Big Mike McComb.

E25: "Black Fire" (March 16, 1958) ★ ★ ★: Bret and an acquaintance switch identities in an Agatha Christie–like whodunit, as an old man's heirs start to die one by one. Fun episode that is the first centered on Bret that Bart introduces and narrates (Kelly doesn't receive credit).

E26: "Burial Grounds of the Gods" (March 30, 1958): Bart story.

E27: "Seed of Deception" (April 13, 1958) ★ ★ ★: In a small town, Bret is mistaken for Wyatt Earp and when Bart arrives, he is mistaken for Doc Holliday. One of the better episodes featuring both brothers.

SEASON 2

E1: "The Day They Hanged Bret Maverick" (September 21, 1958) ★ ★ ★: Bret is framed for robbery and murder and awaits his execution. The dates on Bret's gravestone are April 7 (Garner's birthday) and

September 21 (the day the episode first aired). During the closing credits, lyrics to *Maverick* theme song are performed for the first time.

E2: "The Lonesome Reunion" (September 28, 1958) ★ ★ ★: Another female cons Bret while trying to track down $120,000 that her missing husband helped steal. Although Jack Kelly does not appear in the episode, his voice does—as he reads aloud a letter that Bart has left Bret.

E3: "Alias Bart Maverick" (October 5, 1958): Bart story.

E4: "The Belcastle Brand" (October 12, 1958) ★ ★ ★: Bret is saved by a trio of Brits temporarily relocated to Wyoming—and then must return the favor when the quartet are robbed during a "hunting" expedition. Reginald Owen (Ebenezer Scrooge in the 1938 version of *A Christmas Carol*) guest stars.

E5: "High Card Hangs" (October 19, 1958): Bart story.

E6: "Escape to Tampico" (October 26, 1958) ★ ★ ★½: A wronged family hires Bret to lure a suspected killer, Steve Corbett, back to the States from Mexico, and a woman named Amy may be the latest in the long line of females out to hoodwink and bamboozle Bret, not to mention Steve. A good episode with a few plot twists—but perhaps too many musical interludes.

E7: "The Judas Mask" (November 2, 1958): Bart story.

E8: "The Jail at Junction Flats" (November 9, 1958) ★½: Bret breaks Dandy Jim Buckley out of jail only to need the favor returned. Subpar episode is still notable for a couple of reasons: Dan Blocker, soon to appear as Hoss Cartwright on *Bonanza* appears briefly in the episode's beginning. Efrem Zimbalist Jr., son of a violinist and opera singer, displays his own singing talents, but his character grows tedious.

E9: "The Thirty-Ninth Star" (November 16, 1958): Bart story.

E10: "Shady Deal at Sunny Acres" (November 23, 1958) ★ ★ ★ ★: Bret is swindled out of $15,000 by an unscrupulous banker and declares he will be repaid. While Bret seems to casually bide his time following through on his declaration ("I'm working on it."), his brother Bart and assorted associates enact a scheme to out-swindle the banker who did Bret wrong. Classic episode in the series, featuring a who's who of recurring characters including Dandy Jim Buckley, Samantha Crawford, Gentleman Jack Darby, and Big Mike McComb. First episode of season 2 featuring both brothers.

E11: "Island in the Swamp" (November 30, 1958) ★½: Bret is imprisoned on an island in the bayou. Not a particularly memorable episode.

E12: "Prey of the Cat" (December 7, 1958): Bart story.

E13: "The Spanish Dancer" (December 14, 1958): Bart story.

E14: "Holiday at Hollow Rock" (December 28, 1958) ★ ★ ★: Attending an annual horse race where he intends to place a sizable bet, Bret encounters a crooked sheriff.

E15: "Game of Chance" (January 4, 1959) ★ ★ ★: A pair of French con artists use a pearl necklace to swindle Bart out of $10,000, and then fool Bret as well. Episode is narrated by Jack Kelly and Garner.

E16: "Gun-Shy"⁸ (January 11, 1959) ★ ★ ★½: Bret travels to Ellwood, Kansas, in search of $500,000 worth of gold. This parody of *Gunsmoke*—with Marshal Mort Dooley, Doc Stucke, Amy Ward, and Clyde Diefendorfer standing in for Matt Dillon, Doc, Kitty, and Chester—works better for viewers familiar with the original series. Top acting honors go to Walker Edmiston as Clyde, who delivers a funny imitation of Dennis Weaver's Chester—though without a limp (not at *first*).⁹

E17: "Two Beggars on Horseback" (January 18, 1959) ★ ★ ★½: This episode features brother versus brother as Bret and Bart race to cash in their banknotes before the last remaining branch closes. Another episode featuring a scheming woman who's not as bad as she seems.

E18: "The Rivals" (January 26, 1959) ★ ★½: On a bet, Bret switches places with a young aristocrat who wants to woo a woman with his integrity rather than his wealth. Future *Maverick* cast member Roger Moore guest stars as John Vandergelt II in this okay story. Bart appears briefly in the episode, in the first and final scene. The opening scene is the first and only time all three actors appear together on the series.

E19: "Duel at Sundown" (February 1, 1959) ★ ★½: A friend of Bret convinces him to extend his visit in hopes of distracting his starstruck daughter from the town's sharp-shooting bully. Average episode with a brief appearance of Bart. The bully is played by Clint Eastwood.

E20: "Yellow River" (February 8, 1959): Bart story.

E21: "The Saga of Waco Williams" (February 15, 1959) ★ ★ ★: With a hidden motive, Bret rides into town with recent acquaintance Waco Williams, who has a secret of his own.

E22: "Brasada Spur" (February 22, 1959): Bart story.

E23: "Passage to Fort Doom" (March 8, 1959): Bart story.

E24: "Two Tickets to Ten Strike" (March 15, 1959) ★ ★½: Bret arrives in town and is immediately railroaded out of it for no apparent reason.

E25: "Betrayal" (March 22, 1959): Bart story.

E26: "The Strange Journey of Jenny Hill" (March 29, 1959) ★ ★½: Bret follows a concert singer on a tour that seems to have no end—but why?

SEASON 3

E1: "Pappy" (September 13, 1959) ★★★½: Bret and Bart investigate why an eighteen-year-old woman would marry their father, Beau. Garner is quite amusing playing his character's pappy, though the ending credits simply cite "?" in the role. Jack Kelly also appears very briefly as Beau's brother Bentley (cited in the credits as "Himself").

E2: "Royal Four Flush" (September 20, 1959): Bart story.

E3: "The Sheriff of Duck 'n' Shoot" (September 27, 1959) ★★★½: Bret is blackmailed into becoming a town sheriff and does a pretty fine job (shades of *Support Your Local Sheriff!* to come) until he is conned by a trio of thieves. Bart makes another late episode appearance.

E4: "You Can't Beat the Percentage" (October 4, 1959): Bart story.

E5: "The Cats of Paradise" (October 11, 1959) ★★★: Bret is duped by a young woman whose fiancé is the town's superstitious—not to mention corrupt—sheriff (Buddy Ebsen).

E6: "A Tale of Three Cities" (October 18, 1959): Bart story. Ben Gage, who played Marshal Mort Dooley in the "Gun-Shy" parody of *Gunsmoke*, returns as a town sheriff.

E7: "Full House" (October 25, 1959) ★★★½: Bret is mistaken for the villainous Foxy Smith and must contend with a rogues' gallery of real-life criminals, including Belle Starr, Cole Younger, Jesse James, Black Bart, and Billy the Kid (Joel Grey). Gordon Jones, Garner's *Shoot-Out at Medicine Bend* costar, appears as a sheriff. Another outstanding episode in which Garner truly shines.

E8: "The Lass with the Poisonous Air" (November 1, 1959): Bart story.

E9: "The Ghost Soldiers" (November 8, 1959) ★★★: After a Sioux tribe has decimated an army fort, Bret and a handful of soldiers stave off a return attack. Atypical episode in which not a single card is dealt—much less seen—and hostile Native Americans prominently figure.

E10: "Easy Mark" (November 15, 1959): Bart story.

E11: "A Fellow's Brother" (November 22, 1959) ★★★: Bret is mistaken for robbery and murder, which doesn't dissuade a young man from admiring him. Jack Kelly makes a last scene appearance, but otherwise Bart does not figure in the episode.

E12: "Trooper Maverick" (November 29, 1959): Bart story.

E13: "Maverick Springs" (December 6, 1959) ★★: Bret concocts an investment scheme to recover a swindled man's half ownership of an estate—ultimately requiring the participation of Bart. Average episode with an unconvincing con.

E14: "The Goose Drownder" (December 13, 1959): Bart story.

E15: "A Cure for Johnny Rain" (December 20, 1959) ★★½: Bret is deputized in order to help a town capture a highwayman—a beloved resident who is also a black-out drunk.

E16: "The Marquesa" (January 3, 1960): Bart story.

E17: "Cruise of the Cynthia B." (January 10, 1960) ★★★: Bret is one of seven owners of a riverboat, some of whom fall victim to foul play.

E18: "Maverick and Juliet" (January 17, 1960) ★★½: Bret offers to settle a decades-long feud between two families by taking part in a poker game that could also cost him his life. His opponent: Bart.

E19: "The White Widow" (January 24, 1960): Bart story.

E20: "Guatemala City" (January 31, 1960) ★★½: Bret falls for a woman, who suddenly disappears—at the same time that a diamond theft occurs—so he's off to find her and maybe collect a reward.

E21: "The People's Friend" (February 7, 1960): Bart story.

E22: "A Flock of Trouble" (February 14, 1960) ★★: Bret is deeded a sheep ranch, which makes him a target of the local cattlemen.

E23: "Iron Hand" (February 21, 1960): Bart story and Robert Redford's screen debut.

E24: "The Resurrection of Joe November" (February 28, 1960) ★★★: During Mardi Gras, Bret is recruited by a childhood acquaintance and her German husband to secure the casket of the woman's beloved major domo.

E25: "The Misfortune Teller" (March 6, 1960) ★★½: Bret rides into the town of Medicine Bow where the locals immediately want to lynch him—for a swindle someone else perpetrated in his name. Average episode with an amusing prologue. Bret also reveals his date of birth as May 11, which contradicts the first episode of season 2, which indicates April 7 (Garner's actual birthday) on a grave marker.

E26: "Greenbacks, Unlimited" (March 13, 1960) ★★★: Bret is hired to conduct some "detective work" the law can't handle, and for his efforts a bank will pay all of his expenses, plus a $1,000 bonus if he succeeds. Bret's last solo adventure and the penultimate episode for Garner offers his character a *Rockford Files*–like assignment. As his pappy used to say, "He who fights and runs away, lives to run away another day."

SEASON 4

E10: "The Maverick Line" (November 20, 1960) ★ ★: The Maverick
brothers inherit a stagecoach line from their recently deceased uncle,
which makes them targets for murder. Garner's last episode is unfortunately a weak one, played too much for laughs, but it's fitting that Bret
once again must face a conniving, if pretty, female.

30

NICHOLS

(1971–1972)

After more than a decade of making features, James Garner was looking for a property that could return him to television. He found a candidate in an offbeat series that, like *Maverick*, offered an idiosyncratic spin on the traditional western: *Nichols*. As with many of Garner's projects of the 1960s, the series was produced by the actor's company, Cherokee Productions.

The show's creator, Frank Pierson, was well acquainted with offbeat westerns, having written and produced for the popular series *Have Gun—Will Travel* in the late 1950s, as well as earning an Oscar nomination for cowriting the 1965 comic western *Cat Ballou*. In addition to creating *Nichols*, Pierson served as the show's producer, contributed stories to a few episodes, and even directed a handful, including the pilot.

Set just before World War I, *Nichols* may have displayed the usual trappings of a western—a small-town locale with a saloon, stables, and plenty of horses—but these staples of a fading era were juxtaposed with recent developments of the modern world: telephones, automobiles, and a Harley Davidson motorcycle. What the town didn't have was a proper jail, so a storage room in the basement of the Salter Hotel served as a makeshift holding pen. Such a setting seemed apt for a man with lofty dreams, and Nichols (he only went by his last name) was just such a man.

After serving eighteen years in the army, Nichols abandons the military and returns to the town of his youth, where he aims to get rich, by whatever means possible. But in the decades since his departure, life in the town

Set in 1914 Nevada, *Nichols* was a television western ahead of its time. *NBC / Photofest © NBC*

has changed, symbolized by the new car that arrives on the train with him. While the town still bears the Nichols family name, not much else from his youth has survived, including his stake in the family ranch. After holding his own against the town's wealthiest—and wiliest—citizen, Ma Ketcham, Nichols is blackmailed by her into becoming the sheriff. His qualifications? He "suits" Ma, despite his aversion for violence. The position had previously been held by a sniveling dimwit named Mitch, whom Ma designates as Nichols's deputy. In addition to reluctantly usurping Mitch's authority, Nichols draws the romantic attention of Ruth, a barmaid Ma had planned to marry her eldest son, a handsome but slow-witted bully—whom everyone calls Ketcham, including his mother.

In his own way, Nichols may have been a maverick but by no means is he Bret. While Garner's poker player character from the earlier series engaged in cons, they were often employed to right a wrong. Not so Nichols. At times he behaves as a man of principles, but those principles are often situational at best. On the one hand, he often administers justice befitting an officer of the law. At other times, he breaks the very laws he has been hired to enforce, especially when it comes to the pursuit of riches.

Perhaps it was the main character's lack of a steady moral code that doomed the series. While Garner and others may have believed *Nichols* was ahead of its time, it might also be said that the show was behind the times. Unlike *Maverick*, which premiered when audiences couldn't get enough westerns at the local movie house or at home, the television landscape had changed drastically by the time *Nichols* arrived. By the early 1970s, westerns had begun to fade from the scene, and television was virtually a ghost town where the genre was concerned.

Traditional westerns and the like had become passé, whether out of network design or as a result of the American public's shifting tastes—but most likely a combination of both. CBS, which had thrived on such shows, became particularly aggressive in its programming strategy. Before the fall of 1971, the network had axed several series that were deemed too rural, including former top ten hits *Green Acres* and *Mayberry R.F.D.*, as well as *Hee Haw* and *Lassie*.[1] Gone, too, was *The Beverly Hillbillies*, a show that had once ruled the Nielson ratings and was still perched in the top thirty when it received the death blow. The show and its kin appealed to viewers who were "too heavily concentrated in rural areas to suit Madison Avenue advertisers."[2] Although the network still relied on *Gunsmoke* to anchor its Monday nights, the long-running series was the sole western on CBS's schedule. In fact, only three westerns were holdovers on the networks that fall. NBC's *Bonanza*, which had been a top ten staple for a decade—including three years at the peak—had fallen in the ratings and its 1972 season would be its last. On ABC, the lone western was *Alias Smith and Jones*, a midseason replacement that debuted in January of 1971. The series' creative personnel boasted Roy Huggins as writer and executive producer, and the show starred a pair of likable leads. *Smith and Jones* may have lasted longer than three seasons had not one its stars, Peter Duel, committed suicide.

Into this desolate landscape rode *Nichols*. Strangely, it wasn't the only series set in the western territories circa 1914 to debut that fall. *Bearcats*, a short-lived show about two thrill seekers traveling by car, arrived on CBS just one *hour* before the first episode of *Nichols* on NBC. In another curious coincidence, *Bearcats* was created by Douglas Heyes, who had written and directed many of the best *Maverick* episodes in the show's first two seasons—but Heyes couldn't prevent the show from getting canceled within two months of its debut.

Nichols didn't last much longer. Besides the questionable morality of its lead character, the show was hindered by other quirks: in particular, the scripts often emphasized character over plot, and a lack of strong stories may have failed to hold the attention of its viewers. It seemed that the producers also didn't know what to make of the series regulars, constraining them to one-dimensional characterizations. Perhaps that explains why many of the episodes highlighted a new character every week, some more successfully drawn than others.

While not all of the episodes in this series constitute essential viewing, several of them are worthy candidates. To be sure, *Nichols* is not for every taste, especially for those who can only see James Garner cast in a particular light. But that doesn't mean the show should be dismissed wholesale. Throughout the twenty-four episodes, the actor's charisma remains intact, and his chemistry with his costars never wavers, particularly with Margot Kidder, despite their twenty-year age difference. And some of the story lines do service the more fully etched characters, satisfying viewers in want of personality *and* plot. Based on the final episode of the series, the showrunners may have recognized the need for more of this balance—and most especially in a lead character to root for—but a plot twist arrives just a little too late to save *Nichols* from its fate.

It's futile to lament what was not to be, since the success of *Nichols* may have jeopardized Garner's second attempt to return to series television. Had *Nichols* survived, it could well have interrupted the trajectory of Garner's prospects, and the actor may not have struck television gold twice. And who knows? The lessons Garner and his compatriots may have learned from this failed enterprise may have influenced their decisions when conceiving and executing Garner's next—and most famous—creation.

Indeed, *Nichols* served as a bridge between the actor's two most successful series, drawing on talent from both *Maverick* and *The Rockford Files*. Marion Hargrove, who wrote several episodes of *Maverick* also contributed to an episode of *Nichols*. More significantly, three principals involved with *Nichols* would also play major roles on Garner's later show. Meta Rosenberg, who had been Garner's agent, received executive producer credit on *Nichols*, a title she would also receive on *The Rockford Files*. Juanita Bartlett, who made her television writing debut on *Nichols*—penning several episodes—would write three dozen of *The Rockford Files* as well as earn producer credit for the final season of the detective series. Most visibly connected to both *Nichols* and *The Rockford Files* was actor Stuart Margolin, who plays a weaselly character on both programs. As deputy sheriff, Mitchell, Margolin displays many of the characteristics he would develop as Angel Martin on *The Rockford Files*, though his spineless Mitch on *Nichols* was not nearly as shifty as Angel—or nearly as appealing.

For viewers not inclined to watch all of the episodes of *Nichols*, they do need to catch the pilot, which establishes all five of the major characters, as well as outlines the show's premise. Of the remaining episodes, some succeed more than others. Episodes designated with 2½ stars or more are recommended viewing.

SEASON I

E1: "Nichols" (September 16, 1971) ★★½: After eighteen years in the army, Nichols returns to the hometown named for his kin and learns that his family and homestead are out of reach. But the town's matriarch, Ma Ketcham, extorts Nichols into taking a job he may be perfectly suited for—or not: sheriff.

E2: "The Siege" (September 23, 1971) ★★: A Mexican revolutionary comes to town for dental work and cuts the citizens off from contact with the outside world.

E3: "The Indian Giver" (September 30, 1971) ★★½: A Princeton-educated Apache claims to own the deed to the Ketcham ranch.

E4: "The Paper Badge" (October 7, 1971) ★★★: After Mitch breaks his leg, Ketcham is deputized and takes his new role too seriously.

E5: "Gulley vs. Hansen" (October 14, 1971) ★★: Two old adversaries engage in a final showdown, provoked by Ketcham and Mitch.

E6: "Deer Crossing" (October 21, 1971) ★★½: An Apache intends to hunt the same deer that Ketcham has set his sights on.

E7: "The Specialists" (October 28, 1971) ★★: Nichols assembles a handful of former associates to help him steal $200,000 in gold. Inexplicable episode in which Nichols intentionally breaks the law *just to break it* and in the process, a man gets killed.

E8: "Peanuts and Crackerjacks" (November 4, 1971) ★★: Baseball aficionado Nichols puts together a squad to challenge an army corps of engineers.

E9: "Ketcham Power" (November 11, 1971) ★★: An acting troupe arrives in town the same day as a young lawman who offers Nichols his unwelcome assistance. Curious title for the episode doesn't really make sense.

E10: "The One-Eyed Mule's Time Has Come" (November 23, 1971) ★: After an earthquake, Nichols is trapped inside a destroyed house with a young man and a mule while a trio of thieves threaten them. Tedious episode.

E11: "Away the Rolling River" (November 30, 1971) ★★: An old army pal of Nichols comes to town with larcenous schemes on his mind. Another episode in which Nichols breaks several laws.

E12: "Where Did Everybody Go?" (December 7, 1971) ★★★: Three brothers looking for trouble challenge Nichols, who handles the situation in his own inimitable way. One of the better entries in the series, this one references two *Maverick* episodes, particularly "Shady Deal at Sunny Acres" in which Nichols sits on a porch rocking chair and declares, "I'm working on it." He also displays his gun-twirling skills à la the third season episode "Full House."

E13: "The Marrying Fool" (December 28, 1971) ★★½: Ruth returns from vacation with a fiancé—Charley Doyle, inventor . . . and bigamist. Another episode that features a quirky guest character.

E14: "Eddie Joe" (January 4, 1972) ★★½: The hotel chef, Eddie Joe, is really a convicted felon under an assumed name, and his luck is about to run out. Paul Winfield guest stars in an episode that recalls Garner's film *Skin Game*.

E15: "Zachariah" (January 11, 1972) ★★: Nichols takes advantage of his uncle Zachariah, whose stolen loot helps his nephew make an investment that just might not pay off.

E16: "The Unholy Alliance" (January 18, 1972) ★★★: Nichols is mistaken for a safecracker by a gang of thieves who put him to the test. Fun episode undermined by an unnecessary ending.

E17: "Sleight of Hand" (February 1, 1972) ★ ★ ★: Nichols goes into partnership with a stranger, who has half the map to a gold mine tattooed on the palm of his hand.

E18: "Wings of an Angel" (February 8, 1972) ★ ★: An aviator unintentionally thwarts Nichols in his pursuit of a killer, so the sheriff recruits the pilot to help him finish the job. Series regular John Beck plays the pilot, for no clear reason.

E19: "Man of the Cloth" (February 15, 1972) ★ ★ ★½: In pursuit of a man whom many claim to be Jesse James, Nichols dons the clothes of a preacher and forges an uneasy alliance with a fellow bounty hunter. Fun episode made all the more enjoyable by guest stars Jack Elam, Fran Ryan, and Charles McGraw—not to mention the sight of Garner in preacher garb riding his Harley Davidson. The highlight of the series.

E20: "Fight of the Century" (February 22, 1972) ★ ★: Nichols is challenged to find a local man dumb enough to take on a world champion boxer.

E21: "Bertha" (February 29, 1972) ★ ★: Desperate for $500, Nichols offers to run the town brothel, while Bertha's daughter comes to visit.

E22: "Man's Best Enemy" (March 7, 1972) ★ ★: Guarding a killer in the hotel storeroom gets complicated by Mitchell's dog, a hound that can't be controlled.

E23: "Wonder Fizz Flies Again" (March 14, 1972) ★ ★: Nichols is duped into taking on a mission that requires the assistance of his acquaintance Orv, pilot of the *Wonder Fizz*. John Beck reprises his role of Orv.

E24: "All in the Family" (May 16, 1972) ★ ★ ★: Tragedy strikes the town of Nichols, and the sheriff's brother, Jim, seeks justice.

31

THE ROCKFORD FILES

(1974–1980)

After the cancellation of *Nichols*, James Garner returned to the big screen, appearing in three features—*They Only Kill Their Masters*, *The Castaway Cowboy*, and *One Little Indian*, the latter two for Disney. But the actor still had his sights on television, a desire he shared with his good friend, Luis Delgado. Delgado's association with the actor dated back to the Garner's *Maverick* days.[1] Delgado was also the brother-in-law of *Maverick* creator Roy Huggins,[2] so Garner asked Delgado to convey to the producer his interest in doing another series. Huggins had kept busy since *Maverick*, creating several successful series including *77 Sunset Strip*, *Run for Your Life*, and one of the most successful dramas of the 1960s, *The Fugitive*, starring Garner's old Warner Bros. contract buddy, David Janssen. Since terminating his association with Warner Bros., Huggins found a home at Universal Television, which would eventually produce *The Rockford Files*.

Upon learning of Garner's desire to return to television, Huggins quickly wrote a story and gave it to Stephen J. Cannell to develop a script. Cannell was a young writer who had written for several series in the early 1970s, including *Ironside*, *Adam-12*, and *Columbo*. Most recently, Cannell had worked on a pair of short-lived police series—*Chase*, a show he co-created, and *Toma*, which he produced. Though a short-lived show, *Toma* afforded Cannell the opportunity to work with Huggins, who wrote ten episodes of the series, not to mention Juanita Bartlett, who also wrote for the program.[3] According to Cannell, the character of Rockford originally had been written

Noah Beery Jr. as Rocky, with Garner in *The Rockford Files*. NBC / *Photofest* © NBC

for an episode of *Toma*, and his last name was one that Huggins discovered by thumbing through the Universal Studios phone directory.

Cannell sent the script to Garner, who appreciated that Jim Rockford, like Bret Maverick, was an antihero. Garner agreed to do *The Rockford Files*, asking Cannell to be brought on not just as a writer but as a producer as well. A pilot, "Backlash of the Hunter," was produced and aired March 27, 1974, on NBC. After the success of the pilot, NBC committed the show to the network's fall lineup, and the series debuted on Friday night, September 13th.

James Scott Rockford is a Los Angeles–based licensed private investigator (PI) who owns his own firm, the Rockford Agency. Before he earned his detective's license, Rockford served five years in San Quentin prison for armed robbery, a crime he didn't commit. Unlike most convicts who claim innocence, Rockford was eventually pardoned by the governor and set free. Although Rockford takes his investigations seriously, he nevertheless retains his sense of humor. Sometimes it's self-deprecating, but more often than not, his barbs are aimed at the wrong people at the wrong time—especially when he directs his stinging remarks at those only too willing to inflict bodily harm upon him.

In an effort to steer clear of the police whenever possible, Rockford avoids active cases. On occasion he reluctantly breaks this rule, usually on behalf of friends. His fee is $200 per day plus expenses, though on many cases, he fails to collect payment. Despite the hazardous nature of his occupation, Jim frequently goes to great lengths to avoid dangerous situations. Though he owns a handgun, he doesn't hold a permit for it, so he retrieves the weapon from his cookie jar only on rare occasions. Rockford lives in a comfortable, albeit grungy-looking trailer that sits at the edge of a parking lot at 29 Cove Road in Malibu, California, off the Pacific Coast Highway.

Besides Rockford, two regulars appeared throughout the series. Jim's father, Joseph "Rocky" Rockford (Noah Beery Jr.), a semiretired truck driver, is always trying to convince Jim to get out of the PI business, especially when it gets too dangerous. Jim has an ally in the Los Angeles police department, detective Dennis Becker (Joe Santos), whose complicated relationship with Jim provides some of the series more memorable exchanges. Dennis helps Jim on his cases, mostly by running down license plate numbers or providing classified information from police reports. The dynamic of their friendship often puts them at odds, especially when Jim compromises Dennis's position at the precinct. But Dennis also grudgingly respects Jim's investigative instincts, and on occasion, requires his buddy's assistance.

If Jim's relationship with Dennis is complicated, his association with Angel Martin is often exasperating. Evelyn "Angel" Martin (Stuart Margolin), a perennial, but not terribly successful con artist, had served prison time with Jim, and true to his nature, is always looking for the next get-rich scheme. Such scams often get him into hot water with either the mob or the police and sometimes both—not to mention making life difficult for Jim. Despite efforts to distance himself from his "friend," Rockford often gets dragged into Angel's corrupt world.

Jim's on again–off again romance with Beth Davenport (Gretchen Corbett) is no less complicated than his other relationships. As Jim's attorney, Beth usually has Jim's back, but as with Angel and Dennis, she sometimes needs to call on the man she refers to as the "best private investigator money can buy." Despite the couple's affinity, the relationship never progresses beyond a casual arrangement.

Other characters appear on an infrequent basis throughout the series, many of them Dennis Becker's associates at the police department. Becker reports to Lieutenant Doug Chapman (James Luisi), whose disdain for Rockford hinges as much on Rockford's line of work as it does on Jim's history as an ex-con. Lieutenant Diel (Tom Atkins) is another of Becker's superiors, though the character was not seen after the third season.

Captain McEnroe and Officer Billings were two peripheral characters played by two people close to James Garner. Captain McEnroe was portrayed by Garner's older brother Jack, who also portrayed other characters on the show, everything from a janitor to a sheriff. Good friend Luis Delgado played another minor character, Officer Billings. Because Cherokee Productions produced the series, Garner frequently employed other actors and members of the crew he had worked with earlier in his movie and television projects.

Besides regulars Rocky and Dennis and semi-regulars Angel and Beth, viewers could expect some common elements in most, if not all, of the episodes:

- An opening credits sequence that features an ever-changing voice-over: as the camera pans over Jim's desk, it reveals an unfinished game of solitaire; a framed picture of Jim's father, Rocky; and a black, push button phone perched atop an answering machine. After two rings, Garner's voice announces: "This is Jim Rockford. At the tone, leave your name and message. I'll get back to you." And with each new episode, viewers were treated to a different message, usually laced with humor and sometimes menace. And often, the call reinforces Jim's precarious financial situation. Once the message concludes, the show's signature theme song kicks in, an up-tempo rock instrumental—and eventual top ten hit.[4]
- A car chase, more often than not featuring Jim's gold Pontiac Firebird.[5] Rockford's dexterity behind the wheel often gets him out of many precarious situations. One common move that Jim employed was the "J-turn," a maneuver in which the car spins around 180 degrees. The signature move became so recognized with the show that stunt drivers, police officers, and others often referred to it as the "Rockford spin."[6]
- An altercation, often a fistfight, in which Jim is just as likely to lose as win—or at the very least, leave him wincing from his wounds.
- Less frequently, a miniature printing press (stored in Jim's glove compartment) used to create business cards for Rockford's aliases like "Jimmy Joe Meeker" or "Jim Taggart."
- Leisurely opening credits, often concluding well into the episode, after significant action has taken place.

What viewers looked forward to most were the engaging story lines, the keen scripts, and most of all, James Garner as Jim Rockford. Indeed, the success of *The Rockford Files* can be attributed to two constants: the magnetic charisma of its star and some of the sharpest scripts in television history. Whether the plots proved simple, complex, or downright convoluted, the dialogue was particularly crisp, especially for a detective series. And Garner was a master at delivering his lines—no matter what was required of them. Whether the line needed to convey a sense of irony, wit, or sarcasm—or all of the above—it didn't matter. Garner delivered. But he was just as adept at communicating frustration and anger, or even more subtle emotions like bemusement or lament. For a man who claimed his acting skills relied on listening, Garner had few peers when it came to making speeches. Whether his speeches were vented in succinct bursts of annoyance or required a more elaborate speech, Garner always conveyed them with authenticity.

Fortunately, the actor could depend on a reliable pool of writers over the course of the show's run to maintain the level of excellence that matched Garner's acting skills. Accounting for the majority of those scripts were the series cocreators, Cannell and Huggins—the latter of whose credits were attributed to John Thomas James[7]—as well as regular contributors and eventual producers of the series, Juanita Bartlett and David Chase.

Cannell would go on to create or cocreate several shows after *The Rockford Files*, including *Wiseguy*, *21 Jump Street*, and *The Commish*, while Bartlett wrote for several more shows including another beloved detective series, *Spenser: For Hire*. Of course, Chase, who had written several *Rockford* episodes featuring the mob—Italian and otherwise—for *The Rockford Files*, would later parlay his fascination with the mafia by creating *The Sopranos* (in the pilot episode, Chase pays homage to *The Rockford Files* when the show's theme plays in the background during one scene).

During its six-season run, the series received eighteen Emmy nominations, including three for Outstanding Drama Series from 1978 to 1980 and fifteen for acting. Of Garner's five nominations for Outstanding Lead Actor, he was awarded the top prize once, in 1977. Curiously, the series also earned four Lead Actress nominations, all for single-episode performances: Rita Moreno, who portrayed Rita Capkovic in three episodes, received back-to-back nominations in 1978 and '79, winning the first year, but losing in 1979 to Mariette Hartley for her role on *The Incredible Hulk*. The following year, Hartley was nominated again, this time for a *Rockford Files* episode. Hartley and fellow *Rockford* nominee Lauren Bacall lost the lead actress race to *Dallas* matriarch Barbara Bel Geddes.

The remaining acting nominations were distributed among the show's supporting players: Joe Santos received his lone nomination in 1979, while Noah Beery Jr. received three nominations, in 1977, 1979, and 1980. In 1979, both actors lost to fellow *Rockford Files* cast member Stuart Margolin for his reoccurring character, Angel. Margolin repeated the win in 1980, making his record two for two.

In addition to the four acting Emmys, the show's most impressive win was the award for Best Drama series in 1978. To date, *The Rockford Files* is the *only* private detective series to win the Emmy in that category.[8]

Despite a slew of Emmy and Golden Globe nominations, none of them were in the writing category. However, the series did receive five nominations in the episodic drama series category from the Writers Guild of America: "So Help Me God" (Juanita Bartlett) in 1976; "Quickie Nirvana" (David Chase) and "Beamer's Last Case" (Booker Bradshaw and Calvin Kelly: story; Stephen J. Cannell: teleplay) in 1978; "The House on Willis Avenue" (Stephen J. Cannell) in 1979; and "Love Is the Word" (David Chase) in 1980.

On January 10, 1980, *The Rockford Files* came to an abrupt end, halfway through its sixth season. Though Garner would have gladly continued, his aching body said otherwise. However, as with his other iconic character, Bret Maverick, the actor would get another opportunity to play the beloved detective. Nearly fifteen years after the last original episode aired, Garner reprised his role as Jim Rockford in a number of television films. Many of the series regulars also returned, including Joe Santos, Stuart Margolin, and Gretchen Corbett. Unfortunately, Noah Beery Jr. was too ill to participate and passed away on November 1, 1994, just twenty-six days before the first movie aired.

Though the eight TV movies were only moderately successful at rekindling the spirit of the original series, viewers were more than pleased to welcome Rockford back. In addition to the popularity of the films, Garner proved that he still had the respect of his peers, earning back-to-back nominations in 1995–1996 for Outstanding Performance by a Male Actor in a TV Movie or Miniseries from the Screen Actors Guild. On April 20, 1999, audiences paid a final farewell to Jim Rockford.

Garner's work in more than two dozen films and television movies is a testament to his superlative—and one could claim—underrated skills as actor. One could argue that it's somewhat unfortunate many of those productions are overshadowed by his two most beloved shows. But one could also contend, with little resistance, that *The Rockford Files* captured the essence of James Garner—his charisma, his generosity, and most of all, his integrity—more than any other film, show, or miniseries. And for that reason alone, *The Rockford Files* is *the* most essential viewing in the actor's long career.

Listed next are the episodes, by season, of James Garner's crowning achievement.

SEASON I

Pilot: "Backlash of the Hunter" (March 27, 1974) ★★: A young woman asks Jim Rockford to help solve her father's murder.

E1: "The Kirkoff Case" (September 13, 1974) ★★★: A wealthy client hires Rockford to prove he had nothing to do with his father's murder.

E2: "The Dark and Bloody Ground" (September 20, 1974) ★★★½: Rockford's lawyer and occasional girlfriend, Beth Davenport, hires him to look into the death of her friend.

E3: "The Countess" (September 27, 1974) ★★★★: A woman who acquired her royal title via marriage is being blackmailed because of her past relationship with the mob.

E4: "Exit Prentiss Carr" (October 4, 1974) ★★★: Rockford looks into the death of a friend's husband after the case is closed by the police, who consider it a suicide.

E5: "Tall Woman in Red Wagon" (October 11, 1974) ★★★: A reporter asks Jim to look into the suspicious death of a friend.

E6: "This Case Is Closed" (October 18, 1974) ★★★★: Rockford is hired by a woman's father to investigate his daughter's fiancé.

E7: "The Big Ripoff" (October 25, 1974) ★★★: Rockford suspects a man staged his death to collect the insurance money.

E8: "Find Me if You Can" (November 1, 1974) ★★★: A mysterious woman hires Rockford to see if he can discover her real identity and track her down.

E9: "In Pursuit of Carol Thorne" (November 8, 1974) ★★★: Rockford is hired by a man and a woman who pose as parents trying to locate a man they say is their son, but it turns out to be a chase for stolen money.

E10: "The Dexter Crisis" (November 15, 1974) ★★: A wealthy businessman wants Rockford to locate his mistress, and the woman's roommate tags along during the search.

E11: "Caledonia—It's Worth a Fortune" (December 6, 1974) ★★★★: Rockford helps a convict's wife search for a buried fortune in a small town.

E12: "Profit and Loss, Part 1: Profit" (December 20, 1974) ★★★★: After Jim is accused of filing a false police report, he is hired to dig deeper into a conglomerate's shady practices.

E13: "Profit and Loss, Part 2: Loss" (December 27, 1974) ★★½: In the weaker conclusion to a two-episode story, Rockford's investigation into an unscrupulous conglomerate forces him to spend a little too much time behind the wheel.

E14: "Aura Lee, Farewell" (January 3, 1975) ★★★: Rockford is once again hired by a sometime girlfriend (Sara Butler), but this time it is to investigate the death of her employee.

E15: "Sleight of Hand"[9] (January 17, 1975) ★★: After Rockford's search for a girlfriend, Karen Mills, ends in tragedy, he investigates the mysterious mob-related circumstances about her death.

E16: "Counter Gambit" (January 24, 1975) ★★★: A former fellow inmate hires Rockford to spy on an ex-girlfriend, but it turns out the ex-con steals a necklace from the woman and Rockford gets framed for the theft.

E17: "Claire" (January 31, 1975) ★★★: Rockford's former girlfriend needs his help to get out of trouble with a loan shark.

E18: "Say Goodbye to Jennifer" (February 7, 1975) ★★★: An old army buddy of Rockford asks him look into the death of a model.

E19: "Charlie Harris at Large" (February 14, 1975) ★★★: Rockford is hired by a friend, who is accused of killing his wife, to locate a woman who can provide an alibi for the friend.

E20: "The Four-Pound Brick" (February 21, 1975) ★★★: Rocky hires Jim to investigate the suspicious death of a police officer who is the son of Rocky's friend.

E21: "Just by Accident" (February 28, 1975) ★★: Rockford investigates a murder involving car insurance scammers.

E22: "Roundabout" (March 7, 1975) ★★: Rockford is hired by an insurance company to locate a beneficiary whose life may be in danger.

SEASON 2

E1: "The Aaron Ironwood School of Success" (September 12, 1975) ★★: A boyhood friend of Rockford entangles him in a self-empowerment scam.

E2: "The Farnsworth Stratagem" (September 19, 1975) ★★★: Dennis Becker invests in a real estate syndicate scam and asks Rockford to help him get out of it.

E3: "Gear Jammers" (September 26, 1975) ★★: After Rocky unwittingly observes an illegal transaction, he becomes sought after by Rockford and the men looking to silence him.

E4: "Gear Jammers, Part II" (October 3, 1975) *½: This is the conclusion of a thin story that might have been improved if kept contained to one episode.

E5: "The Deep Blue Sleep" (October 10, 1975) ★★★: Rockford's attorney, Beth Davenport, hires him to track down her missing friend, a model.

E6: "The Great Blue Lake Land and Development Company" (October 17, 1975) ★★: After Jim leaves money in a land developer's safe, a man who steals it turns up dead—making Rockford the number one suspect.

E7: "The Real Easy Red Dog" (October 31, 1975) ★★: Rockford investigates the death of a woman, but his client is pretending to be the dead woman's sister.

E8: "Resurrection in Black and White" (November 7, 1975) ★★★: A reporter hires Rockford to find proof that a man accused of murdering his girlfriend is innocent.

E9: "Chicken Little Is a Little Chicken" (November 14, 1975) ★★★: Angel tries to run a scam and hides money in Rockford's car.

E10: "2 into 5.56 Won't Go" (November 21, 1975) ★★: After the suspicious death of a colonel Jim served under, Rockford uncovers a smuggling operation involving military officers.

E11: "Pastoria Prime Pick" (November 28, 1975) ★★★: Rockford finds himself stranded in a small town and gets involved in both a scandal and a frame-up.

E12: "The Reincarnation of Angie" (December 5, 1975) ★★★: Rockford is hired by the sister of a stockbroker whose death may have resulted from a stock certificate scam.

E13: "The Girl in the Bay City Boys Club" (December 19, 1975) ★★★: Rockford portrays a newspaper publisher to uncover a rigged gambling operation. The only episode directed by Garner, and the only directing credit of his career.

E14: "The Hammer of C Block" (January 9, 1976) ★★: To pay off a debt, Jim investigates the death of a woman whose murder is pinned on an ex-con acquaintance of Rockford's.

E15: "The No-Cut Contract" (January 16, 1976) ★★★: A minor league football player accuses Jim of blackmailing him but then needs Rockford's help to elude a mob hit.

E16: "A Portrait of Elizabeth" (January 23, 1976) ★★★: A client of Beth Davenport hires Rockford under the guise of investigating a bogus check scheme.

E17: "Joey Blue Eyes" (January 30, 1976) ★ ★ ★: Beth asks Jim to look into an unethical restaurant deal of another friend of hers.

E18: "In Hazard" (February 6, 1976) ★ ★ ★: Beth becomes a target for murder, leaving Jim to figure out which of her clients has put her life in jeopardy.

E19: "The Italian Bird Fiasco" (February 13, 1976) ★ ★: Rockford is hired by an export-import broker to bid on a relic, which is really a ploy for something more illegal.

E20: "Where's Houston?" (February 20, 1976) ★ ★: After the granddaughter of Rocky's friend is presumed kidnapped, the grandfather winds up dead.

E21: "Foul on the First Play" (March 12, 1976) ★ ★: Jim's former parole officer, Marcus Hayes, is now a private detective and hires Rockford.

E22: "A Bad Deal in the Valley" (March 19, 1976) ★ ★ ★: A former girl-friend of Rockford uses him in a counterfeit money scheme.

SEASON 3

E1: "The Fourth Man" (September 24, 1976) ★ ★ ★: A flight attendant friend of Jim recognizes a passenger who turns out to be a hitman, and now she becomes one of his targets.

E2: "The Oracle Wore a Cashmere Suit" (October 1, 1976) ★ ★: A psychic's "visions" get Rockford into trouble with the police and drug dealers.

E3: "The Family Hour" (October 8, 1976) ★ ★ ★: Jim must locate a father who left his daughter on the footsteps of Rockford's trailer.

E4: "Feeding Frenzy" (October 15, 1976) ★ ★ ★: The father of Jim's friend wants to return money he stole, but the friend is kidnapped for ransom.

E5: "Drought at Indianhead River" (November 5, 1976) ★ ★: Angel has a mob hit contract put on him.

E6: "Coulter City Wildcat" (November 12, 1976) ★ ★ ★: Rocky owns oil rights, but someone will go to extremes to acquire them.

E7: "So Help Me God" (November 19, 1976) ★ ★ ★ ★: Appearing before a grand jury, Rockford feels he is being treated unjustly, so he exercises his constitutional rights and stands up to the judicial system.

E8: "Rattlers' Class of '63" (November 26, 1976) ★: Angel marries into a crime family he is trying to scam and needs Rockford to rescue him.

E9: "Return to the 38th Parallel" (December 10, 1976) ★ ★ ★: A down-on-his-luck buddy from Jim's days in Korea uses Rockford to locate a stolen Ming vase.

E10: "Piece Work" (December 17, 1976) **: On an insurance claim case, Rockford inadvertently gets roped into a gun-smuggling ring.

E11: "The Trouble with Warren" (December 24, 1976) ***: Beth Davenport needs Jim to intervene on behalf of her cousin who is accused of murder.

E12: "There's One in Every Port" (January 7, 1977) ***: Rockford is swindled by friends and aims to turn the tables.

E13: "Sticks and Stones May Break Your Bones, but Waterbury Will Bury You" (January 14, 1977) **: Rockford and other PIs try to stop an unscrupulous private investigator from putting them out of business.

E14: "The Trees, the Bees and T. T. Flowers" (January 21, 1977) ***: An unscrupulous developer wants to evict Rocky's friend, T.T., from his land, so Jim steps in.

E15: "The Trees, the Bees and T. T. Flowers," Part II (January 28, 1977) ***: After Jim helps Rocky's friend escape from psychological torture, the land developer resorts to even deadlier means to eliminate the old man, as well as Rockford and his father.

E16: "The Becker Connection" (February 11, 1977) **: Dennis Becker is framed, and Rockford helps to clear his name.

E17: "Just Another Polish Wedding" (February 18, 1977) **: Jim gets an ex-cellmate a job with a fellow PI, but the colleague hones in on a case Rockford is already investigating.

E18: "New Life, Old Dragons" (February 25, 1977) **: Rockford is hired by the sister of a missing Vietnamese man kidnapped by former army rangers.

E19: "To Protect and Serve" (March 11, 1977) ***: Rockford is hired to find a missing woman who is also being sought by New York mobsters.

E20: "To Protect and Serve," Part II (March 18, 1977) ***: A police groupie puts Jim and a woman hiding from mobsters in jeopardy.

E21: "Crack Back" (March 25, 1977) ***: During a trial in which she is defending a football player, Beth Davenport is being terrorized.

E22: "Dirty Money, Black Light" (April 1, 1977) **: Rocky's house is being used as a drop for illegal money.

SEASON 4

E1: "Beamer's Last Case" (September 16, 1977) ***: Fred Beamer, a wannabe private investigator, pretends to be Rockford, and he gets them both in trouble with the mob.

E2: "Trouble in Chapter 17" (September 23, 1977) ★ ★ ★: Rockford is hired by an author who claims that feminists want to kill her.

E3: "The Battle of Canoga Park" (September 30, 1977) ★ ★: Rockford needs to clear his name when his gun is used to commit a murder.

E4: "Second Chance" (October 14, 1977) ★ ★ ★: A former fellow inmate needs Jim to find a missing singer, which gets Rockford involved in a crooked music syndicate.

E5: "The Dog and Pony Show" (October 21, 1977) ★ ★ ★: Rockford helps a woman with a mental illness who thinks she's being followed.

E6: "Requiem for a Funny Box" (November 4, 1977) ★ ★: A has-been comedian wants Jim to protect him from his ex-partner who ends up dead, which gets Rockford framed for murder.

E7: "Quickie Nirvana" (November 11, 1977) ★ ★ ★: Rockford helps a hippie who has become a target of thugs who are after her money.

E8: "Irving the Explainer" (November 18, 1977) ★ ★ ★: Rockford is hired by a woman to track down a painting stolen during the Nazi Germany era.

E9: "The Mayor's Committee from Deer Lick Falls" (November 25, 1977) ★ ★: Three businessmen from Michigan hire Rockford under the guise of a fire engine purchase, but their real goal is murder.

E10: "Hotel of Fear" (December 2, 1977) ★ ★: Angel becomes the target of a hitman.

E11: "Forced Retirement" (December 9, 1977) ★ ★: Rockford assists Beth's friend, who is preyed upon by unscrupulous businessmen.

E12: "The Queen of Peru" (December 16, 1977) ★ ★: Rockford's insurance company client hires him to help with ransom exchange for a stolen diamond.

E13: "A Deadly Maze" (December 23, 1977) ★ ★: Rockford is hired by a man posing as the husband of a missing wife, but something quite different is actually happening.

E14: "The Attractive Nuisance" (January 6, 1977) ★ ★: Rocky opens a diner with a friend, but after a break-in, Rockford finds out the partner used to be in the mob.

E15: "The Gang at Don's Drive-in" (January 13, 1978) ★ ★: Rockford is hired by an author friend to do research for his new book about a murder of the writer's classmate.

E16: "The Paper Palace" (January 20, 1978) ★ ★: Jim comes to the rescue of his friend, Rita Capovic, to find out why she is being threatened—and by whom.

E17: "Dwarf in a Helium Hat" (January 27, 1978) ★ ★: Jim is mistaken for a man who's a target of the mob.

E18: "South by Southeast" (February 3, 1978) ★★: Rockford is misidentified by the FBI as one of its agents on an undercover case. The episode was inspired by the 1959 Alfred Hitchcock classic *North by Northwest*.

E19: "The Competitive Edge" (February 10, 1978) ★★★★: While working on a missing person case, Rockford rattles some members of a club, who then kidnap him and put him in a mental hospital.

E20: "The Prisoner of Rosemont Hall" (February 17, 1978) ★★: Rockford investigates the disappearance of a friend's son, who is a fraternity pledge.

E21: "The House on Willis Avenue" (February 24, 1978) ★★★★: Rockford teams up with a fellow PI, Richie Brockelman, to determine if a colleague died by accident or was murdered.[10]

SEASON 5

E1: "Heartaches of a Fool" (September 22, 1978) ★★: After being duped into hauling a load of contraband sausages, Rocky needs Jim to prove his innocence.

E2: "Rosendahl and Gilda Stern Are Dead" (September 22, 1978) ★★★: Jim's friend, Rita Capovic, needs his help to clear her of a murder charge.

E3: "The Jersey Bounce" (October 6, 1978) ★★: Rocky's punk neighbors are causing trouble, and Rockford takes matters into his own hands, but at a cost.

E4: "White on White and Nearly Perfect" (October 20, 1978) ★★: Rockford teams up with a slick private eye to rescue the kidnapped daughter of an industrialist.

E5: "Kill the Messenger" (October 27, 1978) ★★: Rockford helps Dennis Becker investigate the death of the deputy chief's wife.

E6: "The Empty Frame" (November 3, 1978) ★★: Rockford investigates the theft of a painting by pseudo-militants.

E7: "Three-Day Affair with a Thirty-Day Escrow" (November 10, 1978) ★★: Rockford reluctantly enters an Arab family's affairs involving a missing daughter whom the family said shamed them.

E8: "A Good Clean Bust with Sequel Rights" (November 17, 1978) ★★★: Rockford must babysit a former cop whose likeness is part of a toy line.

E9: "Black Mirror" (November 24, 1978) ★★★: Rockford protects a female client from a stalker.

E10: "A Fast Count" (December 1, 1978) ★★: Rockford invests in a boxer and must clear the boxer's manager accused of bribery and murder.

E11: "Local Man Eaten by Newspaper" (December 8, 1978) ★★: Rockford investigates a tabloid after an article is published about a doctor's patients.

E12: "With the French Heel Back, Can the Nehru Jacket Be Far Behind?" (January 5, 1979) ★★: Jim's model friend is murdered, and he enters the world of high fashion to find the killer.

E13: "The Battle-Ax and the Exploding Cigar" (January 12, 1979) ★★: Rockford is accused of being a gun smuggler and must clear his name.

E14: "Guilt" (January 19, 1979) ★★★: Jim investigates the attempted murder of an old love, while Rocky tries to fan the nonexistent flames of romance.

E15: "The Deuce" (January 26, 1979) ★★★: Rockford is called to jury duty, and because he questions the defendant's guilt, he is hired to prove the man's innocence.

E16: "The Man Who Saw the Alligators" (February 10, 1979) ★★: A gangster who blames Rockford for his incarceration wants revenge.

E17: "The Return of the Black Shadow" (February 17, 1979) ★★★: Out to dinner, Jim and his date are attacked.

E18: "A Material Difference" (February 24, 1979) ★★: Angel poses as a hitman and gets Rockford caught up in his scheme.

E19: "Never Send a Boy King to Do a Man's Job" (March 3, 1979) ★★★: Rockford helps the father of fellow detective, Richie Brockelman, recoup money from an unscrupulous business deal.

E20: "A Different Drummer" (April 13, 1979) ★★: After Jim winds up in the hospital, he questions an organ donor program and the doctor running it.

SEASON 6

E1: "Paradise Cove" (September 28, 1979) ★★: Rockford is sued by a former sheriff with a questionable past.

E2: "Lions, Tigers, Monkeys and Dogs" (October 12, 1979) ★★★½: Rockford is hired by a princess to find out who is trying to kill her friend.

E3: "Lions, Tigers, Monkeys and Dogs," Part II (October 19, 1979) ★★★: Jim continues his investigation among high society, leading to an unexpected outcome.

E4: "Only Rock 'n' Roll Will Never Die" (October 19, 1979) ★★★ Rockford is hired to locate a music producer.

E5: "Only Rock 'n' Roll Will Never Die," Part II (October 26, 1979) ★★★: After Rockford locates the body of a missing music producer, his investigation leads to the killers.

E6: "Love Is the Word" (November 9, 1979) ★★★: Jim's former flame, Megan, asks his help to clear her fiancé of murder.

E7: "Nice Guys Finish Dead" (November 16, 1979) ★★: Rockford and Lance White help clear a wannabe detective of murder.

E8: "The Hawaiian Headache" (November 23, 1979) ★★: Rockford becomes a courier for a secret mission on behalf of the government.

E9: "No Fault Affair" (November 30, 1979) ★★: Rita tries to leave her old profession, and Rockford helps with her transition.

E10: "The Big Cheese" (December 7, 1979) ★★★: A buddy who entrusts Jim with information on a mobster is killed, and Rockford unwittingly teams up with an IRS agent to solve the murder.

E11: "Just a Coupla Guys" (December 14, 1979) ★★: Rockford heads to New Jersey, and encounters a couple of amateur detectives who are investigating the attempted murder of an ex-mobster.

E12: "Deadlock in Parma" (January 10, 1980) ★★★: While on vacation, Jim becomes a proxy voter for a small-town referendum, and along with the proxy comes trouble.

APPENDIX A: FILMOGRAPHY

FILMS AND MADE-FOR-TELEVISION MOVIES

Toward the Unknown (1956, Warner Bros.) ★★
Director: Mervyn LeRoy. *Screenplay:* Beirne Lay Jr.
Cast: William Holden (Major Lincoln Bond), Lloyd Nolan (Brigadier General Bill Banner), Virginia Leith (Connie Mitchell), James Garner (Lieutenant Colonel Joe Craven)
Specs: 115 minutes; color
Availability: DVD (Warner Archive Collection)
Holden leads a group of supersonic test pilots in this melodramatic film that is notable mainly as Garner's feature debut. Garner's role is brief, but his charm and personality are clearly evident.

The Girl He Left Behind (1956, Warner Bros.) ★★
Director: David Butler. *Screenplay:* Guy Trosper, based on the novel by Marion Hargrove
Cast: Tab Hunter (Andy Shaeffer), Natalie Wood (Susan Daniels), David Janssen (Captain Genero), James Garner (Preston)
Specs: 103 minutes; black and white
Availability: DVD (Warner Archive Collection)
Spoiled student Andy flunks out of college, forcing him to join the army. Garner plays one of his fellow recruits whose foolish mistake leads to Andy's redemption. Wood is good; the movie is not.

Shoot-Out at Medicine Bend (1957, Warner Bros.) ★★½
  Director: Richard L. Bare. *Screenplay:* John Tucker Battle, D. D. Beau-
    champ
  Cast: Randolph Scott (Captain Devlin), James Garner (Sergeant John
    Maitland), James Craig (Ep Clark), Gordon Jones (Private Will Clegg),
    Angie Dickinson (Priscilla King), Dani Crayne (Nell Garrison)
  Specs: 87 minutes; black and white
  Availability: DVD (Warner Archive Collection)
  Three army men whose uniforms have been stolen pose as peaceful
    Quakers. In town, they look for evidence to catch a crooked business-
    man whose faulty rifles have led to several deaths.

Sayonara (1957, Warner Bros.) ★★½
  Director: Joshua Logan. *Screenplay:* Paul Osborn, based on the novel by
    James Michener
  Cast: Marlon Brando (Major Gruver), Red Buttons (Joe Kelly), Miiko
    Taka (Hana-Ogi), James Garner (Captain Bailey), Ricardo Montalban
    (Nakamura), Miyoshi Umeki (Katsumi)
  Specs: 147 minutes; color
  Availability: DVD (MGM); Blu-ray (Twilight Time)
  Officers stationed in Japan defy the military's rules of fraternizing with
    the locals. The film's indictment of xenophobia is undermined by the
    yellow casting of Latino Montalban as a kabuki performer.

Darby's Rangers (1957, Warner Bros.) ★★
  Director: William A. Wellman. *Screenplay:* Guy Trosper, suggested by
    the book by Major James Altieri
  Cast: James Garner (William Orlando Darby), Jack Warden (Saul
    Rosen), Stuart Whitman (Hank Bishop), Murray Hamilton (Sims
    Delancey), Edward Byrnes (Lieutenant Arnold Ditman), Etchika
    Choureau (Angelina De Lotta)
  Specs: 122 minutes; black and white
  Availability: DVD (Warner Archive Collection)
  This is an almost disrespectful account of real-life Colonel William
    Darby, a World War II commander, and his American battalion.
    Though Garner earns his first top billing, the film focuses more on
    the romantic exploits of his men, sometimes in embarrassingly bad
    vignettes.

Up Periscope (1959, Warner Bros.) ★★½

Director: Gordon Douglas. *Screenplay:* Richard H. Landau, based on the novel by Robb White

Cast: James Garner (Lieutenant Kenneth Braden), Edmond O'Brien (Cmdr. Paul Stevenson), Alan Hale Jr. (Pat Malone), Carleton Carpenter (Lieutenant Phil Carney), Andra Martin (Sally Johnson)

Specs: 111 minutes; color

Availability: DVD (Warner Home Video)

Submarine Commander Stevenson's mission is to transport Kenneth Braden to a Japanese-occupied island where the lieutenant can secure signal codes that will help the allies win the war.

Cash McCall (1960, Warner Bros.) ★★★

Director: Joseph Pevney. *Screenplay:* Lenore Coffee, Marion Hargrove, based on Cameron Hawley's novel

Cast: James Garner (Cash McCall), Natalie Wood (Lory Austen), Dean Jagger (Grant Austen), Nina Foch (Maude Kennard), Henry Jones (Gilmore Clark)

Specs: 102 minutes; color

Availability: DVD (Warner Home Video)

Cash McCall is a corporate raider who falls in love with the daughter of a businessman, whose company McCall wants to buy.

The Children's Hour (1961, MGM; the Mirisch Company) ★★★

Director: William Wyler. *Screenplay:* John Michael Hayes, Lillian Hellman, based on Hellman's play

Cast: Audrey Hepburn (Karen Wright), Shirley MacLaine (Martha Dobie), James Garner (Dr. Joe Cardin), Miriam Hopkins (Miss Lily Mortar), Fay Bainter (Mrs. Amelia Tilford), Karen Balkin (Mary Tilford), Veronica Cartright (Rosalie Wells)

Specs: 107 minutes; black and white

Availability: DVD and Blu-ray (Kino Lorber)

In this remake of William Wyler's 1936 film *These Three*, a rumor spread by a vindictive girl may have an element of truth to it. The scandalous subject of the original play is restored for the 1961 version.

Boys' Night Out (1962, MGM) ★★

Director: Michael Gordon. *Screenplay:* Ira Wallach; adaptation by Marion Hargrove, based on a story by Arne Sultan, Marvin Worth

Cast: Kim Novak (Cathy), James Garner (Fred Williams), Tony Randall (George Drayton), Howard Duff (Doug Jackson), Howard Morris (Howard McIllenny)

Specs: 112 minutes; color

Availability: DVD (Warner Archive Collection)

Garner's character is the only bachelor among a group of friends who rent an in-town place to hang out during the week. Typical 1960s comedy that should be better than it is.

The Great Escape (1963, United Artists; the Mirisch Company) ★★★★

Director: John Sturges. *Screenplay:* James Clavell, W. R. Burnett, based the book by Paul Brickhill

Cast: Steve McQueen (Virgil Hilts), James Garner (Hendley), Richard Attenborough (Roger Bartlett), James Donald (Ramsey), Charles Bronson (Danny), Donald Pleasence (Blythe), James Coburn (Sedgwick), Angus Lennie (Ives)

Specs: 172 minutes; color

Availability: DVD and Blu-ray (MGM)

Prisoners in a World War II German stalag tunnel make many attempts—and finally succeed to escape their captors.

The Thrill of It All (1963, Universal) ★★★

Director: Norman Jewison. *Screenplay:* Carl Reiner, based on a story by Larry Gelbart, Carl Reiner

Cast: Doris Day (Beverly Boyer), James Garner (Gerald Boyer), Arlene Francis (Mrs. Fraleigh), Edward Andrews (Gardiner Fraleigh), Elliot Reid (Mike Palmer), Carl Reiner (Actor)

Specs: 108 minutes; color

Availability: DVD (Universal)

A doctor's wife becomes the spokeswoman for a soap company, resulting in less time with her husband and children.

The Wheeler Dealers (1963, MGM; Filmways) ★★½

Director: Arthur Hiller. *Screenplay:* George J. W. Goodman, Ira Wallach, based on a novel by George J. W. Goodman

Cast: James Garner (Henry Tyroon), Lee Remick (Molly Thatcher), Phil Harris (Ray Jay Fox), Chill Wills (Jay Ray Spinelby), Jim Backus (Bullar Bear), Louis Nye (Stanislas), John Astin (Hector Vanson), Elliott Reid (Leonard), Patricia Crowley (Eloise Cott)

Specs: 105 minutes; color

Availability: DVD (Warner Archive Collection)

A Texas businessman who has run out of money travels to New York City to convince his investors to fund his ventures.

Move Over, Darling (1963, 20th Century Fox) ★★

Director: Michael Gordon. *Screenplay:* Hal Kanter, Jack Sher, based on a screenplay by Bella Spewack, Samuel Spewack; story by Bella Spewack, Samuel Spewack, Leo McCarey

Cast: Doris Day (Ellen Arden), James Garner (Nicholas Arden), Polly Bergen (Bianca Steele), Thelma Ritter (Grace Arden), Chuck Connors (Stephen Burkett)

Specs: 103 minutes; color

Availability: DVD (20th Century Fox)

A woman who has been missing for seven years and has just been declared legally dead arrives to find her husband about to remarry. This remake of the 1940 Leo McCarey film *My Favorite Wife*, starring Cary Grant and Irene Dunne, fails to live up to the original.

The Americanization of Emily (1964, MGM) ★★★★

Director: Arthur Hiller. *Screenplay:* Paddy Chayefsky, based on the novel by William Bradford Huic

Cast: James Garner (Lieutenant Commander Charles E. Madison), Julie Andrews (Emily Barham), Melvyn Douglas (Admiral William Jessup), James Coburn (Lieutenant Commander Paul "Bus" Cummings), Joyce Grenfell (Mrs. Barham)

Specs: 115 minutes; black and white

Availability: DVD and Blu-ray (Warner Home Video)

Charlie Madison is a "dog-robber" who thrives on keeping his commanding officer happy, until the failing admiral sends Charlie on a suicide mission—to film the invasion of Omaha Beach on D-day.

36 Hours (1964, MGM; made in cooperation with Cherokee Productions) ★★½

Director: George Seaton. *Screenplay:* George Seaton, Carl K. Hittleman, Luis H. Vance (story), based on the story "Beware of the Dog" by Roald Dahl

Cast: James Garner (Major Jefferson Pike), Eva Marie Saint (Anna Hedler), Rod Taylor (Major Walter Gerber), Werner Peters (Otto (Schack), John Banner (Ernst)

Specs: 115 minutes; black and white

Availability: DVD and Blu-ray (Warner Archive Collection)

Days before the D-day invasion, a top-ranking officer is kidnapped, drugged, and fooled into thinking the war is over by Nazi schemers. The Germans have very little time to trick the kidnapped officer into revealing the Allied plans. The first of Garner's Cherokee Productions.

The Art of Love (1965, a Universal–Ross Hunter–Cherokee Picture) ★ ★
Director: Norman Jewison. *Screenplay:* Carl Reiner
Cast: James Garner (Casey Barnett), Dick Van Dyke (Paul Sloane), Elke Sommer (Nikki Dunnay), Angie Dickinson (Laurie Gibson), Carl Reiner (Rodin)
Specs: 99 minutes; color
Availability: unavailable
When Paul Sloane, an unsuccessful painter, realizes that his art will increase in value after he dies, he fakes his death, with the help of his friend, Casey.

A Man Could Get Killed (1966, a Universal-Cherokee Production) ★ ★
Directors: Ronald Neame, Cliff Owen. *Screenplay:* Richard Breen, T.E.B. Clarke, based on the novel *Diamonds for Danger* by David Esdaile Walker
Cast: James Garner (William Beddoes), Melina Mercouri (Aurora), Sandra Dee (Amy Franklin), Anthony Franciosa (Steve)
Specs: 99 minutes; color
Availability: unavailable
In this comedy, an American businessman (Garner) is mistaken for an international spy.

Duel at Diablo (1966, United Artists; a Nelson-Engel-Cherokee Production) ★ ★
Director: Ralph Nelson. *Screenplay:* Michael M. Grilikhes, Marvin H. Albert, based on Albert's novel *Apache Rising*
Cast: James Garner (Jess Remsberg), Sidney Poitier (Toller), Bibi Andersson (Ellen Grange), Dennis Weaver (Willard Grange), Bill Travers (Lieutenant Scotty McAllister)
Specs: 104 minutes; color
Availability: DVD and Blu-ray (Kino Lorber)
Frontier scout Remsberg leads a cavalry through Apache land where the troops must stave off an attack. This is an unconventional western in which the race of Poitier's character is not mentioned, but then again,

the film also doesn't account for Bibi Andersson's Swedish accent or that fact that Travers, who plays a lieutenant in the American cavalry, speaks with a Scottish accent.

Mister Buddwing (1966, MGM; a DDD-Cherokee Production) ★ ★
> *Director:* Delbert Mann. *Screenplay:* Dale Wasserman, based on the novel *Buddwing* by Evan Hunter
> *Cast:* James Garner, Angela Lansbury, Katharine Ross, Suzanne Pleshette, Jean Simmons (unnamed characters)
> *Specs:* 99 minutes; black and white
> *Availability:* DVD (Warner Archive Collection)
> In this peculiar film, amnesiac Garner slowly regains his memory and encounters several nameless females who might provide him with answers. Garner cited this as the worst picture he ever made, but it's not nearly as insipid as *How Sweet It Is!* or *Tank*.

Grand Prix (1966, MGM; a coproduction of Joel Productions-JFP and Cherokee Productions) ★ ★ ★
> *Director:* John Frankenheimer. *Screenplay:* Robert Alan Aurthur
> *Cast:* James Garner (Pete Aron), Yves Montand (Jean-Paul Sarti), Eva Marie Saint (Louise Frederickson), Toshiro Mifune (Izo Yamura), Brian Bedford (Scott Stoddard), Jessica Walter (Pat Stoddard)
> *Specs:* 176 minutes; color
> *Availability:* DVD and Blu-ray (Warner Home Video)
> The personal lives of Formula 1 drivers are revealed as they compete on the circuit. An amateur race car driver himself, Garner enjoyed making this film the most.

Hour of the Gun (1967, the Mirisch Corporation) ★ ★
> *Director:* John Sturges. *Screenplay:* Edward Anhalt
> *Cast:* James Garner (Wyatt Earp), Jason Robards (John "Doc" Holliday), Robert Ryan (Ike Clanton), Albert Salmi (Octavius Roy), Charles Aidman (Horace Sullivan)
> *Specs:* 101 minutes; color
> *Availability:* DVD and Blu-ray (MGM)
> Wyatt Earp's brother is gunned down and can't perform his duties as city marshal. After an election is held to replace him, the new marshal is killed by the same gang. Wyatt Earp has been commissioned by the US government as a federal marshal to capture the outlaws.

How Sweet It Is! (1968, National General Pictures; a Cherokee Production) ½

  Director: Jerry Paris. *Screenplay:* Garry Marshall, Jerry Belson, based on the novel *The Girl in the Turquoise Bikini* by Muriel Resnik

  Cast: James Garner (Grif Henderson), Debbie Reynolds (Jenny Henderson), Maurice Ronet (Phillipe Maspere), Donald Losby (Davey Henderson), Paul Lynde (ship purser)

  Specs: 98 minutes; color

  Availability: DVD (Warner Archive Collection)

  A traveling photographer is sent to Europe on assignment, so he brings along his wife and son, hoping for an opportunity to bond as a family. While the opening credits for this failed attempt at groovy comedy are painful, the end credit footage of Garner, Reynolds, and Losby is truly absurd.

The Pink Jungle (1968, a Universal-Cherokee Production) ★

  Director: Delbert Mann. *Screenplay:* Charles Williams, based on the novel *Snake Water* by Alan Williams

  Cast: James Garner (Ben Morris), George Kennedy (Sammy Reiderbeit), Eva Renzi (Alison Duguesne), Michael Ansara (Raul Ortega), George Rose (Captain Stopes)

  Specs: 104 minutes; color

  Availability: unavailable

  A fashion photographer on assignment in South America gets mixed up with diamond hunters, but scoring diamonds is the least of his interests. Garner admitted that financial gain was his primary motivation for making the film.

Support Your Local Sheriff! (1969, MGM; Cherokee Productions) ★ ★ ★

  Director: Burt Kennedy. *Screenplay:* William Bowers

  Cast: James Garner (Jason McCullough), Joan Hackett (Prudy Perkins), Walter Brennan (Pa Danby), Harry Morgan (Mayor Olly Perkins), Jack Elam (Jake), Bruce Dern (Joe Danby), Henry Jones (Henry Jackson)

  Specs: 92 minutes; color

  Availability: DVD (Warner Bros.); Blu-ray (Twilight Time)

  A stranger in town accepts an offer to become sheriff mostly for the money.

Marlowe (1969, MGM; Katzka-Berne Productions, Inc., and Cherokee Productions) ★ ★ ★½

  Director: Paul Bogart. *Screenplay:* Stirling Silliphant, based on the novel *The Little Sister* by Raymond Chandler

Cast: James Garner (Philip Marlowe), Gayle Hunnicutt (Mavis Wald), Carroll O'Connor (Lieutenant Christy French), Rita Moreno (Dolores Gonzales), Sharon Farrell (Orfamay Quest), William Daniels (Mr. Crowell), Paul Stevens (Dr. Vincent Lagardie)
Specs: 96 minutes; color
Availability: DVD (Warner Home Archive Collection)
Private detective Philip Marlowe learns that the two cases he's working on may be connected.

A Man Called Sledge (1970, Columbia Pictures) ★
Director: Vic Morrow. *Screenplay:* Vic Morrow, Frank Kowalski
Cast: James Garner (Luther Sledge), Dennis Weaver (Erwin Ward), Claude Akins (Hooker), John Marley (old man), Laura Antonelli (Ria)
Specs: 92 minutes; color
Availability: DVD (Columbia Pictures)
Luther Sledge is an outlaw who goes after a big score: a safe full of gold secured in a prison. Poor excuse for a spaghetti western in which Garner plays a rare bad guy.

Support Your Local Gunfighter (1971, United Artists; Cherokee-Brigade Productions) ★★
Director: Burt Kennedy. *Screenplay:* James Edward Grant
Cast: James Garner (Latigo), Suzanne Pleshette (Patience), Jack Elam (Jug May), Harry Morgan (Taylor), Joan Blondell (Jenny), Henry Jones (Ez)
Specs: 93 minutes; color
Availability: DVD (Kino Lorber); Blu-ray (Twilight Time)
This film has the same director, star, and many cast members from Garner's 1969 film *Support Your Local Sheriff!* but this is not a sequel. And it's not as good, either. One might be inclined to blame the screenwriter, but he died five years before the film was made.

Skin Game (1971, Warner Bros.; a Cherokee Production) ★★★½
Directors: Paul Bogart. *Screenplay:* Peter Stone (under the pseudonym "Pierre Marton"), based on the story by Richard Alan Simmons
Cast: James Garner (Quincy Drew), Lou Gossett Jr. (Jason O'Rourke), Susan Clark (Ginger), Brenda Sykes (Naomi), Edward Asner (Plunkett), Andrew Duggan (Calloway), Henry Jones (Sam)
Specs: 102 minutes; color
Availability: DVD (Warner Archive Collection)
Two con men, one white and one a free black man, scam buyers out of their money after they believe they have purchased a slave.

They Only Kill Their Masters (1972, MGM) ★★½
  Director: James Goldstone. *Screenplay:* Lane Slate
  Cast: James Garner (Abel Marsh), Katharine Ross (Kate), Hal Holbrook
    (Dr. Watkins), Harry Guardino (Captain Streeter), Tom Ewell (Wal-
    ter), Peter Lawford (Campbell), Edmond O'Brien (George), June Al-
    lyson (Mrs. Watkins)
  Specs: 97 minutes; color
  Availability: DVD (Warner Bros.)
  Abel Marsh, a laid-back police chief in a small California town, inves-
    tigates the murder of a woman who has apparently been mauled to
    death by her own dog, a Doberman pinscher named Murphy. Along
    with Marlowe, the role of Marsh foreshadows Garner's most famous
    character, Jim Rockford, the antihero hero.

One Little Indian (1973, Walt Disney Pictures) ★★
  Director: Bernard McEveety. *Screenplay:* Harry Spalding
  Cast: James Garner (Keyes), Vera Miles (Doris), Pat Hingle (Captain
    Stewart), Clay O'Brien (Mark), Morgan Woodward (Sergeant Raines),
    Jodie Foster (Martha), Jay Silverheels (Jimmy Wolf)
  Specs: 91 minutes; color
  Availability: DVD (Disney)
  In this western, Garner's character goes AWOL from the cavalry, but
    while on the lam, he comes across an Indian boy trying to find his home.

The Castaway Cowboy (1974, Walt Disney Productions) ★½
  Director: Vincent McEveety. *Screenplay:* Don Tait
  Cast: James Garner (Lincoln Costain), Vera Miles (Henrietta MacAvoy),
    Robert Culp (Calvin Bryson), Eric Shea (Booton MacAvoy), Gregory
    Sierra (Marruja)
  Specs: 91 minutes; color
  Availability: DVD (Disney)
  A cowboy is rescued out at sea by a boy, and in turn the cowboy helps
    the boy's family.

The New Maverick (1978, Warner Bros.; a Cherokee Production) ★★
  Director: Hy Averback. *Teleplay:* Juanita Bartlett
  Cast: James Garner (Bret Maverick), Charles Frank (Ben Maverick),
    Jack Kelly (Bart Maverick), Susan Blanchard (Nell McGarahan), Eu-
    gene Roche (Judge Austin Crupper), Susan Sullivan (Alice Ivers)
  Specs: 90 minutes; color

Availability: DVD (Warner Bros.)

Bret and Bart's nephew Ben, a Harvard dropout, follows in his uncles' footsteps as a gambler and con man.

HealtH (1980, Lion's Gate) ★★

Director: Robert Altman. *Screenplay:* Frank Barhydt, Robert Altman, Paul Dooley

Cast: Carol Burnett (Gloria Burbank), Glenda Jackson (Isabella Garnell), James Garner (Harry Wolff), Lauren Bacall (Esther Brill), Paul Dooley (Gil Gainey)

Specs: 105 minutes; color

Availability: unavailable

A political satire set at a health food convention, this film features the usual Altman characteristics.

The Fan (1981, *Paramount*) ★

Director: Edward Bianchi. *Screenplay:* Priscilla Chapman, John Hartwell, based on the novel by Bob Randall

Cast: Lauren Bacall (Sally Ross), James Garner (Jake Berman), Maureen Stapleton (Belle Goldman), Michael Biehn (Douglas Breen), Hector Elizondo (Inspector Andrews)

Specs: 95 minutes; color

Availability: DVD (Paramount)

Deranged loner stalks a movie star.

The Long Summer of George Adams (1982, Warner Bros. Television) ★★½

Director: Stuart Margolin. *Teleplay:* John Gay, based on the book by Weldon Hill (William R. Scott)

Cast: James Garner (George Adams), Joan Hackett (Norma Adams), Alex Harvey (Ernie), Juanin Clay (Ann Sharp), David Graf (Olin Summers), Anjanette Comer (Mrs. Post)

Specs: 93 minutes; color

Availability: DVD (Warner Home Archive Collection)

In 1950s Oklahoma, George Adams, a longtime employee of the railroad, confronts an uncertain future.

Victor/Victoria (1982, MGM) ★★★½

Director: Blake Edwards. *Screenplay:* Blake Edwards, based on the screenplay for *Viktor und Viktoria* by Rheinhold Schünzel

Cast: Julie Andrews (Victoria Grant), James Garner (King Marchand), Robert Preston (Carroll "Toddy" Todd), Lesley Ann Warren (Norma Cassady), Alex Karras (Squash Bernstein)
Specs: 133 minutes; color
Availability: DVD (Warner Archive Collection)
In 1930s Paris, a down-on-her luck singer poses as a man and becomes a drag queen star.

Tank (1984, Universal Pictures) ½
Director: Marvin J. Chomsky. *Screenplay:* Dan Gordon
Cast: James Garner (Zack Carey), Shirley Jones (LaDonna Carey), C. Thomas Howell (Billy Carey), Jenilee Harrsion (Sarah)
Specs: 114 minutes; color
Availability: DVD (Universal)
Army veteran Garner gets into hot water with a small-town sheriff and takes his case to the road—inside a tank. This movie is actually worse than it sounds and ranks as one of Garner's weakest films, despite his chemistry with Shirley Jones.

Heartsounds (1984, AVCO Embassy) ★★★½
Director: Glenn Jordan. *Teleplay:* Fay Kanin, based on the book by Martha Weinman Lear
Cast: Mary Tyler Moore (Martha Lear), James Garner (Harold Lear), Sam Wannamaker (Moe Silverman), Wendy Crewson (Judy), David Gardner (Barney Knapp)
Specs: 150 minutes; color
Availability: unavailable
A doctor suffers a heart attack and must face the challenges of his own mortality and frailties, with the loving support of his wife.

The Glitter Dome (1984, HBO) ★½
Director: Stuart Margolin. *Teleplay:* Stanley Kallis, based on the novel by Joseph Wambaugh
Cast: James Garner (Al Mackey), Margot Kidder (Willie), John Lithgow (Marty Welborn), John Marley (Captain Woofer), Stuart Margolin (Herman Sinclair)
Specs: 95 minutes; color
Availability: unavailable
Veteran Hollywood detective and his psychologically damaged partner solve the murder of a wealthy studio head.

Space (1985, Paramount Television) ★ ★
  Directors: Joseph Sargent, Lee Phillips. *Teleplay:* James A. Michener,
    Stirling Silliphant, Richard Berg, based on Michener's novel
  Cast: James Garner (Senator Norman Grant), Susan Anspach (Elinor
    Grant), Blair Brown (Penny Pope), Bruce Dern (Stanley Mott), Harry
    Hamlin (John Pope)
  Specs: 78 minutes; color
  Availability: unavailable
  This five-part miniseries covers the development of the space program
    after World War II. Nominated for an Emmy as Outstanding Limited
    Series, *Space* lost to *Jewel in the Crown.*

Murphy's Romance (1985, Columbia Pictures) ★ ★ ★
  Director: Martin Ritt. *Screenplay:* Harriet Frank Jr., Irving Ravetch,
    based on the novella by Max Schott
  Cast: Sally Field (Emma Moriarty), James Garner (Murphy Jones), Brian
    Kerwin (Bobby Jack Moriarty), Corey Haim (Jake Moriarty), Dennis
    Burkley (Freeman Coverly)
  Specs: 108 minutes; color
  Availability: DVD (Columbia Pictures)
  Widower Murphy Jones may seem too old for divorcee Emma Moriarty,
    who is trying to build a new life for her and her son, but Murphy and
    Emma are drawn to each other.

Promise (1986, Hallmark Hall of Fame; Garner-Duchow Productions) ★ ★ ★½
  Director: Glenn Jordan. *Teleplay:* Richard Friedenberg; story by Ken-
    neth Blackwell and Tennyson Flowers, and Richard Friedenberg
  Cast: James Garner (Bob Beuhler), James Woods (D. J. Beuhler), Piper
    Laurie (Annie Gilbert), Peter Michael Goetz (Stuart), Michael All-
    dredge (Gibb), Alan Rosenberg (Dr. Pressman)
  Specs: 97 minutes; color
  Availability: DVD (Warner Archive Collection)
  An older brother must address the challenges of taking care of his
    younger brother who suffers from schizophrenia.

Sunset (1988, Tri-Star Pictures) ★½
  Director: Blake Edwards. *Screenplay:* Blake Edwards; story by Rod Amateau
  Cast: Bruce Willis (Tom Mix), James Garner (Wyatt Earp), Malcolm Mc-
    Dowell (Alfie Alperin), Mariel Hemingway (Cheryl King), Kathleen
    Quinlan, Jennifer Edwards

Specs: 102 minutes; color

Availability: DVD (Sony Pictures Home Entertainment)

A murder in silent-era Hollywood has occurred, and it's up to a silent-film cowboy and an aging marshal to solve it. Intriguing premise that fails to deliver, despite Garner's second portrayal of Earp (*Hour of the Gun*).

My Name Is Bill W. (1989, Hallmark Hall of Fame; Garner-Duchow Productions) ★ ★½

Director: Daniel Petrie. *Teleplay:* William G. Borchert

Cast: James Woods (William Wilson), JoBeth Williams (Lois Wilson), Gary Sinise (Ebby Thatcher), James Garner (Dr. Bob Smith)

Specs: 99 minutes; color

Availability: DVD (Warner Archive Collection)

This film tells the story of William Wilson, who cofounded Alcoholics Anonymous, with the support of his wife, Lois, and the help of fellow alcoholic Robert Smith.

Decoration Day (1990, Hallmark Hall of Fame) ★ ★ ★½

Director: Robert Markowitz. *Teleplay:* Robert W. Lenski, based on the novella by John William Corrington

Cast: James Garner (Albert Sidney Finch), Judith Ivey (Terry Novis), Ruby Dee (Rowena), Bill Cobbs (Gee Penniwell), Laurence Fishburne (Michael Waring), Jo Anderson (Loreen Wendell), Norm Skaggs (Billy Wendell)

Specs: 100 minutes; color

Availability: DVD (Artisan Home Entertainment)

A retired judge is asked to figure out why his estranged childhood friend, an African American, refuses to accept a Congressional Medal of Honor for an act of bravery during World War II.

The Distinguished Gentleman (1992, Hollywood Pictures) ★ ★

Director: Jonathan Lynn. *Screenplay:* Marty Kaplan, Jonathan Reynolds

Cast: Eddie Murphy (Thomas Jefferson Johnson), Lane Smith (Dick Dodge), Sheryl Lee Ralph (Miss Loretta), Joe Don Baker (Olaf Andersen), James Garner (Jeff Johnson)

Specs: 112 minutes; color

Availability: DVD (Hollywood Pictures Home Video)

When a congressman suddenly dies, a con man is recruited to take his place. Another marginally funny Eddie Murphy movie, this one featuring little more than a cameo by Garner, who probably shouldn't have bothered.

Fire in the Sky (1993, Paramount Pictures) ★ ★
   Director: Robert Lieberman. *Screenplay:* Tracy Torme, based on the book *The Walton Experience* by Travis Walton
   Cast: D. B. Sweeney (Travis Walton), Robert Patrick (Mike Rogers), Craig Sheffer (Allan Dallis), Peter Berg (David Whitlock), Henry Thomas (Greg Hayes), James Garner (Frank Watters)
   Specs: 109 minutes; color
   Availability DVD (Warner Archive Collection)
   A logger goes missing and the townsfolk suspect his friends of foul play, but the real cause may be not of this world. Supposedly based on a true story, this film is less about alien abduction and more about how friends can turn on each other. Garner is quite good as a skeptical investigator.

Barbarians at the Gate (1993, HBO Films) ★ ★ ★
   Director: Glenn Jordan. *Teleplay:* Larry Gelbart, based on the book by Bryan Burrough, John Helyar
   Cast: James Garner (F. Ross Johnson), Jonathan Pryce (Henry Kravis), Peter Reigert (Peter Cohen), Joanna Cassidy (Linda Robinson), Fred Dalton Thompson (Jim Robinson), Leilani Sarelle (Laurie Johnson), Matt Clark (Edward Horrigan Jr.), Jeffrey DeMunn (H. John Greeniaus), David Rasche (Ted Forstmann), Ron Canada (Vernon Jordan)
   Specs: 102 minutes; color
   Availability: DVD (HBO)
   Satirical take on the true story of the buyout bid of R. J. Nabisco by its ostentatious president, F. Ross Johnson.

Breathing Lessons (1994, Hallmark Hall of Fame) ★ ★ ★
   Director: John Erman. *Teleplay:* Robert W. Lenski, based on the book by Anne Tyler
   Cast: James Garner (Ira Moran), Joanne Woodward (Maggie Moran), Kathryn Erbe (Fiona), Joyce Van Patten (Serena), Eileen Heckart (Mabel), Paul Winfield (Daniel Otis), Tim Guinee (Jesse), Jean Louisa Kelly (Daisy), Stephi Lineburg (Leroy), Henry Jones (Sam Moran)
   Specs: 97 minutes; color
   Availability: DVD (Hallmark Hall of Fame)

This gentle film chronicles a weekend in the lives of a long-married couple who rediscover how much they really mean to each other.

Maverick (1994, Warner Bros.) ★ ★ ★
  Director: Richard Donner. *Screenplay:* William Goldman, based on the television series *Maverick* created by Roy Huggins
  Cast: Mel Gibson (Bret Maverick), Jodie Foster (Annabelle Bransford), James Garner (Zane Cooper), Graham Greene (Joseph), Alfred Molina (Angel), James Coburn (Commodore)
  Specs: 121 minutes; color
  Availability: DVD (Warner Home Video)
  Bret Maverick is headed to a high-stakes riverboat poker tournament in four days. In his quest to secure the final $3,000 of the $25,000 buy-in, he encounters an unconventional lawman and a pretty woman who has a way with cards herself.

The Rockford Files: I Still Love L.A. (1995, Universal Television; MGB Productions) ★ ★
  Director: James Whitmore Jr. *Teleplay:* Juanita Bartlett
  Cast: James Garner (Jim Rockford), Joanna Cassidy (Kit), Joe Santos (Lieutenant Dennis Becker), Stuart Margolin (Angel Martin), Geoffrey Nauffts (Josh), Shannon Kenny (Dorie)
  Specs: 93 minutes; color
  Availability: DVD (Universal Home Video)
  Jim Rockford is employed by his ex-wife Kit, a defense attorney, to help her clients, a pair of siblings accused of killing their mother. In addition to reuniting actors Garner, Margolin, and Santos, the first of eight *Rockford* movies featured a script by show producer Bartlett. Despite the involvement of Bartlett and other behind the scenes principals from the original show—cocreator Stephen J. Cannell, fellow producers David Chase and Charles Floyd Johnson—the return of Rockford didn't quite capture the flavor or fun of the original series. Still, Garner received a Screen Actors Guild nomination for the film.

The Rockford Files: A Blessing in Disguise (1995, Universal Television; MGB Productions) ★
  Director: Jeannot Szwarc. *Teleplay:* Stephen J. Cannell
  Cast: James Garner (Jim Rockford), Renee O'Connor (Laura Sue Dean), Joe Santos (Lieutenant Dennis Becker), Stuart Margolin (Angel Martin), Richard Romanus (Vincent Penguinetti)

Specs: 89 minutes; color
Availability: DVD (Universal Home Video)
Jim Rockford reluctantly becomes the bodyguard for an actress whose breakout film is targeted by religious zealots. The teleplay by series cocreator Cannell takes clichéd jabs at Hollywood agents and producers, not to mention the religious right. Despite being the weakest entry of the series revival, Garner received his second Screen Actors Guild nomination for playing Rockford.

Streets of Laredo (1995, RHI Entertainment) ★ ★
Director: Joseph Sargent. *Teleplay:* Larry McMurtry, based on his novel
Cast: James Garner (Woodrow Call), Sissy Spacek (Lorena), Sam Shepard (Pea Eye), Wes Studi (Famous Shoes), Charles Martin Smith (Ned Brooksire), George Carlin (Billy Williams)
Specs: 300 minutes; color
Availability: DVD (RHI Entertainment)
This miniseries is the sequel to the highly acclaimed *Lonesome Dove*, which was an adaption of McMurtry's Pulitzer Prize–winning novel. Garner is fine in the role originated by Tommy Lee Jones, but he imitates Jones's speech patterns, which is a bit disconcerting. The rest of the cast performs ably, including stand-up genius Carlin in a rare dramatic role.

The Rockford Files: If the Frame Fits . . . (1996, Universal Television; MGB Productions) ★ ★
Director: Jeannot Szwarc. *Teleplay:* Juanita Bartlett
Cast: James Garner (Jim Rockford), Dyan Cannon (Jess Wilding), Joe Santos (Lieutenant Dennis Becker), Gretchen Corbett (Beth Davenport), Tom Atkins (Commander Diehl), James Luisi (Captain Chapman), Stuart Margolin (Angel Martin)
Specs: 93 minutes; color
Availability: DVD (Universal Home Video)
Enticed by a client who is willing to pay far more than his usual fee, Rockford investigates a domestic case, which is typically off limits. As a result, he is charged with the murder of a fellow private investigator. The third *The Rockford Files* film is one of the best, in part because series regulars Jim, con man Angel Martin (Margolin), and Lieutenant Becker (Santos) are joined by three other recurring characters, attorney Beth Davenport van Zandt (Corbett), Lieutenant Chapman (Luisi), and Commander Diehl (Atkins). The screenplay by longtime

Rockford producer and writer Bartlett captured much of the spirit of the original series, and Garner is also at his best playing his most memorable role.

The Rockford Files: The Godfather Knows Best (1996, Universal Television; MGB Productions) ★½
Director: Tony Wharmby. *Teleplay:* David Chase
Cast: James Garner (Jim Rockford), Joe Santos (Lieutenant Dennis Becker), Damian Chapa (Scotty Becker), Maxwell Caulfield (Ian Levin), Pat Finley (Peggy Becker), Barbara Carrera (Elizabeth Fama), Dan Lauria (Lieutenant Gencher), Stuart Margolin (Angel Martin)
Specs: 89 minutes; color
Availability: DVD (Universal Home Video)
Rockford tries to help Dennis Becker's homeless son Scotty, who is implicated in the murder of a fashion designer with ties to the mafia. The fourth installment of *The Rockford Files* movies, this segment features the return of yet another Rockford alum, Becker's wife, Peggy. Series writer and producer David Chase wrote this three years before creating *The Sopranos*, and though this *Rockford* segment features a mafia-related story line, it's not a particularly memorable installment.

The Rockford Files: Friends and Foul Play (1996, Universal Television; MGB Productions) ★
Director: Stuart Margolin. *Teleplay:* Stephen J. Cannell
Cast: James Garner (Jim Rockford), Marcia Strassman (Dr. Trish George), Joe Santos (Lieutenant Dennis Becker), David Proval (Joseph Cartello), James Luisi (Captain Chapman), Wendy Phillips (Babs Honeywell), Gretchen Corbett (Beth Davenport), Stuart Margolin (Angel Martin)
Specs: 92 minutes; color
Availability: DVD (Universal Home Video)
Jim reluctantly assists a waitress from the Sand Castle, the restaurant across the parking lot from his mobile home—with disastrous results. Despite a screenplay by series cocreator Cannell, this is one of the weaker segments of the *Rockford* revivals—at turns maudlin and contrived (Jim goes back to college!).

The Rockford Files: Punishment and Crime (1996, Universal Television; MGB Productions) ★★
Director: David Chase. *Teleplay:* David Chase

Cast: James Garner (Jim Rockford), Kathryn Harrold (Megan Dougherty Adams), Joe Santos (Lieutenant Dennis Becker), Bryan Cranston (Joe Dougherty), Richard Kiley (Frank Dougherty), Stuart Margolin (Angel Martin), Jack Garner (Captain McEnroe)

Specs: 90 minutes; color

Availability: DVD (Universal Home Video)

Jim reunites with an old flame, a woman who has been blind since her teen years. She asks him to help her talent agent cousin, Joe, locate one of his clients, which draws the attention of the Russian mafia. This is the second *Rockford* film focusing on mafia and family loyalties, both courtesy of longtime producer and writer David Chase—who would go on to create *The Sopranos.* Like the best *Rockford* episodes, the film features a complicated plot and some good dialogue—yet it doesn't add up to a very satisfying entry.

My Fellow Americans (1996, Warner Bros.) ★ ★ ★

Director: Peter Segal. *Screenplay:* E. Jack Kaplan and Richard Chapman, and Peter Tolan; story by E. Jack Kaplan, Richard Chapman

Cast: Jack Lemmon (President Russell P. Kramer), James Garner (President Matthew Douglas), Dan Aykroyd (President William Haney), Bradley Whitford (Carl Witnaur), Wilford Brimley (Joe Hollis), John Heard (Vice President Ted Matthews), Lauren Bacall (Margaret Kramer)

Specs: 101 minutes; color

Availability: DVD (Warner Bros. Home Video)

Two former presidents—one Republican, the other a Democrat—are implicated in a scandal that could take down the current administration. In order to prove their innocence, they must secure evidence from a presidential library—while trying to evade assassins.

Dead Silence (1997, HBO) ★½

Director: Daniel Petrie Jr. *Teleplay:* Donald Stewart, based on the novel *A Maiden's Grave* by Jeffrey Deaver

Cast: James Garner (John Potter), Kim Coates (Ted Handy), Marlee Matlin (Melanie Charrol), Lolita Davidovich (Sharon Foster), Charles Martin Smith (Roland Marks)

Specs: 99 minutes; color

Availability: DVD (HBO Video)

Escaped convicts take several deaf children and their teacher hostage. An FBI agent with a slightly tarnished reputation takes charge of the negotiation in this anemic thriller.

The Rockford Files: Murders and Misdemeanors (1997, Universal Television; MGB Productions) ★ ★
  Director: Tony Wharmby. *Teleplay:* Juanita Bartlett
  Cast: James Garner (Jim Rockford), John Amos (Booker Hutch), Joe Santos (Lieutenant Dennis Becker), Isabel Glasser (Brianne Lambert), Conrad Janis (Harvey), Dan Lauria (Commander Gage), Stuart Margolin (Angle Martin)
  Specs: 90 minutes; color
  Availability: DVD (Universal Home Video)
  Rockford agrees to take on the last cases of a fellow convict–turned–private investigator, which gets him into hot water with the police. Originally titled *Shoot-Out at the Golden Pagoda*, the producers must have felt a title change necessary because (1) a shoot-out doesn't actually occur in the film, and (2) the name of the building in question is the "gold," not golden, pagoda. Nevertheless, this penultimate *Rockford Files* film ranks as one of the best.

Twilight (1998, Paramount) ★ ★½
  Director: Robert Benton. *Screenplay:* Robert Benton, Richard Russo
  Cast: Paul Newman (Harry Ross), Susan Sarandon (Catherine Ames), Gene Hackman (Jack Ames), Reese Witherspoon (Mel Ames), Stockard Channing (Lieutenant Verna Hollander), James Garner (Raymond Hope)
  Specs: 96 minutes; color
  Availability: DVD (Paramount Home Video)
  This slow-going but still entertaining neo-noir comes from the director of *Kramer vs. Kramer* and Pulitzer Prize–winning author Richard Russo (*Empire Falls*). Garner plays a fairly small—but pivotal—role.

Legalese (1998, New Line Television) ★ ★
  Director: Glenn Jordan. *Teleplay:* Billy Ray
  Cast: James Garner (Norman Keane), Gina Gershon (Angela Beale), Mary-Louise Parker (Rica Martin), Edward Kerr (Roy Guyton), Kathleen Turner (Brenda Whitlass)
  Specs: 92 minutes; color
  Availability: DVD (New Line)

In *Legalese*, a high-profile lawyer plays behind-the-scenes counsel to a fresh-off-the-farm defense attorney. Not as sharp or as biting as it should have been, this satire of legal maneuverings nonetheless earned Garner a nomination from the Screen Actors Guild.

The Rockford Files: If It Bleeds . . . It Leads (1999, Universal Television; MGB Productions) ★★
> *Director:* Stuart Margolin. *Teleplay:* Reuben Leder; story by Juanita Bartlett, Stephen J. Cannell
> *Cast:* James Garner (Jim Rockford), Rita Moreno (Rita Kapkovic Landale), Joe Santos (Lieutenant Dennis Becker), Gretchen Corbett (Beth Davenport), Hal Linden (Ernie Landale), Stuart Margolin (Angel Martin)
> *Specs:* 90 minutes; color
> *Availability:* DVD (Universal Home Video)
> Jim reunites with Rita Kapkovic, whose husband of twelve years is suspected of being a rapist. The final *Rockford Files* movie is among the better ones.

One Special Night (1999, Green-Epstein Productions) ★★½
> *Director:* Roger Young. *Teleplay:* Nancey Silvers, based on the play *A Winter Visitor* by Jan Hartman
> *Cast:* James Garner (Robert Woodward), Julie Andrews (Catherine Howard), Patricia Charbonneau (Lori Campbell), Stacy Grant (Jaclyn Woodward), Stewart Bick (Jeff Campbell)
> *Specs:* 92 minutes; color
> *Availability:* DVD (MTI Home Video)
> Thanksgiving time: When Robert goes to visit his wife at a hospice, he meets Catherine, a widow who is visiting her deceased husband's old room. But Robert's wife is in in no condition to leave and he's without a car, so Catherine offers him a ride home during a winter storm. After they crash, the two find refuge in an abandoned cabin. This was the third and final movie appearance with Garner and Andrews together.

Space Cowboys (2000, Warner Bros.) ★★
> *Director:* Clint Eastwood. *Screenplay:* Ken Kaufman, Howard Klausner
> *Cast:* Clint Eastwood (Frank Corvin), Tommy Lee Jones (Hawk Hawkins), Donald Sutherland (Jerry O'Neill), James Garner (Tank Sullivan), Marcia Gay Harden (Sara Holland)

Specs: 130 minutes; color

Availability: DVD (Warner Home Video)

Four navy hot shots back in their day must temporarily come out of retirement to repair a broken satellite. Friends Garner and Eastwood worked together on an episode of *Maverick*.

The Last Debate (2000, Paramount Television) ★★

Director: John Badham. *Teleplay:* Jon Maas, based on the novel by Jim Lehrer

Cast: James Garner (Mike Howley), Peter Gallagher (Tom Chapman), Audra McDonald (Barbara Manning), Donna Murphy (Joan Naylor), Dorian Harewood (Brad Lily)

Specs: 96 minutes; color

Availability: unavailable

Political maneuverings by media figures occur at a debate just days before the presidential election.

Roughing It (2002, Hallmark Entertainment) ★★

Director: Charles Martin Smith. *Teleplay:* Steven H. Berman, based on the book by Mark Twain

Cast: Robin Dunne (Samuel Clemens), Ned Beatty (Slade), Jill Eikenberry (Livy Clemens), Adam Arkin (Henry), James Garner (Mark Twain)

Specs: 96 minutes; color

Availability: DVD (Echo Bridge Home Entertainment)

Mark Twain delivers his daughter's graduation commencement address, which serves as the framework to recount adventures he experienced as a young man.

Divine Secrets of the Ya-Ya Sisterhood (2002, Warner Bros.) ★

Director: Callie Khouri. *Screenplay:* Callie Khouri, Mark Andrus, based on the novel by Rebecca Wells

Cast: Sandra Bullock (Sidda), Ellen Burstyn (Vivi), Fionnula Flanagan (Teensy), James Garner (Shep Walker), Cherry Jones (Buggy), Ashley Judd (young Vivi), Shirley Knight (Necie), Maggie Smith (Caro)

Specs: 116 minutes; color

Availability: DVD (Warner Home Video)

A playwright's strained relationship with her mother is threatened even more so by the older woman's friends who are anxious to reveal her troubled past. An impressive cast is wasted, and Garner as Sandra

Bullock's father is no exception. Some viewers may enjoy this film, but we found this adaptation of the best-selling novel an excruciating experience to watch.

The Notebook (2004, New Line Cinema) ★ ★ ★
Director: Nick Cassavetes. *Screenplay:* Jeremy Leven; adaptation by Jan Sardi, based on the novel by Nicholas Sparks
Cast: Ryan Gosling (Noah Calhoun), Rachel McAdams (Allie Hamilton), James Garner (Duke), Gena Rowlands (Allie Calhoun), James Marsden (Lon Hammond), Sam Shepard (Frank Calhoun), Joan Allen (Anne Hamilton)
Specs: 124 minutes; color
Availability: DVD (New Line Video)
At a nursing home facility, Duke, a man in his seventies, reads from a journal to a fellow resident, a woman who suffers from Alzheimer's disease. The story Duke reads to her is about the tangled romance between Noah Calhoun and Allison that took place decades earlier.

The Ultimate Gift (2006, Ultimate Gift, LLC) ★
Director: Michael O. Sajbel. *Screenplay:* Cheryl McKay, based on the novel by Jim Stovall
Cast: Drew Fuller (Jason Stevens), Bill Cobbs (Theophilus Hamilton), Abigail Breslin (Emily Rose), Ali Hillis (Alexia), Brian Dennehy (Gus), Lee Meriwether (Miss Hastings), James Garner (Howard "Red" Stevens)
Specs: 116 minutes; color
Availability: DVD (20th Century Fox)
A spoiled man must pass a series of tests devised by his late grandfather in order to inherit the deceased man's wealth.

ANIMATED FEATURES, SHORTS, AND DIRECT TO VIDEO PRODUCTIONS

Atlantis: The Lost Empire (2001, Disney) ★ ★
Director: Gary Trousdale, Kirk Wise. *Screenplay:* Tab Murphy; additional material by David Reynolds; story by Kirk Wise, Gary Trousdale, Joss Whedon, Bryce Zabel, Jackie Zabel, Tab Murphy
Cast (voices): Michael J. Fox (Milo James Thatch), Corey Burton (Gaetan "the Mole" Moliere), James Garner (Commander Lyle Tiberius

Rourke), Claudia Christian (Helga Katrina Sinclair), John Mahoney
(Preston B. Whitmore)
Specs: 95 minutes; color
Availability: DVD (Walt Disney Studios Home Entertainment)
Milo Thatch and others seek out the lost world of Atlantis.

The Land before Time X: The Great Longneck Migration (2003, Universal Cartoon Studios) ★
> *Director:* Charles Grosvenor. *Screenplay:* John Loy. *Characters:* Judy
> Freudberg, Tony Geiss
> *Cast (voices):* John Ingle (Narrator/Cera's Dad), Alec Medlock (Littlefoot), Kenneth Mars (Grandpa), Miriam Flynn (Grandma), Anndi
> McAfee (Cera), James Garner (Pat)
> *Specs:* 94 minutes; color
> *Availability:* DVD (Universal Studios Home Entertainment)
> Young brontosaurus Littlefoot, his grandparents, and friends must leave
> their homeland. One of many direct-to-video sequels to the 1988 feature *The Land before Time.*

Al Roach: Private Insectigator (2004, ObieCo Entertainment) ★
> *Director:* Obie Scott Wade. *Screenplay:* Jordan Beswick, Michael Maler,
> Obie Scott Wade
> *Cast (voices):* James Garner (Al Roach), Michelle Forbes (Dede Dragonfly), Kathy Kinney (Betty Earwiggins), Freddy Rodriguez (The Fly on
> the Wall), Gregg Berger (Professor Bugdonovich)
> *Specs:* 7 minutes; black and white
> A noir spoof about Hollywood insects.

Battle for Terra (2007, Lionsgate Films) ★ ★
> *Director:* Aristomenis Tsirbas. *Screenplay:* Evan Spiliotopoulos; story by
> Aristomenis Tsirbas
> *Cast (voices):* Chad Allen (Terrian Scientist), Rosanna Arquette (Professor Lina), Bill Birch (Terrian 2), Brooke Bloom (Technician Quinn),
> James Garner (Doron)
> *Specs:* 85 minutes; color
> *Availability:* DVD (Lionsgate Home Entertainment)
> In this animated feature, a peaceful alien planet must save itself from
> destruction—and humans.

First Night (2007, Montoya Films) ★
  Director: Martin Spanjers. *Screenplay:* Matthew Bozin
  Cast (voices): Billy Aaron Brown (John), James Garner (Dr. Curtis), Rome Brooks (Chloe), Howard Alonzo (Dealer), Mark Arnold (Officer)
  Specs: 14 minutes; color
  A young man enters rehab.

Superman/Shazam! The Return of Black Adam (2010, Warner Bros., DC Entertainment) ★
  Director: Joaquim Dos Santos. *Screenplay:* Michael Jelenic (Jerry Siegel, Joe Shuster [Superman creators] and C. C. Beck, Bill Parker [Captain Marvel creators])
  Cast (voices): Zach Callison (Billy Batson), James Garner (Shazam), Josh Keaton (Punk), Danica McKellar (Sally), George Newbern (Superman/ Clark Kent)
  Specs: 25 minutes; color
  Availability: DVD (Warner Bros.)
  Black Adam has his sights on Captain Marvel, but he has to get through Superman first.

TELEVISION ROLES

Cheyenne (ABC)
  Season 1, episode 1 (September 20, 1955): "Mountain Fortress." Role: Lieutenant Brad Forsythe
  Season 1, episode 7 (January 24, 1956): "Decision." Role: Lieutenant Lee Rogers

Warner Bros. Presents (ABC)
  Season 1, episode 28 (March 27, 1956): "Explosion." Role: Unknown

Cheyenne (ABC)
  Season 1, episode 15 (May 29, 1956): "The Last Train West." Role: Bret

Conflict (ABC)
  Season 1, episode 5 (November 13, 1956): "The People against McQuade." Role: Jim Curtis
  Season 1, episode 6 (November 27, 1956): "Man from 1997." Role: Red Donnelly

Zane Grey Theater (**CBS and NBC**)
   Season 1, episode 13 (December 28, 1956): "Star over Texas." Role:
   Lieutenant Jim Collins

Conflict (**ABC**)
   Season 1, episode 9 (January 8, 1957): "Girl on the Subway." Role: unknown

Cheyenne (**ABC**)
   Season 2, episode 12 (February 12, 1957): "War Party." Role: Willis
   Peake

Maverick (**ABC**)
   Seasons 1–4, fifty-two episodes (September 22, 1957–November 20,
   1960). Role: Bret Maverick

Sugarfoot (**ABC**)
   Season 1, episode 7 (December 10, 1957): "Misfire." Role: Bret Maverick

Angel (**CBS**)
   Season 1, episode 19 (February 23, 1961): "The French Lesson." Role:
   Jim

Nichols (**NBC**)
   Season 1, twenty-four episodes (September 16, 1971–March 14, 1972).
   Role: Nichols

The Rockford Files (**NBC**)
   Seasons 1–6, 123 episodes including pilot (March 27, 1974–January 10,
   1980). Role: Jim Rockford

Young Maverick (**CBS**)
   Season 1, episode 1 (November 8, 1979): "Clancy." Role: Bret Maverick

Bret Maverick (**NBC**)
   Season 1, eighteen episodes (December 1, 1981–May 4, 1982). Role:
   Bret Maverick

Man of the People (NBC)
Season 1, twelve episodes (two unaired) (September 15, 1991–July 13, 1992). Role: Jim Doyle

God, the Devil and Bob (CBS)
Season 1, thirteen episodes (nine unaired) (March 9, 2000–March 28, 2000). Role: God

Chicago Hope (CBS)
Season 6, episode 19 (April 13, 2000): "Miller Time." Role: Hubert "Hue" Miller
Season 6, episode 20 (April 20, 2000): "Thoughts of You"
Season 6, episode 21 (April 27, 2000): "Everybody's Special at Chicago Hope"
Season 6, episode 22 (May 4, 2000): "Have I Got a Deal for You"

First Monday (CBS)
Season 1, thirteen episodes (January 15, 2002–May 3, 2002). Role: Chief Justice Thomas Brankin

8 Simple Rules (ABC)
Seasons 2–3, forty-five episodes (November 4, 2003–April 15, 2005). Role: Jim Egan

APPENDIX B:
AWARDS AND HONORS

ACADEMY AWARDS

Nomination

1986   Best Actor in a Leading Role   *Murphy's Romance*

EMMY AWARDS

Nominations (winner in bold)

1959   Best Actor in a Leading Role (Continuing   *Maverick*
        Character) in a Dramatic Series
1976   Outstanding Lead Actor in a Drama Series   *The Rockford Files*
1977   Outstanding Lead Actor in a Drama   *The Rockford Files*
        Series
1978   Outstanding Lead Actor in a Drama Series   *The Rockford Files*
1979   Outstanding Lead Actor in a Drama Series   *The Rockford Files*
1980   Outstanding Lead Actor in a Drama Series   *The Rockford Files*
1982   Outstanding Lead Actor in a Drama Series   *Bret Maverick*
1985   Outstanding Lead Actor in a Limited   *Heartsounds*
        Series or Special
1987   Outstanding Lead Actor in a Miniseries   *Promise*
        or Special

1987	**Outstanding Drama/Comedy Special**	*Promise*
1989	Outstanding Supporting Actor in a Miniseries or Special	*My Name Is Bill W.*
1989	Outstanding Drama/Comedy Special	*My Name Is Bill W.*
1991	Outstanding Lead Actor in a Miniseries or Special	*Decoration Day*
1993	Outstanding Lead Actor in a Miniseries or Special	*Barbarians at the Gate*
1994	Outstanding Lead Actor in a Miniseries or Special	*Breathing Lessons*

GOLDEN GLOBES

Nominations (winner in bold)

1958	**Most Promising Newcomer—Male**	*Sayonara*
1964	Best Actor—Comedy or Musical	*The Wheeler Dealers*
1978	Best Actor in a Television Series—Drama	*The Rockford Files*
1979	Best Actor in a Television Series—Drama	*The Rockford Files*
1980	Best Actor in a Television Series—Drama	*The Rockford Files*
1982	Best Performance by an Actor in a Television Series—Comedy or Musical	*Bret Maverick*
1985	Best Performance by an Actor in a Miniseries or Motion Picture Made for Television	*Heartsounds*
1986	Best Performance by an Actor in a Motion Picture—Comedy or Musical	*Murphy's Romance*
1987	Best Performance by an Actor in a Miniseries or Motion Picture Made for Television	*Promise*
1991	**Best Performance by an Actor in a Miniseries or Motion Picture Made for Television**	***Decoration Day***
1994	**Best Performance by an Actor in a Miniseries or Motion Picture Made for Television**	***Barbarians at the Gate***
1995	Best Performance by an Actor in a Miniseries or Motion Picture Made for Television	*Breathing Lessons*

SCREEN ACTORS GUILD

Nominations (winner in bold)

1995	Outstanding Performance by a Male Actor in a TV Movie or Miniseries	*The Rockford Files: I Still Love L.A.*
1996	Outstanding Performance by a Male Actor in a TV Movie or Miniseries	*The Rockford Files: A Blessing in Disguise*
1999	Outstanding Performance by a Male Actor in a TV Movie or Miniseries	*Legalese*
2005	Outstanding Performance by a Male Actor in a Supporting Role	*The Notebook*
2005	**Lifetime Achievement Award**	

MISCELLANEOUS AWARDS

Television Critics Association Award

2010   Career Achievement

Hollywood Walk of Fame

1960   Star (6927 Hollywood Blvd)

TV Guide Best Of

In *TV Guide*'s fortieth anniversary issue (April 17, 1993), James Garner was cited as the best television actor over the previous four decades.

NOTES

THE CAREER OF JAMES GARNER

1. Bare, Richard L. *Confessions of a Hollywood Director*. Lanham, MD: Scarecrow Press, 2001. Page 265.

2. Walker was not the tallest actor to headline a western in the 1950s. That distinction belonged to six-foot-seven James Arness, *Gunsmoke*'s Marshal Matt Dillon.

3. Kelly had appeared in the second episode of *Sally*, the show *Maverick* knocked off the airwaves in their head-to-head scheduling.

4. The two other non-western top ten programs during the 1958–1959 season were the sitcom *The Real McCoys* (ranked eighth) and the celebrity game show *I've Got a Secret* at number nine.

5. Roger Moore appeared on the series in an earlier episode ("The Rivals," which first aired on January 25, 1959), but not as Beau. He played a British playboy named John Vandergelt. The season 2 episode featured both Garner and Kelly, so it was the only episode in which all three actors appeared.

6. A few years after the demise of *Nichols*, Pierson would receive a third Oscar nomination—for *Dog Day Afternoon*—this time winning.

7. Reruns aired at different times and/or different days during the show's run, but original episodes aired at the 9:00 p.m. Friday time period.

8. The highest-ranked series to debut that fall was *Chico and the Man*, which also bowed on Friday, September 13, 1974, just before *The Rockford Files*.

9. The phone number was also 555-9000.

10. The most elaborate opening sequences were produced by *The Simpsons*, beginning with a new chalkboard punishment for Bart that had to be written one hundred times, different sax solos performed by Lisa, and finally, when the family gathered in front of the television set just before the credits appeared on an animated television screen.

11. Seasons 1–3 and 5 had twenty-two episodes each, and season 4 had twenty-one.

12. His first was the 1978 TV movie, *The New Maverick*, a pilot for a series that starred Charles Frank. Garner also made a cameo appearance on the first episode of what turned out to be a very short-lived series (only eight episodes were broadcast).

13. A year after the release of *The Ultimate Gift*, the actor appeared in a fourteen-minute short, "First Night."

14. As quoted in *Hollywood Reporter*. "Hollywood Mourns James Garner." *Hollywood Reporter* staff, July 20, 2014.

CHAPTER 1

1. In a February 1938 contest sponsored by newspaper columnist Ed Sullivan, Gable was voted the King of Hollywood (Myrna Loy was voted queen).

2. *Bridgeport Telegram* staff. "'Shoot-Out' at Warner." *Bridgeport Telegram*, May 3, 1957.

3. Dani Crayne briefly resumed her acting career twenty years later in a 1978 television movie, *Standing Tall*, under her married name, Dani Janssen, and after that only appeared in three more films.

CHAPTER 2

1. This was the first of two Michener adaptations Garner appeared in over his career. Seventeen years after the release of *Sayonara*, Garner starred in the miniseries *Space*, based on Michener's 1982 novel.

2. Yellow casting is the practice of hiring non-Asian actors to play Asian roles.

3. Kanfer, Stefan. *Somebody: The Reckless Life and Remarkable Career of Marlon Brando*. New York: Knopf, 2008. Page 147.

4. *Variety* staff. "Review: *Sayonara*." *Variety*, December 31, 1956.

5. Crowther, Bosley. "Brando Stars in *Sayonara*; Off-Beat Acting Marks Film at Music Hall." *New York Times*, December 6, 1957.

6. Shared with John Saxon (*This Happy Feeling*) and Patrick Wayne (*The Searchers*).

7. "Sayonara (1957-12-05)." BoxOfficePro. http://pro.boxoffice.com/movie/14839/sayonara. Accessed November 6, 2017.

8. O. Reilly, Sean. "*Sayonara.*" In *The Encyclopedia of Racism in American Films*. Edited by Salvador Murguia. Lanham, MD: Rowman & Littlefield, 2018. Page 502.

CHAPTER 3

1. Weiler, A. H. "*Up Periscope* at Roxy." *New York Times*, March 5, 1959.

2. Garner, James, and Jon Winokur. *The Garner Files*. New York: Simon & Schuster, 2011. Page 253.

3. Carpenter, Carleton. *The Absolute Joy of Work: From Vermont to Broadway, Hollywood, and Damn Near around the World*. Albany, GA: BearManor Media, 2016. Page 210.

CHAPTER 4

1. Strait, Raymond. *James Garner: A Biography*. New York: St. Martin's Press, 1985. Page 132.

2. Strait, *James Garner*, 139.

3. Lambert, Gavin. *Natalie Wood: A Life*. New York: Knopf, 2004. Page 149.

4. Throughout *The Girl He Left Behind*, Hunter's self-absorbed character antagonizes his fellow recruits until the end of the film, when he saves a reckless Garner from getting himself killed in an army maneuver—and thus earns the respect of his commanding officers.

5. Although Garner had received top billing in *Darby's Rangers*, his on-screen presence was no more significant than other actors in the film, as it focused on fragmented exploits of various soldiers during World War II.

6. Thompson, Howard. "*Cash McCall* Explores Business World." *New York Times*. January 28, 1960.

7. *Hollywood Reporter*, as quoted in Strait, *James Garner*, 153.

8. *The Motion Picture Herald*, as quoted in Strait, *James Garner*, 153.

9. Garner, James, and Jon Winokur. *The Garner Files*. New York: Simon & Schuster, 2011. Page 252.

CHAPTER 5

1. The first person to win an Oscar under Wyler's tutelage was Walter Brennan, who received the first statue in the newly established category of Best Supporting Actor for *Come and Get It* in 1937. Two years later, Bette Davis and Fay Bainter

would receive Oscars for Best Actress and Best Supporting Actress, respectively, for Wyler's film, *Jezebel*.

2. It would take a decade (from Walter Brennan in 1937 to March in 1947) for Wyler films to secure the wins in all four acting categories. Three decades would pass before Scorsese films would complete the quartet: from Ellen Burstyn for *Alice Doesn't Live Here Anymore* in 1975 to Cate Blanchett in *The Aviator* in 2005. Amazingly, Ashby, who directed only eleven features, achieved this rare accomplishment in just over four years: Lee Grant in *Shampoo* (1976), Jon Voight and Jane Fonda in *Coming Home* (1979), and Melvyn Douglas in *Being There* (1980).

3. Herman, Jan. *A Talent for Trouble: The Life of Hollywood's Most Acclaimed Director, William Wyler*. New York: Putnam, 1995. Page 413.

4. Herman, *A Talent for Trouble*, 417.

5. *Variety* staff. "The Children's Hour." *Variety*, December 31, 1960.

6. Balio, Tino. *United Artists: The Company That Changed the Film Industry, Volume 2 (1951–1978)*. Madison: University of Wisconsin Press, 2009. Page 171.

7. DeRosa, Steven. *Writing with Hitchcock: The Collaboration of Alfred Hitchcock and John Michael Hayes*. New York: Faber and Faber, 2001. Page 212.

8. As quoted in DeRosa, *Writing with Hitchcock*, 212.

9. Clarke, Cath, Dave Calhoun, Tom Huddleston, Ben Walters, and Guy Lodge. "The 50 Best Gay Movies: The Best in LGBT Film-Making." *TimeOut London*, March 15, 2017. https://www.timeout.com/london/film/the-50-best-gay-movies-the-best-in-lgbt-film-making. Accessed December 26, 2017.

10. Coates, Tyler, and Dave Holmes. "The 50 Best LGBT Movies Ever Made." *Esquire*, June 8, 2017. http://www.esquire.com/entertainment/movies/g3392/best-gay-lgbt-movies-of-all-time/. Accessed December 26, 2017.

CHAPTER 6

1. "Paul Brickhill, 74, Author of War Novels." *New York Times*, April 26, 1991.

2. Lovell, Glenn. *Escape Artist: The Life and Films of John Sturges*. Madison: University of Wisconsin Press, 2008. Page 222.

3. *Variety* staff. "Review: The Great Escape." *Variety*, December 31, 1963.

4. Crowther, Bosley. "P.O.W.'s in 'Great Escape': Inmates of Nazi Camp Are Stereotypical Steve McQueen Leads Snarling Tunnelers." *New York Times*, August 8, 1963.

5. "The Great Escape (1963)." The Numbers. http://www.the-numbers.com/movie/Great-Escape-The#tab=summary. Accessed October 9, 2017.

6. "The Great Escape (1963)."

7. The other nominees were *It's a Mad, Mad, Mad, Mad World* (154 minutes), *The Cardinal* (175 minutes), and *Cleopatra* (192 minutes).

8. Santas, Constantine, et al. *The Encyclopedia of Epic Films*. Lanham, MD: Rowman & Littlefield, 2014. Page 260.

9. Garner, James, and Jon Winokur. *The Garner Files*. New York: Simon & Schuster, 2011. Page 83.

10. Ahead of *The Magnificent Seven* on the AFI survey were *Star Wars* (John Williams), *Gone with the Wind* (Max Steiner), *Lawrence of Arabia* (Maurice Jarre), *Psycho* (Bernard Herrmann), *The Godfather* (Nino Rota), *Jaws* (John Williams), and *Laura* (David Raksin).

11. Lawson, Matt, and Laurence E. MacDonald. *100 Greatest Film Scores*. Lanham, MD: Rowman & Littlefield, 2018.

12. In the season 4 episode of *The Simpsons* titled "A Streetcar Named Marge," Maggie the baby is sent to a day-care center—Ayn Rand's School for Tots—where she engineers a successful procurement of pacifiers. Though the scene ends with Maggie tossing a ball in her playpen—à la Steve McQueen's character—her resourcefulness also references the scrounger that Garner plays in *The Great Escape*.

CHAPTER 7

1. Jewison, Norman. *This Terrible Business Has Been Good to Me*. Toronto: Key Porter Books, 2004. Page 74.

2. Jewison, *This Terrible Business*, 75.

3. Jewison, *This Terrible Business*, 82.

4. Quoted in Edelman, Rob, and Audrey Kupferberg. *Matthau: A Life*. Lanham, MD: Taylor Trade, 2002. Page 127.

5. Crowther, Bosley. "*The Thrill of It All* Opens at Music Hall—Doris Day Stars in Carl Reiner Comedy." *New York Times*, August 2, 1963.

6. *Variety* staff. "Review: *The Thrill of It All*." *Variety*, December 31, 1962.

7. "The Thrill of It All." The Films of Doris Day. http://www.dorisday.net/the-thrill-of-it-all/. Accessed May 30, 2017.

8. "The Thrill of It All (1963)." The Numbers. http://www.the-numbers.com/movie/Thrill-of-it-All-The#tab=summary. Accessed December 26, 2017.

CHAPTER 8

1. Crowther, Bosley. "Manipulating Financial Deals: *The Wheeler Dealers* Opens at Music Hall." *New York Times*, November 15, 1963.

2. "*Wheeler Dealers* Spin Some Fun." *Cleveland Press*, November 23, 1963.

3. Garner, James, and Jon Winokur. *The Garner Files*. New York: Simon & Schuster, 2011. Page 254.

CHAPTER 9

1. Considine, Shaun. *Mad as Hell: The Life and Work of Paddy Chayefsky*. New York: Random House, 1994. Page 215.

2. Hiller, Arthur. *The Americanization of Emily* DVD. Special Features. Audio Commentary.

3. Garner, James, and Jon Winokur. *The Garner Files*. New York: Simon & Schuster, 2011. Page 84.

4. Hiller, *The Americanization of Emily*, audio commentary.

5. *The Americanization of Emily* is the second antiwar film of 1964 graced by character actor Keenan Wynn. In both films, Wynn plays a military man, though his Colonel "Bat" Guano in *Dr. Strangelove* ranks much higher than the unnamed seaman he plays in *Emily*.

6. In one of her earliest on-screen roles, Diana Rigg plays one of the girls in the motor pool. In her very brief scene at the beginning of the film, Garner appears to call her Pat, which is the same name as the head of the motor pool, played by Linda Marlowe, so a continuity error may have occurred during the filming.

7. Crowther, Bosley. "*The Americanization of Emily* Arrives." *New York Times*, October 28, 1964.

8. *Variety* staff. "Review: *The Americanization of Emily*." *Variety*, December 31, 1963.

9. Hiller, *The Americanization of Emily*, audio commentary.

10. Correspondence with Gigi Garner and Stephen Ryan, March 12, 2018.

11. Chayefsky, Paddy. *The Collected Works of Paddy Chayefsky: The Screenplays Volume 1*. New York: Applause Books, 1995. Page 222.

12. Garner and Winokur, *The Garner Files*, 254.

13. Hiller, *The Americanization of Emily*, audio commentary.

CHAPTER 10

1. Norma was the first name of Lancaster's wife at the time.

2. Strait, Raymond. *James Garner: A Biography*. New York: St. Martin's Press, 1985. Page 216.

3. Quinlan, David. *Quinlan's Film Directors*. London: Batsford, 1999. Page 309.

4. Sturrock, Donald. *Storyteller: The Authorized Biography of Roald Dahl*. New York: Simon & Schuster, 2010. Page 407.

5. The remake starred Corbin Bernsen as Pike. Bernsen is best known for playing Arnie Becker on *L.A. Law*.

6. George Davis won Oscars for *The Robe* and *The Diary of Anne Frank*, and Edward Carfagno won for *Julius Caesar* and *Ben-Hur*, as well as *The Bad and the Beautiful*, a film about contemporary Hollywood.

7. Henry Grace would earn his thirteenth—and last—Oscar nomination on another Garner film, *Mister Buddwing*, in 1967.

8. Gill, Brendan. "The Current Cinema: Two Labyrinths." *New Yorker*, April 10, 1965.

9. *New Yorker* staff. "Goings on about Town, Motion Pictures: *36 Hours*." *New Yorker*, June 19, 1965.

10. Crowther, Bosley. "Contrived Trapping of Spies: Perlberg-Seaton Offer *36 Hours*, a Drama." *New York Times*, January 29, 1965.

11. *Variety* staff. "Review: *36 Hours*." *Variety*, December 31, 1964.

12. Martin, Mick, and Marsha Porter. *DVD & Video Guide 2004*. New York: Ballantine Books, 2003. Page 1, 116.

CHAPTER 11

1. Garner, James, and Jon Winokur. *The Garner Files*. New York: Simon & Schuster, 2011. Page 102.

2. *Variety* staff. "Review: *Grand Prix*." *Variety*, December 31, 1965.

3. Crowther, Bosley. "Screen: Flag Is Down at Warner for *Grand Prix*: Drama of Auto Racers Stars Yves Montand Story of Love and Roar 4 Other Films Bow." *New York Times*, December 22, 1965.

4. Mastroianni, Tony. "Racing Cars Star in *Grand Prix*." *Cleveland Press*, February 8, 1967.

5. "Top-US-Grossing Feature Films Released 1966-01-01 to 1966-12-31." IMDb. http://www.imdb.com/search/title?sort=boxoffice_gross_us&title_type=feature&year=1966,1966. Accessed November 8, 2017.

6. From 1948 through 1952, the nominations were announced quarterly.

7. Italian director Michaelangelo Antonioni was the lone 1967 Oscar nominee to not receive a corresponding DGA nod, for his film *Blow-Up*.

8. Though the Hollywood Foreign Press, which bestows the Golden Globes, did not actually specify *Grand Prix* in its nominations, Sabato's only other film in 1966 was an Italian feature, *Lo Scandalo*, while Walter made two features that year, *Grand Prix* and *The Group*.

CHAPTER 12

1. One of William Bowers's other credits was the television film *Sidekicks* (1974), a small-screen remake of Garner's 1971 film *Skin Game*, with Louis Gossett Jr. repeating his role from the earlier film.

2. *Variety* staff. "Review: *Support Your Local Sheriff!*" *Variety*, December 31, 1968.

3. Dalton, Stephen. "James Garner: An Appreciation." *Hollywood Reporter*, July 20, 2014.

4. Canby, Vincent. "*Support Your Local Sheriff*: Film Serves Up Dollop of Three-Line Jokes." *New York Times*, April 9, 1969.

5. Despite the inconsistent use of the exclamation point at the end of the film's title, it does appear in the most important place of all—the opening credits of the film.

6. In the year before, another western with an exclamation in the title debuted at number one, *Bandolero!*

7. "The Best Comedy Westerns of All Time." Flickchart. http://www.flickchart .com/Charts.aspx?genre=Comedy+Western. Accessed October 14, 2017.

8. "The 10 Funniest Comedy Westerns." IGN, May 28, 2014. http://www.ign .com/articles/2014/05/28/the-10-funniest-comedy-westerns. Accessed December 26, 2017.

9. The only actor who *might* be reprising his role is Dick Haynes, who plays an unnamed bartender in both films.

CHAPTER 13

1. An unfinished novel, *Poodle Springs*, was completed by Robert B. Parker, author of another series of successful novels about a private investigator, Spenser. Chandler had written the first four chapters of the novel, which was published in 1989.

2. The song sung over the opening credits, "Little Sister," echoed the title of the film's source novel, *The Little Sister*.

3. Stirling Silliphant, quoted in Clark, Al. *Raymond Chandler in Hollywood*. Los Angeles: Silman-James Press, 1996. Page 156.

4. Paul Bogart would make his biggest name in television a year after *Marlowe*, directing nearly one hundred episodes of *All in the Family* and winning four more Emmys.

5. Strait, Raymond. *James Garner: A Biography*. New York: St. Martin's Press, 1985. Page 257.

6. Garner, James, and Jon Winokur. *The Garner Files*. New York: Simon & Schuster, 2011. Page 258.

7. Standish, Myles. "The New Films: A Comedy Private Eye." *St. Louis Post-Dispatch*, October 31, 1969.

8. Greenspun, Roger. "Screen: In the Tradition of 'Marlowe': Work by Paul Bogart Begins Local Run." *New York Times*, October 23, 1969.

9. "Marlowe." *TimeOut London*. https://www.timeout.com/london/film/marlowe-1969. Accessed September 12, 2017.

10. Garner and Winokur, *The Garner Files*, 258.

11. Although the character of Steelgrave is central to Chandler's novel, his first name is never given. Presumably it was Silliphant who added it while writing the screenplay.

CHAPTER 14

1. Prior to *Skin Game*, "Pierre Marton" wrote the Gregory Peck thriller *Arabesque* (1966) and later the television movie *One of My Wives Is Missing* (1976).

2. Moore was preceded by Hattie McDaniel (*Gone with the Wind*), Ethel Waters (*Pinky*), and Dorothy Dandridge (*Carmen Jones*).

3. Kael, Pauline. "Goings on about Town." *New Yorker*, October 9, 1971.

4. *Variety*, as quoted in Strait, Raymond. *James Garner: A Biography*. New York: St. Martin's Press, 1985. Page 272.

5. Fretts, Bruce. "Why James Garner Was a Game Changer." Fretts on Film, July 24, 2014. https://frettsonfilm.com/2014/07/24/why-james-garner-was-a-game-changer/. Accessed December 26, 2017.

6. Greenspun, Roger. "White and Black Play the *Skin Game* in Film." *New York Times*, October 1, 1971.

CHAPTER 15

1. Thompson, Howard. "They Only Kill Their Masters." *New York Times*, November 23, 1972.

2. Ebert, Roger. "The Movies: They Only Kill . . .'" *Chicago Sun-Times*, November 22, 1972.

CHAPTER 16

1. Maltin, Leonard. *Leonard Maltin's Movie and Video Guide, 1994*. New York: Signet, 1993. Page 749.

2. *People* staff. "Picks and Pans Review: *The Long Summer of George Adams*." *People*, January 18, 1982.

3. Quoted in Strait, Raymond. *James Garner: A Biography*. New York: St. Martin's Press, 1985. Page 355.

CHAPTER 17

1. *Variety* staff. "Review: *Victor/Victoria*." *Variety*, December 31, 1981.

2. Canby, Vincent. "*Victor Victoria*: A Blake Edwards Farce." *New York Times*, March 19, 1982.

3. *Cabaret* debuted on February 13, 1972, *Victor/Victoria* arrived March 19, 1982.

4. The notable exception to staged musical numbers in *Cabaret* is the singing of "Tomorrow Belongs to Me," sung by Hitler Youth, one of the most powerful scenes in a musical.

5. Toward the end of his career, Garner did provide voicework for a number of fantasy/science fiction animated projects, but he did not appear in any live-action science fiction, fantasy, or horror films or television programs.

6. Andrews, Julie. "Foreword." In *The Garner Files*, by James Garner and Jon Winokur. New York: Simon & Schuster, 2011. Page x.

CHAPTER 18

1. Lear, Norman. *Even This I Get to Experience*. New York: Penguin Press, 2014. Page 343.

2. O'Connor, John. "*Heartsounds* Takes an Unblinking Look at Doctors." *New York Times*, September 30, 1984.

3. Marill, Alvin H. *Movies Made for Television, 1964–2004*. Lanham, MD: Scarecrow Press, 2005. Page 153.

4. Maltin, Leonard. *Movie and Video Guide 1994*. New York: Signet, 1993. Page 537.

5. "Heartsounds." Peabody Awards. http://www.peabodyawards.com/award -profile/heartsounds. Accessed December 27, 2016.

6. Martha Lear, quoted in Strait, Raymond. *James Garner: A Biography*. New York: St. Martin's Press, 1985. Page 366.

7. Garner, James, and Jon Winokur. *The Garner Files*. New York: Simon & Schuster, 2011. Page 268.

CHAPTER 19

1. O'Connor, Thomas. "Martin Ritt: Human Relationships and Moral Choices Fuel His Movies." *New York Times*, January 12, 1986.

2. The trio of Ritt, Ravetch, and Frank would make one more film together, *Stanley and Iris* (1990), another movie about a couple finding love.

3. Garner, James, and Jon Winokur. *The Garner Files*. New York: Simon & Schuster, 2011. Page 203.

4. Ebert, Roger. "'Romance' Stays Predictably Good, Authenticity Makes Plot, Dialogue Work." *Chicago Sun-Times*, January 17, 1986.

5. Maltin, Leonard. *Leonard Maltin's 2014 Movie Guide*. New York: Signet, 2013. Page 967.

6. "1985 Domestic Grosses." Box Office Mojo. http://www.boxofficemojo.com/ yearly/chart/?yr=1985. Accessed October 23, 2016. Had the film been released in 1986, it would have ranked thirty-four among the top films of the year.

7. *Watch What Happens: Live.* March 10, 2016 (11:18 p.m.).

8. In his memoir, Garner says he was fifty-eight, but the movie began filming in February 1985—when Garner was still fifty-six and several weeks before his birthday on April 7.

9. Garner wasn't the only one to "age" for the film. Charles Lane, who had just turned eighty before filming, plays the town's "oldest citizen," the eighty-eight-year-old Mr. Abbott. The actor would eventually surpass the age of his character—and then some—when he died in 2007 at the age of 102.

10. Garner and Winokur, *The Garner Files*, 204.

11. Frank, Jr., Harriet, and Irving Ravetch. *Murphy's Romance* screenplay. Columbia Pictures. 1985.

12. Garner and Winokur, *The Garner Files*, 203.

CHAPTER 20

1. Gendel, Morgan. "Garner Shifts Gears in Hallmark's *Promise*." *Los Angeles Times*, December 13, 1986.

2. Rosenberg, Howard. "James Garner in *Promise*, Film on Schizophrenia." *New York Times*, December 12, 1986.

3. Maltin, Leonard. *Leonard Maltin's Movie and Video Guide, 2003.* New York: Signet, 2002. Page 1,113.

4. Sragow, Michael. "Promise." *New Yorker*, February 23, 1998.

5. *Decoration Day* DVD. Special Features: Biographies, James Garner. Page 3.

6. "Promise." Peabody Awards. http://www.peabodyawards.com/award-profile/promise. Accessed December 28, 2016.

7. Gendel, Morgan. As quoted in "Garner Shifts Gears in Hallmark's *Promise*." *Los Angeles Times*, December 13, 1986.

8. Garner, James, and Jon Winokur. *The Garner Files*. New York: Simon & Schuster, 2011. Page 193.

9. Quoted in Gendel, "Garner Shifts Gears."

10. Quoted in Garner and Winokur, *The Garner Files*, 250.

CHAPTER 21

1. Stevens, John W. "Bill W. of Alcoholics Anonymous Dies." *New York Times*, January 26, 1971.

2. "About the Author." WilliamBorchert.com. http://williamborchert.com/author.html. Accessed November 9, 2017.

3. O'Connor, John J. "How One Day at a Time Became a Creed." *New York Times*, April 30, 1989.

4. Maltin, Leonard. *Leonard Maltin's Movie and Video Guide, 1994*. New York: Signet, 1993. Page 876.

5. Martin, Mick, and Marsha Porter. *DVD & Video Guide 2004*. New York: Ballantine Books, 2003. Page 762.

6. "Promise." Peabody Awards. http://www.peabodyawards.com/award-profile/promise. Accessed December 28, 2016.

7. Oddly enough, the two organizations differed in their genre categories. Garner's Emmy nomination was for Outstanding Lead Actor in a Drama Series, while the Golden Globe nomination was for Best Performance by an Actor in a Television Series—Comedy or Musical. He lost to Daniel J. Travanti (*Hill Street Blues*) and Alan Alda (*M°A°S°H*), respectively.

8. Garner, James, and Jon Winokur. *The Garner Files*. New York: Simon & Schuster, 2011. Page 201.

CHAPTER 22

1. "Conversations with James Garner." *Decoration Day* DVD. Special Features. Page 11.

2. "The Making of *Decoration Day*." *Decoration Day* DVD. Special Features.

3. "Conversations with James Garner," 3.

4. "About the Production." *Decoration Day* DVD. Special Features. Page 3.

5. "The Making of *Decoration Day*."

6. "The Making of *Decoration Day*."

7. "About the Production," 2.

8. "The Making of *Decoration Day*."

9. Maltin, Leonard. *Leonard Maltin's Movie and Video Guide, 1994*. New York: Signet, 1993. Page 337.

10. O'Connor, John. "James Garner as a Curmudgeon Pulled Back into Life." *New York Times*, November 30, 1990.

11. O'Connor, "James Garner as a Curmudgeon."

12. "Ratings Archive—November 1990." TV-aholic. http://tvaholics.blogspot.com/2010/07/ratings-archive-november-1990.html. Accessed January 15, 2017.

CHAPTER 23

1. Malarcher, Jay. *The Classically American Comedy of Larry Gelbart*. Lanham, MD: Scarecrow Press, 2003. Page 233.

2. Gelbart, Larry. *Laughing Matters: On Writing M°A°S°H, Tootsie, Oh, God!, and a Few Other Funny Things*. New York: Random House, 1998. Page 105.

3. Archerd, Army. "*Barbarians* Excels on Bare Bones Budget." *Variety*, March 11, 1993.

4. Scott, Tony. "Review: HBO Pictures' *Barbarians at the Gate*." *Variety*, March 17, 1993.

5. Maltin, Leonard. *Leonard Maltin's Movie and Video Guide, 1994*. New York: Signet, 1993. Page 76.

6. O'Connor, John J. "Those Good Old Takeover Days." *New York Times*, March 18, 1993.

7. Rosenberg, Howard. "Who Knew Greed Could Be So Fun?" *Los Angeles Times*, March 19, 1993.

8. Since *Barbarians at the Gate* and *Stalin*, the Emmy for Drama Special has gone to HBO an additional eighteen times.

9. In a category that featured drama and comedy series as well as specials, the critics chose *Barbarians at the Gate* over runners-up *Cheers*, *Homicide: Life on the Streets*, *Seinfeld*, and *The Simpsons*.

10. The other contenders for Outstanding Achievement in Drama were *Homefront*, *Homicide: Life on the Street*, *Law & Order*, and *Prime Suspect 2*.

11. Garner, James, and Jon Winokur. *The Garner Files*. New York: Simon & Schuster, 2011. Page 269.

CHAPTER 24

1. Robert Lenski would later adapt another Tyler novel, *Saint Maybe*, for Hallmark in 1998.

2. Garner, James, and Jon Winokur. *The Garner Files*. New York: Simon & Schuster, 2011. Page 206.

3. Maltin, Leonard. *Leonard Maltin's Movie and Video Guide, 2003*. New York: Signet, 2002. Page 75.

4. O'Connor, John J. "A Leisurely Tour of Anne Tyler's Small Miracles." *New York Times*, February 4, 1994.

5. Martin, Mick, and Marsha Porter. *DVD & Video Guide 2004*. New York: Ballantine Books, 2003. Page 144.

6. O'Connor, "A Leisurely Tour."

7. Bernstein, Roberta. "Review: Hallmark Hall of Fame *Breathing Lessons*." *Variety*, February 3, 1994.

8. Craddock, Jim, ed. *VideoHound's Golden Movie Retriever 2011*. Farmington Hills, MI: Gale Research, 2011. Page 170.

9. Garner and Winokur, *The Garner Files*, 207.

10. Interview with James Garner. *Los Angeles Times*, February 6, 2014.

CHAPTER 25

1. Unless one includes Steven Soderbergh's *Traffic*, which was based on the six-part miniseries *Traffik*, produced for British television in 1989 (Channel 4).

2. Goldman, William. *Which Lie Did I Tell? More Adventures in the Screen Trade*. New York: Vintage, 2001. Page 59.

3. Goldman, *Which Lie Did I Tell?* 60.

4. "Behind the Scenes." *Maverick* DVD, 2011.

5. "Behind the Scenes."

6. Jack Kelly had yet another opportunity to play Bart Maverick, appearing in the 1991 Kenny Rogers television movie *The Gambler Returns: The Luck of the Draw*.

7. "Behind the Scenes."

8. Ebert, Roger. "A Winning Hand: New *Maverick*, Other Westerns Find Their Home on the Range." *Chicago Sun-Times*, May 20, 1994.

9. James, Caryn. "*Maverick:* So Quick, So Suave and Oh So Spineless." *New York Times*, May 20, 1994.

10. Sterritt, David. "*Maverick* Gallops onto the Big Screen." *Christian Science Monitor*, May 20, 1994.

11. Fox, David J. "*Maverick* Wins Big Pot at the Box Office." *Los Angeles Times*, May 23, 1994.

12. Although there is some disagreement among sources—Box Office Mojo (http://www.boxofficemojo.com/genres/chart/?id=western.htm; accessed December 26, 2017) and the *Los Angeles Times* (http://beta.latimes.com/entertainment/envelope/cotown/la-et-ct-top-grossing-american-movie-westerns-20130702-photogallery.html; accessed December 26, 2017), for example—about its placement, *Maverick* consistently ranks among the top ten highest-grossing westerns.

13. "Rogue" is too benign a term to describe Gibson's offscreen character, given the despicable behavior he demonstrated years later, behavior that rightly tarnished his image.

14. Denver Pyle also appeared in a 1952 film called *The Maverick*, and yes, it was a western, of the B type.

CHAPTER 26

1. In addition to the ten films, the actors shared two other film credits: *Kotch* (1973), in which Matthau starred under the direction of Lemmon, and *JFK* (1992), in which both actors have cameos but do not share screen time.

2. Holden, Stephen. "Giving the White House a Couple of Black Eyes." *New York Times*, December 20, 1996.

3. McManus, Kevin. "*My Fellow Americans*." *Washington Post*, December 20, 1996.

4. Ebert, Roger. "'My Fellow Americans' Fails to Deliver on Promise." *Chicago Sun-Times*, December 20, 1996.

5. Dalton, Stephen. "James Garner: An Appreciation." *Hollywood Reporter*, July 20, 2014.

6. McCarthy, Todd. "Review: *My Fellow Americans*." *Variety*, December 8, 1996.

7. "1996 Domestic Grosses." Box Office Mojo. http://www.boxofficemojo.com/yearly/chart/?yr=1996. Accessed January 17, 2017.

8. Talbert, Bob. "Garner's Bored by Brave, Intrigued by Smart." *Detroit Free Press*, January 17, 1981.

CHAPTER 27

1. "Behind the Scenes." *One Special Night* DVD, 2002.

2. "Behind the Scenes."

3. "Behind the Scenes."

4. "Behind the Scenes."

5. Leonard, John. "One Special Night." *New York*, November 29, 1999.

6. Pardi, Robert. "Review of *One Special Night*." *TV Guide*. http://www.tvguide.com/movies/one-special-night/review/136573/. Accessed April 23, 2017.

CHAPTER 28

1. John Cassavetes is only one of eight individuals to receive Oscar nominations for acting, writing, and directing. The others (in chronological order of this achievement) are Orson Welles, John Huston, Woody Allen, Warren Beatty, Kenneth Branagh, Roberto Benigni, and George Clooney.

2. Ebert, Roger. "'Notebook' Tells Beautiful Love Story." *Chicago Sun-Times*, June 25, 2004.

3. Dalton, Stephen. "James Garner: An Appreciation." *Hollywood Reporter*, July 20, 2014.

4. Holden, Stephen. "When Love Is Madness and Life Is a Straitjacket." *New York Times*, June 25, 2004.

5. Thomson, Desson, "Young Love, Old Story." *Washington Post*, June 25, 2004.

6. Hornaday, Anne. "A Tear-Stained *Notebook*; Nick Cassavetes' Saga of Love Lost and Found Tugs at Every Heartstring." *Washington Post*, June 25, 2004.

7. The top ten films of 2004 included *Shrek 2* (at number one), *Spider-man 2* (number two), *The Incredibles* (number five), *Harry Potter and the Prisoner of Azkaban* (number six), and *The Polar Express* (number ten).

8. "2004 Domestic Grosses." Box Office Mojo. http://boxofficemojo.com/yearly/chart/?yr=2004). Accessed February 10, 2013.

9. Garner, James, and Jon Winokur. *The Garner Files*. New York: Simon & Schuster, 2011. Page 264.

CHAPTER 29

1. As quoted in Strait, Raymond. *James Garner: A Biography*. New York: St. Martin's Press, 1985. Page 59.

2. As quoted in Strait, *James Garner*, 59.

3. Leo Gordon also wrote for the series, though his contributions came after Garner left *Maverick*. Though his acting roles far outnumbered his writing credits, Gordon wrote nearly three dozen television episodes and a handful of features. He was also a novelist.

4. Garner himself played four different characters on *Cheyenne*, three in the first season.

5. Garner lost the Emmy to Raymond Burr for his role in *Perry Mason*.

6. In the category of Best Writing of a Western, Heyes lost to eventual *Star Trek*–creator Gene Roddenberry for an episode of *Have Gun—Will Travel* called "Helen of Abajinian."

7. Goldman was no doubt also inspired by the Maverick theme song—introduced in the second season—which includes the lyrics "Fare thee well, Annabelle."

8. Title credit for the episode reads "Gun-shy" while the end credits cite "Gun-Shy."

9. According to series creator, Roy Huggins, the story was by Huggins and written by regular *Maverick* writer Marion Hargrove, but the credits for the episode read "Teleplay by Roy Huggins; story by Douglas Heyes," which seems more likely.

CHAPTER 30

1. Both *Hee Haw* and *Lassie* continued on in syndication after CBS dropped them. *Lassie* lasted three more seasons, while *Hee Haw* continued on for another twenty years.

2. Brooks, Tim, and Earle Marsh. *The Complete Directory to Prime Time Network and Cable TV Shows, 1946–Present*. 9th ed. New York: Ballantine Books, 2007. Page 130.

CHAPTER 31

1. Delgado also appeared in a handful of *Cheyenne* episodes, but none in which Garner appeared.

2. Huggins was married to Delgado's sister, Adele Mara, who had appeared in a trio of *Maverick* episodes herself, most notably the season 1 finale, "Seed of Deception."

3. Charles Floyd Johnson, who would eventually produce *The Rockford Files*, also worked on *Toma*, but not behind the scenes. He acted in two episodes.

4. The song, composed by Mike Post, proved so popular that it was released as a single in the spring of 1975, ultimately peaking at number ten on the August 9 *Billboard* chart.

5. The license plate on Rockford's Firebird, which reads "853 OKG," is attributed to Garner's agent and refers to the date when Garner got his first acting job (August 1953) and the actor's home state and last name: "OK" for Oklahoma and "G" for Garner.

6. It has also been called the "Rockford turn" or the "Rockford."

7. Huggins's writing pseudonym was derived from the first names of his three sons, John, Thomas, and James.

8. Though *NYPD Blue, Law and Order,* and the undeserving *Cagney and Lacey* have won the award for Best Drama, these are all police procedurals, more or less, while *The Rockford Files* is purely a detective series.

9. "Sleight of Hand" is also the name of an episode (17) from Garner's previous series, *Nichols*.

10. This episode featured the first appearance of Richie Brockelman, a character who was spun off into a short-lived series. Cocreated by Stephen J. Cannell and Steven Bochco (*Hill Street Blues, L.A. Law*), *Richie Brockelman: Private Eye*, starring Dennis Dugan, lasted only five episodes.

SELECTED BIBLIOGRAPHY

Balio, Tino. *United Artists: The Company That Changed the Film Industry, Volume 2 (1951–1978)*. Madison: University of Wisconsin Press, 2009.

Barc, Richard L. *Confessions of a Hollywood Director*. Lanham, MD: Scarecrow Press, 2001.

Brooks, Tim, and Earle Marsh. *The Complete Directory to Prime Time Network and Cable TV Shows, 1946–Present*. 9th ed. New York: Ballantine Books, 2007.

Burrough, Bryan, and John Helyar. *Barbarians at the Gate: The Fall of RJR Nabisco*. New York: HarperCollins, 2009.

Carpenter, Carleton. *The Absolute Joy of Work: From Vermont to Broadway, Hollywood, and Damn Near around the World*. Albany, GA: BearManor Media, 2016.

Chayefsky, Paddy. *The Collected Works of Paddy Chayefsky: The Screenplays Volume 1*. New York: Applause Books, 1995.

Clark, Al. *Raymond Chandler in Hollywood*. Los Angeles: Silman-James Press, 1996.

Considine, Shaun. *Mad as Hell: The Life and Work of Paddy Chayefsky*. New York: Random House, 1994.

Craddock, Jim, ed. *VideoHound's Golden Movie Retriever 2011*. Farmington Hills, MI: Gale Research, 2011.

DeRosa, Steven. *Writing with Hitchcock: The Collaboration of Alfred Hitchcock and John Michael Hayes*. New York: Faber and Faber, 2001.

Edelman, Rob, and Audrey Kupferberg *Matthau: A Life*. Lanham, MD: Taylor Trade, 2002.

Finstad, Suzanne. *Natasha: The Biography of Natalie Wood*. New York: Harmony, 2001.

Fishgall, Gary. *Against Type: The Biography of Burt Lancaster*. New York: Scribner, 1995.

Garner, James, and Jon Winokur. *The Garner Files*. New York: Simon & Schuster, 2011.

Gelbart, Larry. *Laughing Matters: On Writing M°A°S°H, Tootsie, Oh, God!, and a Few Other Funny Things*. New York: Random House, 1998.

Goldman, William. *Which Lie Did I Tell? More Adventures in the Screen Trade*. New York: Vintage, 2001.

Herman, Jan. *A Talent for Trouble: The Life of Hollywood's Most Acclaimed Director, William Wyler*. New York: Putnam, 1995.

IMDb.com.

Jewison, Norman. *This Terrible Business Has Been Good to Me*. Toronto: Key Porter Books, 2004.

Kanfer, Stefan. *Somebody: The Reckless Life and Remarkable Career of Marlon Brando*. New York: Knopf, 2008.

Katz, Ephraim. *The Film Encyclopedia: The Complete Guide to Film and the Film Industry*. 7th ed. Revised by Ronald Dean Nolen. New York: Collins Reference, 2012.

Lambert, Gavin. *Natalie Wood: A Life*. New York: Knopf, 2004.

Lawson, Matt, and Laurence E. MacDonald. *100 Greatest Film Scores*. Lanham, MD: Rowman & Littlefield, 2018.

Lear, Norman. *Even This I Get to Experience*. New York: Penguin Press, 2014.

Lovell, Glenn. *Escape Artist. The Life and Films of John Sturges*. Madison: University of Wisconsin Press, 2008.

Malarcher, Jay. *The Classically American Comedy of Larry Gelbart*. Lanham, MD: Scarecrow Press, 2003.

Maltin, Leonard. *Leonard Maltin's Classic Movie Guide*. 3rd ed. New York: Plume, 2015.

———. *Leonard Maltin's Movie and Video Guide, 1994*. New York: Signet, 1993.

———. *Leonard Maltin's Movie and Video Guide, 2003*. New York: Signet, 2002.

Marill, Alvin H. *Movies Made for Television, 1964–2004*. Lanham, MD: Scarecrow Press, 2005.

Martin, Mick, and Marsha Porter. *DVD & Video Guide 2004*. New York: Ballantine Books, 2003.

Murguía, Salvador Jiminez, ed. *The Encyclopedia of Racism in American Films*. Lanham, MD: Rowman & Littlefield, 2018.

Nichols, Peter, ed. The New York Times *Guide to the Best Movies Ever Made*. New York: Times Books, 1999.

Quinlan, David. *Quinlan's Film Directors*. London: Batsford, 1999.

Strait, Raymond. *James Garner: A Biography*. New York: St. Martin's Press, 1985.

Sturrock, Donald. *Storyteller: The Authorized Biography of Roald Dahl*. New York: Simon & Schuster, 2010.

Thomson, David. *A Biographical Dictionary of Film*. 3rd ed. New York: Knopf, 1995.

Wiley, Mason, and Damien Bona. *Inside Oscar*. New York: Ballantine, 1996.

INDEX

ABOUT THE AUTHORS

Stephen H. Ryan earned his master's degree in English pedagogy from Salisbury University, where he taught introduction to composition and literature courses. For several years he was the nonfiction buyer for Crown Books, a national bookstore chain, as well as the managing editor for National Film Network, a documentary distributor. For more than a decade, Stephen has been the senior acquisitions editor for Scarecrow Press/ Rowman & Littlefield, where he oversees the performing arts, popular culture, and literary studies titles.

Paul J. Ryan holds a bachelor's degree in business management from Towson University, is a certified Lean Six Sigma Black Belt, and project management professional. A small business owner and business consultant, Paul has served as a volunteer for organizations such as Junior Achievement and Habitat for Humanity. He is on the graduate school advisory board for Keiser University and is a mentor for his alma mater. Paul manages the blog *Humor in Business* (http://humorseries.blogspot.com/).